HEALING
GENERATIONAL WOUNDS

Restoring Families, Churches and Communities

DOUGLAS W SCHOENINGER, PHD,

JUDITH ALLEN SHELLY, DMIN

XULON PRESS

Healing Generational Wounds
Restoring Families, Churches and Communities
by Douglas W Schoeninger, PhD, Judith Allen Shelly, DMin

Printed in the United States of America.

ISBN 9781498442329

www.xulonpress.com

We dedicate this book to our spouses,
Frances Schoeninger and James Shelly,
who have walked with us and prayed for us
through every step of our journeys with
generational healing and the writing of this book.

Without their love and care this could not be.

Contents

Acknowledgements

Douglas Schoeninger:

My profound gratitude to Frances Schoeninger, my wife, a pioneer in generational healing with me from the early 1980s. We came to insights together as we prayed for clients and sought understanding prayerfully. God gave her an amazing vision journey into the depths of generational transmission, granting her great understanding and strong encouragement to us to persist in the generational healing work. Her support and prayer throughout the writing of this book has been both essential and immeasurable.

The late Kenneth McAll, author of *Healing the Family Tree*, mentored me in family tree healing and was a delightful companion on the journey as Frances, Kenneth and I led annual workshops together. Kenneth, Frances and I initiated an annual gathering of colleagues to explore family tree healing (the family applications of generational healing) together. We were joined over the years by Robert Sears, James Wheeler, Matt, Dennis and Sheila Linn (authors of *Healing the Greatest Hurt*), Ted and Susan TePas and John and Joanna Lehman. These annual meetings continued for many years as a supportive, encouraging circle of inquiry where we tested our growing insights with each other. These meetings, in their origin and continuance, were intertwined with the fellowship and work within the Association of Christian Therapists (now ACTheals) where the teaching of generational healing has been supported, embraced and implemented over the years. Betty Igo, Robert Sears, Austin Joyce, Lou Lussier, Helen Bethel, Denise Dolff and Katsey Long have been especially important collaborators within ACTheals exploring generational healing with me and bringing teaching to all interested members.

Through ACT Elizabeth Brennan became a close friend and mentor in spiritual discernment. Thanks to Betty I became attuned to the presence and action of evil and especially the work of familiar spirits who at times mimic family dynamics.

A special thanks to James Wheeler for years of retreating with me and for providing occasions to teach and research generational healing in his prayer centers in Albuquerque, NM and Long Island, NY.

A hearty thank you to Francis and Judith MacNutt, who gave me personal and theological support when I first presented generational healing in the 1980s to Fishnet Northeast and then for giving Frances and me a teaching platform at Christian Healing Ministries (CHM) in one of their conferences. I still receive appreciation for the teaching in that conference that continued to impact through the outreach of the CHM bookstore.

I have been much blessed by Eileen Schrader and Patricia Deacon for their encouragement as they partnered with my wife Frances and me at the Institute for Christian Healing (ICH) from the mid-1980s to mid-1990s as a research team exploring the lives of our clients generationally and praying for understanding. And much gratitude to Charles Zeiders who picked up the mantle of leading an ICH think tank in recent years and to Julie Wegryn, Robin Caccese, and Herman Riffel who joined us to probe the nature of God's healing work.

I am especially indebted to Barbara Krasner, a treasured colleague and friend, who introduced me to Ivan Boszormenyi-Nagy and Contextual Family Therapy, a profound understanding of family loyalty dynamics and invisible loyalties between and across generations. Barbara mentored me for years leading to a 40 year enduring friendship. Together with Austin Joyce, a close friend and companion with Frances and me in teaching Healing Generational Wounds within the Association of Christian Therapists, we began a weekly writing group we named Community in Dialogue, a circle of trust, where we explore together weekly loyalty dynamics and the critical importance of trust between persons.

My appreciation and grasp of intergenerational loyalty and justice dynamics is rooted with Ivan Nagy and his genius. Barbara Krasner introduced us and Ivan offered me a position in the Family Psychiatry Department at Eastern Pennsylvania Psychiatric Institute in the early 1970s. There I had the privilege of sitting under his tutelage absorbing all I could of his profound insight.

Richard Broholm has encouraged me for 53 years, listening to my thinking and experience and then grasping the nature and importance of healing generational wounds and generously donating funds to support this publication. Our semi-weekly Skype conversations continue to nourish me.

Fernando Colon partnered with me at University of North Carolina as new faculty in the 1960s as we explored and observed each other in our first foray into family therapy work, and he shared with me his journey reconnecting with his biological family in Puerto Rico. His experience taught me the power and significance of multigenerational family ties.

Russ Parker has been a gem of a friend and collegial partner in generational explorations. His book Healing Wounded History inspired me. Our pilgrimages together with my wife Frances and his wife Roz, exploring Celtic roots of Christianity in Scotland, Ireland, Wales and Cornwall, have deepened my appreciation for our ancestors in faith.

Lois Doyle and Bernie Solwey invited Frances and me and Kenneth McAll to teach generational healing in South Dakota and North Dakota. This brought Frances and me into the world of Native American tribal life and opportunities to explore generational healing with Native peoples. Through these initial events came enduring friendships with Lois and Bernie, Joe and Connie Lewis, Potawatomi, Don and Marilyn Bread, Kiowa and Cherokee, Charlene Bolinsky, Kiowa, John David and Gaylene Gomez, Apache and Navaho, and the founding of the All Nations Prayer Warrior Society (ANPWS), an intercessory prayer fellowship praying for the healing of the nations, beginning with Native American tribal nations. I am deeply indebted to Bernie and Lois and all the ANPWS prayer warriors for years of fellowship in powerful intercession for the healing of America's historical wounds.

I am immeasurably grateful to Glenn Wolf, Lenape native, who joined me in the ANPWS and has graced me with friendship and opened to me a depth of union with the natural world and first nation ways.

Through Fernando Colon's encouragement Monica McGoldrick invited me to be a part of faculty the yearly Multicultural Family Therapy conference in New Jersey. By word and example, the way she lives and relates, she has taught me so much about honoring each person, culture, race, gender, sexuality and origins. Through the Culture Conference a friendship has formed with Robin LaDue, a Taidnapam native from Washington State who continues to teach me and bless me with her first nation healing ways.

Thanks to Pamela Clark, and her heart for her Irish ancestors, who sought out Frances and me to join her in leading generational healing workshops for Irish Americans. She opened the world of Irish history to me and the profound suffering that brought many to seek refuge in the US and Canada and the potential for healing these ancestral wounds.

My father Irvin, trekked with me to Germany to connect with our German family and investigate my German grandfather's life and origins. He allowed me to engage him with frequent inquiries about his childhood and emotional wounds, even when this was visibly painful for him. Through him our world of German cousins opened to me resulting in enduring friendship across the Atlantic. Thanks also to my siblings, Sandra, Kenneth and Mary Lynn for engaging family healing processes with me, to my children Kevin and Karin for their lives and for their listening and responding with their insights to my family explorations and writings. To my daughter's husband Scott and his African-American family for their love and embrace, and opening to me the consequences of the historical trauma of slavery and past and present racism; and for participating with me in ANPWS gatherings and intercessions. And now I am blessed by grandchildren who are also inquiring of family legacy. Words are inadequate to express how much this means to me.

Most treasured are the contributions of my psychotherapy clients at the Institute for Christian Healing. There is certainly no book to write without their trust in me and themselves and their courage to walk the journey of healing and plumb the depths of their family relationships and legacies. Thank you to each and all!

Several years ago Judith Shelly my coauthor, friend and colleague on the Board of The Institute for Christian Healing exchanged papers with me, each of us sharing our writings on Healing Generational Wounds. Judy then suggested that we write a book together. What a blessing this has been. Our gifts complement each other so well, Judy's skill with scripture and healing organizations and my experience with healing families. The book I had started and stopped many times over that last 20 years became a wonderful process of writing together. What can I say, working together has been a joy. And bless Jim, her husband, who has stood by and encouraged us, read the manuscript for us and been a prayer warrior with us.

Judith Shelly:

Walking with Doug through the process of documenting, organizing, illustrating and reflecting on our lifetimes of generational healing, both personally and professionally, has be a delightful journey.

My awareness of the need for generational healing began with a crisis within my working environment in the early 1970's. As I sought help, I encountered The Rev. George Callahan, founder of the Institute for Christian Healing. George met with our group in crisis and helped us listen to one another and pray through our differences. He also met with me individually, providing support and encouragement. I ended up enrolling in seminary and studying pastoral counseling. I returned to a greatly healed work environment after graduating with an M.A.R. in pastoral counseling. However, before long many of the same disruptive dynamics began to surface again. It seemed to be the same story with different players within the same organization. These patterns would resolve and then resurface over and over again. My pastoral skills seemed to help, but only temporarily.

Eventually, I went back to seminary for a Doctor of Ministry, focusing on healing wounded systems. In the process, I engaged Dr. Mary Stewart Van Leeuwen, a social psychologist at Eastern University, in an independent study on "Abuse of Power and Control by Women Toward Women." She opened my eyes to the internal literature of religious orders and introduced me to others who were studying this dynamic among mission organizations. Through that study I began to work on developing models for healing organizations that seemed to have long histories of recurring emotional and/ or sexual abuse among their staff. My supervisor, Mary Thompson, encouraged me to plan retreats and other ways to help us work through these periods of crisis. However, despite our best efforts, the patterns continued to resurface. Something seemed to be missing in our attempts to bring healing.

A huge turning point came in 2005 when Mary Thompson said to me, "There's this woman within the organization who prays. We need to go see her." Looking at her with jaded eyes, I simply replied, "You mean there is only one?" We were at a national staff conference and that evening we walked into an empty hotel dining room to find this woman, Mary Anne Voelkel, standing alone. She agreed to meet with us the next day, beginning the most amazing experience of generational healing—both personally and organizationally—that continued over about two years. During that time Mary Anne became my mentor in generational healing prayer while we also worked on compiling teaching manuals on healing prayer and intercession, which we used in staff training.

My job description changed from publications director to "staff spiritual formation and prayer." That introduced me to a whole new peer group of others within the organization in that role. I am especially grateful for the friendships that developed within that group, especially for Lorita and Tom Boyle and Barbara Brown who became my confidants and encouragers.

During this time, my husband Jim and I completed the Christian Healing Ministries School of Healing Prayer and had the privilege of studying under Francis and Judith MacNutt. We continue to use their materials as we facilitate the Schools of Healing Prayer in our area.

Another important influence has been Russ Parker, whom I first met through *Healing Wounded History,* a book I picked up while on Holy Island, Northumberland, England. I marveled aloud to a British friend that this man had written about exactly what I had experienced and was now practicing, so that I really wanted to meet him. She replied that he often went to America and she emailed me when she heard of his next trip. My husband and I connected with Russ at the Fellowship of Christ the Healer in Virginia, and have since become friends and colleagues, working together with Doug and others to re-form the Institute for Christian Healing, exploring obscure Celtic sites, speaking together at conferences and meeting annually for the Fellowship of Christ the Healer.

My husband Jim has been one of our strongest supporters. He is also our family historian and genealogist. Together we have visited the sites where our ancestors lived and walked. We have marveled at our intertwined heritages and appreciated the rich goodness with which our ancestors blessed us. And together we have engaged in generational healing in our churches and communities.

Through living and working with others we have discovered a "missing piece" in facilitating the healing of individuals, families, churches and communities, healing prayer applied to the generational wounding that underlies the presenting problems. This is what we hope to share with you in this book.

Preface

A family may carry a long history of depression or of members disconnecting from each other; or a church goes through a succession of failed pastorates; or members of a Christian organization discover a history of sexual abuse.

Generational healing comes through an intercessory prayer process for healing and freeing families, organizations and communities from wounds and burdens passed generation-to-generation; and freeing and strengthening the God-given gifts and blessings that also pass generation to generation.

God chooses to work through his praying people to bring wounded families, churches, organizations and people groups to Jesus for healing. In this book we describe ways to enter into this healing process, as well as examine the barriers that impede healing. Jesus came to break through these barriers. We look forward to the day when these words from Revelation are fulfilled:

> "See, the home of God is among mortals. He will dwell with them as their God; they will be his peoples, and God himself will be with them; he will wipe every tear from their eyes. Death will be no more; mourning and crying and pain will be no more, for

the first things have passed away." And the one who was seated on the throne said, "See, I am making all things new" (Rev 21:3-5).

In the meantime, we have the privilege—and the joy—of participating in that healing process. Generational healing occurs as a dynamic work of the Holy Spirit urging us to bring ourselves and our legacies, wounds and all, to the altar and into the light of Christ, for God's healing and reconciling purposes to be fulfilled.

Healing Generational Wounds offers a comprehensive method for this generational healing process. We teach specifically how to do it and at the same time provide the Biblical foundations and essential resources, criteria, preparation and theory for engaging generational intercession.

We are writing for all Christians interested in healing, and especially those engaged in healing ministries.

Our passion for this book

Our passion began with a desire to heal ourselves, our families and our communities. We each experienced a growing awareness that the wounds that concerned us were being passed from generation-to-generation. And we were inspired by the inner sense that God wanted to heal these generational wounds.

Our message is extremely important as families, churches, organizations, communities and nations suffer repeating injuries and unreconciled losses. Also, there is a growing consciousness around the world that repentance, forgiveness, healing, and reconciliation for past sins and wounds are essential for peace between people(s) and for persons, communities and nations to survive and thrive. Yet many feel stymied about how to engage a generational healing process. In this book we address this need.

Chapter 1: Awakening to Generational Wounds

God has taught us by revealing his healing process in the specific situations of our lives, in our family, church, and group stories. So we begin this journey with stories. We hope these initial accounts will call to mind your own life experience. In these we introduce the ways generational wounding occurred in a family, a church and a missionary organization. We describe the signs and symptoms of generational wounds and then demonstrate how the same patterns appear in scripture, history and in our lives today.

Chapter 2: Biblical Foundations for Generational Healing

Christians often wonder if and how a particular healing process is grounded in Scripture. Is generational healing biblical? We discovered that, beginning in Genesis, generational healing is clearly at the heart of Scripture and the gospel. Genesis is full of family stories and generation to generation consequences. Here you can enjoy and identify with the generational stories at the beginning and core of our faith history. As we move on to the New Testament we find the mandate to be reconcilers. As the Apostle Paul states,

> So if anyone is in Christ, there is a new creation: everything old has passed away; see, everything has become new! All this is from God, who reconciled us to himself through Christ, and has *given us the ministry of reconciliation*; that is, in Christ God was reconciling the world to himself, not counting their trespasses against them, and entrusting the message of reconciliation to us. (2 Cor 5:17-19)

Chapter 3: Spiritual Resources for Generational Healing

I am just one person, what can I do? What then are the spiritual resources that will strengthen and guide me? We cannot practice generational healing in our own strength, abilities or willpower. While counsel and psychotropic drugs may temporarily relieve symptoms of generational wounding, they do not get to the root of the problem. The wounds recur in the affected person, family, community or organization and reappear in subsequent generations. The wounds and consequences of wounding may recur years and generations after the original source of wounding has died or has been removed from the situation.

Four powerful resources lay the foundation for generational healing and provide wisdom and direction in the process. God's Word, the presence of the Risen Christ, the Cross and Holy Communion bring us into the presence of God and empower us through the Holy Spirit to minister in the authority that Jesus imparted to his followers. In this chapter these resources are presented biblically and theologically in practical terms.

Chapter 4: The Dynamics of Generational Healing

We have often wondered why generational sins and wounds and resulting attitudes can seem so normal, even expected. They become imbedded in our family and group cultures as prejudices, fears, and anticipated outcomes, repeated over and over across generations until they do seem normal. Generation to generation blessings of love and forgiveness also become part of expected family and group practice. We all inherit the good and the bad. Every culture is a mixture of constructive and destructive tendencies, those that promote life and those that diminish life. In generational healing we are touching both injured and blessed aspects of culture.

Our Christian perspective places generational healing in the context of redemption and reconciliation. All lineages and relationships come into union with God in Christ. Confession, forgiveness and repentance lead to healing. Participants in generational healing turn away from that which injures and destroys and toward that which heals and gives life. Ways of seeing, valuing and relating become transformed to express the beautiful, mutually beneficial diversity of life in God.

Chapter 5: How Generational Memories Develop

This chapter examines the dynamics involved in passing blessings and curses through the generations in families and also in communities.

The continuing influence of past experiences across generations implies some sort of inheritance of memories. Our ancestors pass on generational memories through their ways of seeing, valuing and living. Children "feed" from their parents' and other caretakers' perceptions, attitudes, emotions, motivations, beliefs and patterns of relating. These become normative reality for the child. We call this enculturation. Children absorb and invest in their parents' and caretakers' ways of thinking and acting while creating their own ways of perceiving and living, and then pass these patterns to the next generation. Memory serves to transmit, recreate and pass on culture.

In addition to enculturation, ancestral memories (events in generations past) may also persist in their influence through genetic and epigenetic inheritance, group and place memories, the inheritance of justice dynamics, the presence of the departed, the action of the Holy Spirit, the spiritual dynamics of blessing or curse, or the action of evil spirits.

Chapter 6: Accepting Responsibility in Generational Healing

In this chapter we take a look at taking responsibility. What is our responsibility for the impact of something someone else did? In generational healing, we pray about wounds and acts of wounding and subsequent consequences that were set in motion long ago. The original actions often were committed by someone we never knew and who is no longer living. How can we respond to the past event and persons involved in a healing way that frees current and future generations? How do we understand our responsibility for doing this? And how do we view the responsibility of those who preceded us and contributed benefits and burdens?

Chapter 7: A Process for Generational Healing

How do we do engage in generational healing? This chapter describes and illustrates steps for healing generational wounds.

Generational healing is a journey rather than a set procedure. It can progress quickly, but more often, it takes years because there are many facets due to a wide web of relationships over a long time span across generations. Steps we suggest include:

1. awakening to the present influences of the past and calling out to God
2. seeking God's face (listening to God and community)
3. researching the sins, wounds and blessings of the past
4. searching the heart of God for our lineages
5. humbly confessing, personally and representationally
6. apologizing, asking forgiveness and forgiving
7. repenting: renouncing the old and asserting the new
8. rebuking evil, breaking curses and restoring blessings
9. praying for healing: inviting Jesus into our ancestral past to heal and restore
10. reconciling actions

Chapter 8: Healing a Family Lineage

Here we illustrate the generational healing steps in families. God created each person both unique and rooted in a genetic lineage. Being alive in this world depends on God and our biological parents and all those who preceded our parents. Non-biological lineages also shape us. Certainly those who have been adopted, fostered, or raised by step-parents are strongly shaped and influenced by non-biological lineages.

Furthermore, we are born weak and in need of nurturing in order to survive. Given human dependence on care-giving and receiving with parents, grandparents, siblings and other caretakers, how can we strengthen these relationships and the life-giving resources that they transmit? How can we heal and transform the deprivations and injuries that have crippled persons from generation-to-generation? These are our tasks in the generational healing of families. This chapter details the healing steps through two cases of intercession for the healing of family lineages.

Chapter 9: Healing the Lineages of Churches and Organizations

This chapter walks through the steps of the generational healing in a church and in a Christian organization, giving practical suggestions about how to implement the process in the readers own situation.

Generational wounds occur in almost every church and organization. We are all sinful people who have been sinned against; therefore, when we gather as a community we bring our personal wounded histories with us and compound these with the organization's wounded history. These wounds may be buried deep in our personal and corporate history. The initial wounding incidents may be long-forgotten, or only communicated surreptitiously. "Stuffing it," what psychology calls *suppression*, is one of the most common ways of dealing with painful memories. However, even as the memories fade, powerful attitudes and behaviors continue to pass from generation-to-generation and shape the character of the community.

Chapter 10: Enlarging the Focus

At times any of us may feel moved to intercede for healing with a focus that reaches beyond our specific family lineages, churches, or organizations to which we belong.

Everyone and everything has a history—persons, families and organizations, as well as nations, ethnicities, professions and locations. The impact of past events continues to bear powerful influence through both conscious and unconscious memories. Past events and their consequences echo in persons, on the land, in buildings and through national, ethnic, professional and occupational loyalty ties.

This chapter examines the effects of generational wounding on whole people groups, including the effects of legislation on a mental health facility and injustices toward Native Americans and African Americans in our nation's history. Several examples illustrate the powerful potential of generational healing intercessions among and for these people groups.

Chapter 11: Maintaining Generational Health

This chapter reviews the steps of the generational healing journey in the light of preventative generational health, giving readers concrete ways to maintain and continue the healing that has occurred.

Once you have experienced generational healing, further questions quickly surface. How can I help prevent generational wounds from developing in future generations? How can I be sure that I am not wounding others without realizing it? How can I safeguard those who come after me from suffering from wounds like those I experienced? How can I pass on a legacy of faith, truth, goodness, healing and blessing?

Even healed people are wounded and wounding healers. We are constantly learning to be trustworthy and how and when to trust. Frustration, defensiveness and misunderstandings rise up to confront us. However, if we view generational healing as a journey, we see that we are still moving forward, even as we learn new lessons along the way.

Appendices

We conclude with appendices to assist readers with their own generational healing work. The material in these appendices can help in locating and organizing significant family and organizational data. We are grateful to Monica McGoldrick for contributing her genogram mapping of family systems to these appendices.

Appendix A: The Genogram Format for Mapping Family Systems, Monica McGoldrick. How to use genogram symbols to construct a picture of your family systems and lineages.

Appendix B: Suggestions for Gathering Family Information, Douglas Schoeninger. A list of areas to explore when developing your family, church or organizational history of generational blessing and wounding.

Appendix C: Organizing Generational Information, Judith Shelly. A means to view significant patterns in a church or organization.

How to read this book

There are many ways to read this book and engage the generational healing process. Some will be inclined to get at doing the process and then read and study the theory and scriptural foundations later. Others may find understanding the "whys and wherefores" essential to guide the task of doing. Still others may want to start engaging the process in Chapters 7, 8 and 9 and then study the theory and scripture as they proceed and feel the need. We encourage you to find the way that works best for you and to change your approach according to how you experience the material. In any case we invite you to work through the process in your own life and situations as part of engaging this book.

Part I
What is Generational Healing?

Chapter 1

Awakening to Generational Wounds

Maggie, aged 42, worried about her younger brother John. He'd been in the ministry for six years now and his congregation loved him, but John seemed constantly discouraged and was being treated for clinical depression—just like their Dad. Their older sister, Anna, also suffered from depression. Anna's 16 year old son had attempted suicide twice. If Maggie were honest with herself, she'd have to admit that she, too, struggled with depression. One day she sat down with her mother and asked, "Why does depression seem to run in our family? We've always known we are loved, but it just feels like there is a big black cloud over our family."

Maggie's mother held her tightly and said, "Your grandfather was also depressed—ever since he witnessed his own father shooting his mother in a fit of drunken rage. He never really talked about it, but the neighbors knew and we heard that this great-grandfather had served time in prison. That's why we moved away, so you would not have to deal with the old stories."

ॐ

"I the LORD your God am a jealous God, punishing children for the iniquity of parents, to the third and the fourth generation of those who reject me, but showing steadfast love to the thousandth generation of those who love me and keep my commandments" (Ex 20:5-6).

These familiar words from Exodus puzzle many Bible readers. The good news it brings is that the blessing of God's love benefits exponentially more generations of those who love God and keep his commandments than generations affected by iniquity. However, it still does not seem fair that God would punish children for the sins of their parents. In Ezekiel Chapters 16 and 18 God assures Israel that this curse is temporary and that it will be lifted in an everlasting covenant. Yet we still suffer from the consequences of our transgressions and our ancestors' transgressions as they are passed generation to generation. We see the evidence from generation-to-generation all around us as parents who were abused as children abuse their own children, through social irresponsibility and even genetic illnesses that that recur generation-to-generation in families. We also see the effects of generational wounding in churches, communities, organizations, people groups and nations.

Pennsylvania State University Associate Professor Dr. Peter Hatemi states that his recent research has indicated that actual chromosomal damage occurs when children are sexually assaulted. These children also may face tertiary issues such as cancer and drastically shortened life expectancy.[1]

Being Christian does not make us immune from the effects of generational wounding. Sometimes it makes the pain worse. We want to assume that the gospel frees us from generational wounding. Furthermore, we are reluctant to believe that Christians wound one another. So wounded victims often face the isolation created by the Christian community's denial and disbelief. However, because we are human, we are all both victims and perpetrators of generational wounds. Each generation both blesses and wounds the next with the benefits received and the injuries suffered and passed on.

To introduce the scope of this dynamic, we will first tell three more stories. As we do so, we want to make it clear—especially to our clients, friends and colleagues—that all the stories in this book are *true*, but they are not *you*. We are committed to confidentiality. These patterns are so common that we see them over and over again. We have taken liberties in telling these stories to change all information that relates to the personal details, locations or identities of the people involved. We have also combined stories in order to preserve the truths revealed while protecting those involved. If a story feels like your own story, be assured, you are not alone in your experience.

Surprise on a swing

Two children were helping their grandfather, Bill, with spring raking. While Bill hauled bags of leaves to the curb, his grandchildren took turns pushing each other on the bench swing in the yard. When Bill returned Susan was pushing her younger brother, Sam, to heights that frightened him. He kept trying to define his preferred limits, but Susan kept exceeding his range by a considerable margin. Bill intervened, ordering Susan to respect Sam's fears and accede to his wishes. She did not. Bill then stopped her and again explained the importance of respecting her brother's fears.

"I can't do that!" Susan insisted

"Yes, you can learn to do it," Bill patiently explained.

"But Mommy told me that when she was little you used to push her too high on the swing. She was really scared, but you pushed her higher." Susan retorted.

Faced with his own history, Bill became acutely aware of what had been his intolerance of weakness—others and his own. He began to reflect on the ways American culture conditions us to hide our weakness, as if we would be shamed by its exposure. He thought about how images that idolize strength bombard us—in athletics, in advertising, in prayer groups. He realized that American history repeatedly glorified strength and justified conquering with physical might through notions of cultural superiority and manifest destiny. Bill's own African American ancestors' were perceived as inferior because they arrived in this country as slaves. Between these large historical-cultural movements, and his granddaughter's insistence on pushing her brother beyond his limits, stood his father as a child, crying as his mother hit him for showing need, and then his grandfather's suicide in the wake of shaming circumstances he could not control. Here, in microcosm, is the exposure of a destructive cultural value "visited to the third and fourth generations" (Ex 20:5, KJV) and some of its generational roots.

Green Valley Church

When George became pastor of Green Valley Church, he knew it had a long reputation for conflict. The previous pastor was asked to leave, as were several predecessors. The congregational leaders seemed mystified by their long history of "bad pastors." George determined to love the congregation and work toward healing their deep wounds.

The church was founded almost 200 years ago by German immigrants. Many of the older members did not speak English until they started school. Most began as farmers on poor land that had been rejected by the more wealthy "English." Some had even arrived in this country as indentured servants. George noticed immediately that whenever problems arose someone would comment, "Well, we're just dumb Dutch." However, in other ways, the congregation saw themselves as better than their neighbors. They were pietistic, frugal, hardworking, self-sufficient and loyal to family and guardians of their shared traditions. Despite the long line of short pastorates, the congregation adamantly resisted change. Even after new members joined the church, the congregational culture did not change.

The previous pastors varied widely in their theological orientation and pastoral style. They seemed to alternate between ultra-conservative and extremely liberal. Some were staid and formal, others were folksy and informal. Leadership styles ranged from authoritarian to laissez faire. However, each pastor eventually became discouraged and ineffective. The church board would then ask the pastor to leave.

One former pastor, Otto, who preceded the short-term pastorates, stayed for about 20 years. Otto became friends with a self-styled occult healer named Tamok. Otto invited Tamok to attend weekly worship services and sit in the chair across from his own in the chancel. Otto also regularly participated in occult[2] ceremonies with Tamok and took pride in becoming a "Powwow Doctor."[3] Even after Tamok died, the chair was called "Tamok's chair." No one else was allowed to sit in it. When Frank, Otto's successor, heard this history, he removed the chair from the chancel, but it reappeared the next Sunday.

Frank decided that if Tamok's chair was to remain in the chancel, he would use it. He asked a visiting pastor to sit in Tamok's chair during a Sunday morning service. The visiting pastor later mentioned that he felt a cold breeze while sitting in the chair, and an overwhelming sense of someone trying to knock him off the chair.

As George became better acquainted with the congregation, he realized that many members held deep grudges against one another and their own family members. Two brothers, who attended services faithfully, had not spoken to each other for 25 years. They sat on opposite sides of the church and refused to greet each other. The choir gradually dwindled and then dissolved entirely. No one wanted to serve on committees because meetings were so full of tension. The church board meetings usually degenerated into a fierce argument—often about minor issues. There also seemed to be a pattern of undermining anyone who attempted change.

A strange subterfuge within the congregation soon began to grow in intensity. Sunday bulletins, posters for events and supplies for projects would mysteriously disappear, and then reappear after the event. George began to sense a strong destructive spiritual presence in the church building. Several times, he felt as if he were being pushed against a wall, or tripped in the hallway.

Finally, George consulted his denominational officials. They told him that each of the previous pastors serving since Otto had reported very similar concerns. George then resolved to conduct an official exorcism. Those officiating at the exorcism included a denominational official, Pastor George, several neighboring clergy from George's prayer group and a few experienced prayer ministers who were friends of the official. Neither the church board nor congregation was informed about the exorcism. During the exorcism, a large number of spirits were discerned and cast out. However, no one in that group knew about the history with Tamok, nor did anyone discern the presence of his spirit. Things improved dramatically for about six months, and then it became quite evident that all the negative attitudes and behaviors had started up again. George finally resigned in defeat.

After several years of pastoral vacancy and concern that the congregation would fold, the denomination assumed its administration. As Green Valley Church approached its 200th anniversary, Paul, a retiring denominational leader, saw the congregation as a challenge and asked to be assigned to the church. Paul was intrigued by the congregation's history, especially the relationship with Tamok. Paul had also trained as a shaman and sought the church board's permission to build a sweat lodge on church property. The board denied his request.

Although church attendance continued to dwindle, the anniversary celebration drew many lapsed members and former pastors.

Before the service, former Pastor Frank turned to a clergy friend sitting next to him and remarked, "Oh, I see that Tamok's chair is back in place." He then began to talk about the long history of wounding that did not get printed in the anniversary booklet, including sexual abuse, occult ceremonies at the parsonage, deep bitterness toward a neighboring congregation and family feuds. He shook his head and whispered, "Nothing will ever change here." The church continues to struggle.

Gail and the Pan-Africa Mission

Always a leader, Gail graduated from college with honors, and then went on for further study in her profession and in theology. She worked part-time and established a Bible study among her co-workers while she was in graduate school. An enthusiastic evangelist, she knew without question that God had called her to the mission field and did not intend to wait until she got overseas to begin serving as a missionary.

Gail began to attend weekly prayer meetings at the nearby Pan-Africa Mission (PAM) headquarters. Soon her life revolved around mission activities, and she spent a summer in Africa as a short-term missionary. The mission staff encouraged her interest and began grooming her for eventual long-term service. Two years later Gail went to Africa as a fulltime missionary.

Once she arrived on the field, life changed dramatically. At home Gail had been surrounded by friends and family. She was involved with activities in her church, the mission and professional associations. There was always more to do than time to do it. Now she felt so alone. Most of the other missionaries were married and spent their free time with their families. Gail did not speak the language well enough to build friendships with the nationals. She shared a house with Martha, a single missionary in her sixties, who spent weeks in the bush and seldom stayed in the house except to sleep when she was home. Servants prepared the meals and took care of the laundry and cleaning. Within six months Gail had read every book she could find on the compound. With no close friends, she began to sink into depression.

About a year later, Carla, another missionary replaced Martha on the team. She came from a mission compound that had recently been turned over to nationals. Carla had been on the field for about ten years. She was strong, confident, and spoke the language fluently. Gail and Carla clicked immediately. While Gail poured out her feelings of loneliness and frustration with language study, Carla listened and encouraged her. Carla, in turn, shared her pain over leaving a school that she had helped establish, knowing that it might deteriorate in her absence. Gail and Carla formed a warm friendship.

Within a year another single missionary, Joanne, who was about Gail's age, moved into the house. Joanne and Gail discovered they had much in common and immediately felt like kindred spirits. They prayed together for hours, studied the Bible together, and dreamed of ways to expand their ministry. They looked to Carla as a spiritual mentor. At first, Carla seemed flattered and enjoyed her role as teacher and counselor, but eventually things turned sour.

Carla began giving Joanne and Gail a great deal of literature on homosexuality to read. She made frequent innuendoes about their mental health and sexual orientation, and then had the field director confront them about their "inappropriate" friendship. Individually, she confessed to each of them that she had once had a lesbian relationship with another missionary in her previous assignment, warning them to keep her secret.

Carla told the mission field director that she felt Joanne and Gail had an unhealthy relationship and insisted that Joanne move to another house on the compound. She also announced a policy that Joanne and Gail were not allowed to travel together alone. However, she always blamed the field director for these restrictions. She also told the younger women that the field director had noticed that they were dependent on her and each other and seemed to have emotional problems.

While there was no clearly inappropriate physical contact between Carla and the younger missionaries, Carla sometimes used suggestive language and seemed to use touch in a manipulative way, giving or withholding affection to convey her desires. A strange pattern, alternating encouragement with emotional abuse, began to develop. Carla would privately affirm each of the younger women's skills and praise their achievements, then just as they began to feel confident, she would publicly criticize them or set them up for failure. She would pit Joanne and Gail against one another in a subtle competition. Joanne seemed to be her primary target. Feeling battered and discouraged, she did not return to the field after her first home leave.

After Joanne left, Jessica, another younger missionary replaced her. Carla took special interest in Jessica and turned her attacks onto Gail. After several years of Carla's abuse, Gail took an extended home leave, returning only after Carla became a regional director in another country.

Gail remained with the mission and vowed that she would ensure that this abuse of power would never happen again. However, the patterns of abuse continued to recur with different players. Interpersonal relationships would be healthy for about five or six years, and then another incident would occur in which a supervisor became either sexually or emotionally abusive to supervisees. In each situation, the supervisor was seeking power and felt threatened by the supervisee. Often, those supervisees were fired and went on to abuse others in their new context.

Gail continued to seek healing for the mission. She got a master's degree in counseling and carefully studied the dynamics involved in the cycle of abuse. However, that did not stop the dynamic from occurring. Sometimes former missionaries would stir up discontent among the current missionaries. At other times, the abusive behavior seemed to come out of nowhere.

After another major conflict arose, a prayer ministry team trained in generational healing became involved in assisting Gail and the mission leadership team. Current and former missionaries were invited to tell their stories and receive prayer ministry. Mission leaders asked them for forgiveness where that was needed. A genogram was constructed of the entire history of the mission. Points where serious wounding occurred were identified. The mission leaders confessed and asked forgiveness for their transgressions and those of the previous leaders. Inappropriate vows were renounced, curses broken and spirits cast out. A deep healing occurred. Although the mission occasionally encounters interpersonal struggles today, the sting of the generational wounds is gone. Relationships have become healthy and strong.

What's going on here?

In each of the stories, cultural and generational wounds continued to affect behavior and inflict further wounding on subsequent generations. The "generations" can be biological (as in families) or structural, as in organizations, churches, people groups or even nations.

The stories illustrate common patterns that recur in generational wounding. In each case, one or more of the Ten Commandments has been violated, either overtly or covertly. Idolatry, abuse, unfaithfulness, slander, murder (including character assassination) and jealousy are common relationship violations. Other patterns may include one or more of the following:

- A *grasping for power and control* often underlies generational wounding—from playground bullying to sexual harassment to protecting personal or corporate reputation.

- *Patterns of conflict, abuse, sexual sin and emotional distress* appear like pus in a chronic wound. These events often seem unrelated on the surface.

- An *underlying "bitter root"* not based on the current generation's personal experiences frequently occurs. Think of the infamous feud between the Hatfields and the McCoys.

- An *unexplained intractable depression or sense of low self-worth* may pass from generation to generation. This can be especially common among people groups that have been victims of violence and oppression. There can also a deep sense of unresolved grief over a long-forgotten loss.

- A *pervasive spirit of fear or lack of trust* may prevent solid relationships from forming. Workers may distrust management. Leaders may treat their followers with contempt, or even view them as enemies. Marriages fail.

- Generational *wounds do not usually heal with psychological intervention alone*. They *can* be healed by God through spiritual interventions such as deep level healing prayer and deliverance.

- Generational wounds are *often complex and may take time and repeated efforts to heal completely*.

We live in a "fallen" world. We are all wounded people, who live in wounded families, communities and nations. The prophet Jeremiah describes the dynamics of this deep wounding, "From the least to the greatest of them, everyone is greedy for unjust gain; and from prophet to priest, everyone deals falsely. They have treated the wound of my people carelessly, saying, 'Peace, peace,' when there is no peace" (Jer 6:13-14).

Jeremiah also indicates that there is hope for healing, and gives some specific insights into the healing process.

"Thus says the LORD of hosts, the God of Israel: Amend your ways and your doings, and let me dwell with you in this place... For if you truly amend your ways and your doings, if you truly act justly one with another, if you do not oppress the alien, the orphan, and the widow, or shed innocent blood in this place, and if you do not go after other gods to your own hurt, then I will dwell with you in this place, in the land that I gave of old to your ancestors forever and ever" (Jer 7:3-7).

Despite Israel's long history of brokenness and rebellion, God assured them, "I will restore health to you, and your wounds I will heal" (Jer 30:17).

We may not be able to heal our wounds, but God can and does heal. God chooses to work through his praying people to bring wounded families, churches, organizations and people groups to Jesus for healing. In the following chapters, we will describe ways to enter into that healing process, as well as examine the barriers that might impede the healing process. Jesus came to break through those barriers. We look forward to the day when these words from Revelation are fulfilled:

"See, the home of God is among mortals. He will dwell with them as their God; they will be his peoples, and God himself will be with them; he will wipe every tear from their eyes. Death will be no more; mourning and crying and pain will be no more, for the first things have passed away." And the one who was seated on the throne said, "See, I am making all things new" (Rev 21:3-5).

In the meantime, we have the privilege—and the joy—of participating in that healing process. Generational healing is a dynamic work of the Holy Spirit urging us to bring ourselves as we are, wounds and all, to the altar and into the light of Christ, for God's healing and reconciling purposes to be fulfilled.

For Reflection

Read Psalm 139 (below), prayerfully pondering what God is saying to you about your own generational heritage.

O LORD, you have searched me and known me.
² You know when I sit down and when I rise up;
    you discern my thoughts from far away.
³ You search out my path and my lying down,
    and are acquainted with all my ways.
⁴ Even before a word is on my tongue,
    O LORD, you know it completely.
⁵ You hem me in, behind and before,
    and lay your hand upon me.
⁶ Such knowledge is too wonderful for me;
    it is so high that I cannot attain it.
⁷ Where can I go from your spirit?
    Or where can I flee from your presence?
⁸ If I ascend to heaven, you are there;
    if I make my bed in Sheol, you are there.
⁹ If I take the wings of the morning
    and settle at the farthest limits of the sea,
¹⁰ even there your hand shall lead me,
    and your right hand shall hold me fast.
¹¹ If I say, "Surely the darkness shall cover me,
    and the light around me become night,"

[12] even the darkness is not dark to you;

the night is as bright as the day,

for darkness is as light to you.

[13] For it was you who formed my inward parts;

you knit me together in my mother's womb.

[14] I praise you, for I am fearfully and wonderfully made.

Wonderful are your works;

that I know very well.

[15] My frame was not hidden from you,

when I was being made in secret,

intricately woven in the depths of the earth.

[16] Your eyes beheld my unformed substance.

In your book were written

all the days that were formed for me,

when none of them as yet existed.

1. Which of the case studies above struck you as similar to your experience? In what ways do you identify with it?
2. How do you see the effects of generational wounds currently affecting your family, church, work environment or community?
3. Examine your own situation in the light of the patterns listed in this chapter. How do you see these patterns demonstrated?
4. For one situation (family, church, work or community), attempt to trace the wounds back through generations (biological or structural). What patterns do you see?

Chapter 2

Biblical Foundations for Generational Healing

Recently a frantic email arrived from Marjorie, "Someone in my church is praying with people for generational healing. I'm really impressed with the results, but our pastor says it is New Age and it has to stop." Within a week another email arrived from someone in another part of the country with the same concern. Be assured that, while the term *generational healing* is fairly new, it is not "New Age." Jesus came to bring generational healing. As the Apostle Paul attests:

> So if anyone is in Christ, there is a new creation: everything old has passed away; see, everything has become new! All this is from God, who reconciled us to himself through Christ, and has given us the ministry of reconciliation; that is, in Christ God was reconciling the world to himself, not counting their trespasses against them, and entrusting the message of reconciliation to us. (2 Cor 5:17-19)

Generational healing is essentially God reconciling the world to himself and giving us the ministry of reconciliation. The need for generational healing began with Adam and Eve. In the first two chapters of Genesis, we read that God created Adam and Eve *good*, in fact *very good*. God enjoyed bringing every good thing to Adam and giving him the privilege of naming each one. Finally, God gave him a human soul mate, Eve. God put only one restriction on this young couple—*don't eat of the tree of good and evil.* By chapter three, they had both eaten of that tree, causing shame, blame and discord to enter the world. Their relationships with God and each other suffered a deep wounding.

The next generation multiplied the sins of their parents. In a jealous rage, first son Cain murdered his younger brother, Abel. Five generations later sin had spread. Cain's descendant, Lamech, murdered a man who "wounded him." Interestingly, Lamech confided to his wives, "I have killed a man for wounding me, a young man for striking me. If Cain is avenged sevenfold, truly Lamech seventy-sevenfold" (Gen 4:23-24). Thus Lamech justified himself, using his position as Cain's descendant to wreak havoc on others. Human nature drives us to seek vengeance on our enemies—even if only by harboring bitterness in our hearts.

Even as the roots of bitterness pass from generation to generation, so blessings abound from one generation to the next. Adam and Eve had a third son, Seth, who seemed untainted by generational sin. He and his family were greatly blessed and faithful to God. After Seth's son, Enosh, was born, Genesis 4:26 records, "At that time people began to invoke the name of the LORD." Four generations later, his descendant, Enoch, continued the legacy and "walked with God" (Gen 5:21-24). Hundreds of years later, Hebrews 11:5 commended him as a man of faith.

However, the world around the descendants of Seth began to degenerate into great wickedness. God singled out Enoch's great-great grandson, Noah, and his family as the only righteous and faithful people on the face of the earth. Noah built an ark as God instructed, saving his family and two of every living creature. The rains came and the floods rose up, until only Noah and those on board the ark were left. God gave them a fresh start. However, the flood waters had barely receded when Noah got drunk and his youngest son, Ham, seeing Noah naked, sinned so grievously that Noah cursed him and his descendants. Before long, the descendants of Noah were taking the sin of Adam and Eve to new heights by building a soaring tower in Babel to display their power and prowess. God humbled them by garbling their speech so that they no longer understood one another. We still suffer the consequences. There are about 6,500 languages in the world today.[4]

These patterns of faithfulness and sinfulness, blessing and cursing, characterize the history of God's people—in the Scriptures and beyond. The consequences of sin and of faithfulness have clearly passed from generation to generation as curses and blessings. Throughout the biblical story we see God's faithfulness to unfaithful people and his initiatives to restore fellowship. By Second Chronicles, chapter seven, Israel felt secure and united under King Solomon. They had just completed constructing the Temple in Jerusalem. During the dedication ceremony, Solomon prayed passionately and then "fire came down from heaven ... and the glory of the Lord filled the temple" (v. 1). After that powerful public display of his glory, God appeared to Solomon at night saying, "I have heard your prayer...if my people who are called by my name humble themselves, pray, seek my face, and turn from their wicked ways, then I will hear from heaven, and will forgive their sin and heal their land" (v. 14). This message gives us clues as to how God's forgiveness and redemption can become efficacious in our own personal and corporate histories.

The rest of the story in the Hebrew Bible describes God's people falling into such serious sin that God allowed them to be taken into exile. At that point, we see examples of the process described in

Second Chronicles put into action by Daniel, Ezra and Nehemiah—humbling themselves (confession), praying (reopening the conversation with God), seeking God's face (listening to God), turning from their wicked ways (repentance) and experiencing forgiveness and healing, for themselves and their people.

Sadly, after periods of restoration, sinful disobedience invariably started over again. The Bible is unique among religious literature in that it does not gloss over the human failings of God's chosen people—in contrast to God who remains holy, just, loving and faithful. God keeps taking his wayward people back. His forgiveness is not based on their merits, but on God's unceasing love and mercy.

The prophet Jeremiah prophesied truth to a corrupt nation, who did not listen to him. Bewildered, he prayed, asking God for understanding, saying:

> Ah Lord GOD! It is you who made the heavens and the earth by your great power and by your outstretched arm! Nothing is too hard for you. You show steadfast love to the thousandth generation, but repay the guilt of parents into the laps of their children after them, O great and mighty God whose name is the LORD of hosts, great in counsel and mighty in deed; whose eyes are open to all the ways of mortals, rewarding all according to their ways and according to the fruit of their doings. (Jer 32:17-19)

In other words, we suffer the consequences of our sin, which affects our descendants as well. However, God remains holy, just, loving and faithful, restoring us to himself all over again when we repent and turn to him. We continually perpetuate this cycle of sin and return.

Sue's journey

Consider the healing journey of Sue, who in her first job out of college found herself in the middle of a nasty conflict at work in which everyone seemed to turn against one another. A supervisor was emotionally abusing supervisees creating a climate of lies, shame, blame and manipulation. No one trusted anyone. Sue left that job after one year, thinking that she had escaped a uniquely bad situation.

Her next job seemed perfect—until it became evident that one employee was stealing from the company and laying the blame on everyone else. The dishonest employee was fired and things gradually improved. After a few years of enjoying a positive work environment, Sue moved on to a position within the same company that she knew would be challenging. In fact several former employees warned her not to take the position. Most of them were in therapy at the time, trying to heal from the effects of on-the-job emotional abuse. However, Sue was young, idealistic and convinced that she could make a difference.

Within six months, Sue became acutely aware of why her friends had cautioned her about this job. The abuse of power manifested in lies, sexual innuendo, manipulation and denigration. Friendships were torn apart. Responsibilities were delegated without the commensurate authority to complete them. Employees were constantly set up to fail and often publicly shamed. She resigned in defeat, but several years later reconsidered when asked to return in a new role.

As she began her new position, Sue vowed, "I will make sure that the previous dysfunctional patterns will never happen again." A few years later they did happen again—and then again, and again. Each time, Sue was caught off-guard. The conflict seemed to come out of nowhere. Each time, she felt shame, guilt, anger and fear. Old memories resurfaced. She felt powerless to keep her vow. Gradually over the years Sue began to see that subsequent employees were, in fact, experiencing the effects of the original abuse. The abuse had been passed on from one generation of employees to another. Many of the wounded employees who resigned also went on to abuse others in new work environments. Sue became aware of third and fourth generations of wounding, some on other continents. Finally, Sue realized that she could not fix the situation. She even began to see that this pattern is common. She recognized that we are all sinful, wounded human beings living and working with other sinful, wounded human beings. ■

We will never find a perfect family, church, community or workplace. Even Jesus' carefully chosen band of twelve followers was rife with jealousy, power struggles and betrayal. However, through generational healing there is hope for breaking our bondage to imbedded patterns of wounding and sin.

Why does generational sin persist?

Christians are often blindsided by the persistence of generational sin. After all, didn't Jesus conquer sin on the cross? Therefore, shouldn't Christian families, churches and communities be different? The answer is *yes* and *no*. Christians are different in that Jesus has given us tools with which to resolve the effects of generational wounding and the Holy Spirit to empower us to use them. However, we live in an *already-not yet* kingdom. We remain wounded sinners; therefore, we continue to wound others. Why should we be surprised? British lay theologian G.K. Chesterton astutely remarked that original sin is "the only part of Christian theology which can really be proved."[5] All we have to do is look around us — or look within ourselves.

St. Paul wrestled with the reality of persistent sin in his letter to the Romans, recognizing that although God gave the Law to maintain order in society, it was primarily so that we would recognize our own sinfulness and be driven to Christ. He dramatically concluded by saying,

> So I find it to be a law that when I want to do what is
> good, evil lies close at hand. For I delight in the law
> of God in my inmost self, but I see in my members
> another law at war with the law of my mind, making
> me captive to the law of sin that dwells in my mem-
> bers. Wretched man that I am! Who will rescue me
> from this body of death? Thanks be to God through
> Jesus Christ our Lord! So then, with my mind I am
> a slave to the law of God, but with my flesh I am a
> slave to the law of sin. (Rom 7:21-25)

Eugene Peterson clarifies this dynamic by translating verse 25 in the *Message* as, "Parts of me covertly rebel and just when I least expect it they take charge." Previously, Paul had explained the trans-formational process that results from this battle within our souls:

> Therefore, since we are justified by faith, we have
> peace with God through our Lord Jesus Christ, through
> whom we have obtained access to this grace in which
> we stand; and we boast in our hope of sharing the
> glory of God. And not only that, but we also boast
> in our sufferings, knowing that suffering produces
> endurance, and endurance produces character, and
> character produces hope, and hope does not disap-
> point us, because God's love has been poured into our
> hearts through the Holy Spirit that has been given to
> us. (Roman 5:1-5)

We constantly live in a juxtaposition of peace and conflict, grace and vengeance, hope and fear. In the process, our rough edges get smoothed down, our focus moves off of self and onto Jesus and we learn to lean on our heavenly Father as we experience the presence of Jesus in our lives through the power of the Holy Spirit. We cannot orchestrate this process, we simply open ourselves to the presence of God and he works within and between us.

During one of Sue's most discouraging encounters, a colleague shouted at her, "You're hopeless, you'll never change!" Then Sue recalled the words of Paul to the flagrantly sinful Church at Corinth:

> Now the Lord is the Spirit, and where the Spirit of the Lord is, there is freedom. And all of us, with unveiled faces, seeing the glory of the Lord as though reflected in a mirror, are being transformed into the same image from one degree of glory to another; for this comes from the Lord, the Spirit. (2 Cor 3:17-18)

As long as we yield to the Spirit, we are never hopeless. Furthermore, Paul proclaimed,

> For it is the God who said, 'Let light shine out of darkness,' who has shone in our hearts to give the light of the knowledge of the glory of God in the face of Jesus Christ. But we have this treasure in clay jars, so that it may be made clear that this extraordinary power belongs to God and does not come from us. We are afflicted in every way, but not crushed; perplexed, but not driven to despair; persecuted, but not forsaken; struck down, but not destroyed; always carrying in the body the death of Jesus, so that the life of Jesus may also be made visible in our bodies. For

while we live, we are always being given up to death
for Jesus' sake, so that the life of Jesus may be made
visible in our mortal flesh. (2 Cor 4:5-10)

In other words, God uses this process of wounding and healing so
that we can truly recognize the glory of God. The Lord uses cracked
pots. Our experiences with suffering prepare us to become *ministers
of reconciliation* (2 Cor 5:17-21). We are indeed *wounded healers*,
a term coined by the late Henri Nouwen.[6]

Furthermore, even Jesus endured this process. The letter to the
Hebrews explains,

In the days of his flesh, Jesus offered up prayers and
supplications, with loud cries and tears, to the one
who was able to save him from death, and he was
heard because of his reverent submission. Although
he was a Son, he learned obedience through what he
suffered. (Heb 5:7-8)

The Father of our Lord Jesus Christ also hears our cries in the
midst of conflict, pain and suffering.

Engaging the principalities and powers

Generational healing not only deals with the effects of human
sin, but it engages the spiritual world. Original Sin opened the door
for Satan to interfere with human lives. God told the serpent, "I will
put enmity between you and the woman, and between your offspring
and hers; he will strike your head, and you will strike his heel" (Gen
3:15). We still live with the effects of that curse today. Because of
that, Jesus prayed for his disciples (and us):

> Holy Father, protect them in your name that you have given me, so that they may be one, as we are one. While I was with them, I protected them in your name that you have given me. I guarded them...I have given them your word, and the world has hated them because they do not belong to the world, just as I do not belong to the world. I am not asking you to take them out of the world, but I ask you to protect them from the evil one...I ask not only on behalf of these, but also on behalf of those who will believe in me through their word. (Jn 17:11-20)

Peter warned: "Discipline yourselves, keep alert. Like a roaring lion your adversary the devil prowls around, looking for someone to devour" (1 Pet 5:8). Paul gave explicit instructions.

> Put on the whole armor of God, so that you may be able to stand against the wiles of the devil. For our struggle is not against enemies of blood and flesh, but against the rulers, against the authorities, against the cosmic powers of this present darkness, against the spiritual forces of evil in the heavenly places. (Eph 6:11-12)

The armor includes truth, righteous thought and action, proclaiming the gospel of peace, faith/trust, salvation/forgiveness, the authority of the Word of God and prayer.

While many in contemporary Western culture view Satan and his minions as old-fashioned superstition, those with deep generational wounds usually suspect demonic involvement and express relief when it is recognized and addressed. Generational sins often include histories of occult practice, violence, trauma and deeply imbedded bitterness. Those wounds create a vulnerability to demonic oppression that may be passed from one generation to another. Therefore, prayer ministers who practice generational healing keep alert to the "roaring lion," praying for protection and release before and after generational healing sessions. We minister under the authority of Jesus Christ, through the power of the Holy Spirit (Mt 10:7, 8; 28:18-20), not our own. As the disciples discovered the hard way, demons listen only to those who speak in the authority of God, which comes through prayer, confession, repentance, forgiveness and often fasting (see Mk 9:14-28).[7]

Generational healing confronts the spiritual world in the name of Jesus through shining the light of Christ into the dark places in our history and claiming the freedom that Christ won for us on the cross. This is the heart of the gospel in action.

The gospel of peace: seeking shalom

The biblical understanding of generational healing is closely related to salvation and the concept of *shalom*. Often translated as *peace*, shalom actually incorporates all the qualities of a God-centered community—peace, prosperity, rest, safety, security, justice, happiness, health, welfare and wholeness. Christian philosopher Nicholas Wolterstorff speaks of shalom as "the human being dwelling at peace in all his or her relationships: with God, with self, with fellows, with nature."[8] The New Jerusalem described in Revelation 21:2-4 illustrates the meaning of shalom:

> And I saw the holy city, the new Jerusalem, coming down out of heaven from God, prepared as a bride adorned for her husband. And I heard a loud voice from the throne saying, 'See, the home of God is among mortals. He will dwell with them as their God;

they will be his peoples, and God himself will be with
them; he will wipe every tear from their eyes. Death
will be no more; mourning and crying and pain will
be no more, for the first things have passed away.'

The New Testament demonstrates a striking inter-relationship
between healing and salvation. Jesus physically and emotionally
healed people to restore them to a fuller, richer relationship with
God and the faith community. Theologian Jürgen Moltmann explains:
"Healing consists of the restoration of disrupted community, and the
sharing and communication of life. Jesus heals the sick by restoring
their fellowship with God."[9]

Theologian Thomas Droege expands this idea:

Since wholeness is more than physical well-being, the
healings of Jesus also effected changes in the meanings and values of those he encountered. Jesus consistently called people to repentance. He invited people
to turn away from those things that brought division
and disintegration into their lives and to become
responsible for their own health as well as the health
of others.[10]

Such a perspective points to an implicit and central goal of all
healing, restored community—both in the present and generationally
with those who preceded us and those who succeed us. In fact the
level of shalom that we experience today depends to some extent on
the legacies we inherit, and it also influences the lives of those who
come after us. This intersection of time and eternity is illustrated in
the Epistle to the Hebrews (Chapter 11) with multiple examples of
the work of Christ reaching back into previous generations who were
saved by their faith in what had not yet occurred in their time. They

in turn affect our own lives as a great "cloud of witnesses" continues to intercede for us (Heb 12:1-2; Rev 6:9-10; 8:4-5). The witnesses who surround us include those who have gone before us, either biologically or as predecessors in adoptive families, in communities, churches or organizations. Many of those witnesses passed to us a rich inheritance of faith, love and forgiveness. Others have passed to us the consequences of idolatry, persecution, violence, suffering and alienation, as the effects of their woundedness and sinfulness have impacted subsequent generations. These consequences affect us often without our awareness. Moving toward shalom requires healing these generational wounds—"laying aside every weight and the sin that clings so closely"—in order to run the race that is set before us effectively.

Biblical patterns for generational healing

The Bible records several notable examples of generational repentance and healing. Two of the most intriguing accounts appear in Nehemiah and Daniel.

Nehemiah, a Hebrew exile who served as cupbearer for the King of Persia (about 445 BC), heard from some traveling Jews that Jerusalem laid in ruins and the survivors were "in great trouble and shame" (Neh 1:3). Nehemiah recorded, "When I heard these words I sat down and wept, and mourned for days, fasting and praying before the God of heaven" (Neh 1:4). His prayer then turned into confession, not only for his own sin, but for the sins of his family and his nation.

> O LORD God of heaven, the great and awesome God who keeps covenant and steadfast love with those who love him and keep his commandments; let your ear be attentive and your eyes open to hear the prayer of your servant that I now pray before you day and

night for your servants, the people of Israel, confessing the sins of the people of Israel, which we have
sinned against you. Both I and my family have sinned.
We have offended you deeply, failing to keep the commandments, the statutes, and the ordinances that you
commanded your servant Moses. (Neh 1:5-7)

Nehemiah knew that he and his people were suffering both exile
abroad and devastation at home because of their present and generational sin. As he prayed, he recalled the promises God made to Moses
recorded in Scripture (Neh 1:8, 9). His prayer included praise, personal and representational confession (for the people and ancestors),
repentance and reminding God of his promises, making a claim based
in God's covenant with his people. He then determined to return to
Jerusalem to direct the rebuilding of the city wall.

In Jerusalem, Nehemiah organized and led the reconstruction.
When it was completed, he gathered the people to hear the priest Ezra
read from the book of the law. As Ezra read, the people worshiped
God and wept. The next day, family leaders began meeting with
Ezra for Bible study. As they studied, they immediately began rein-
stituting neglected worship practices they discovered in the law. A
spirit of joy spread among the people. A week later, the elders called a
solemn assembly, where they read from the law, worshiped, recalled
God's faithfulness and then confessed the sin of their ancestors and
repented. They clearly recognized that the suffering they presently
experienced had roots in generational sin.

They prayed,

Many years you were patient with them, and warned
them by your spirit through your prophets; yet they
would not listen. Therefore you handed them over to
the peoples of the lands. Nevertheless, in your great

mercies you did not make an end of them or forsake them, for you are a gracious and merciful God. 'Now therefore, our God—the great and mighty and awesome God, keeping covenant and steadfast love—do not treat lightly all the hardship that has come upon us, upon our kings, our officials, our priests, our prophets, our ancestors, and all your people, since the time of the kings of Assyria until today. You have been just in all that has come upon us, for you have dealt faithfully and we have acted wickedly....Here we are, slaves to this day—slaves in the land that you gave to our ancestors to enjoy its fruit and its good gifts.' (Neh 9:30-36)

Daniel found himself in a similar situation. Captured by the Babylonians, he was a bright young Hebrew man placed in a leadership training program in Babylon around the sixth century BC. In studying the prophecies of Jeremiah, he realized that the time for the devastation of Jerusalem was drawing close. He immediately began the same process of prayer, worship, fasting, representational confession and repentance.

Daniel explained,

Then I turned to the Lord God, to seek an answer by prayer and supplication with fasting and sackcloth and ashes. I prayed to the Lord my God and made confession, saying, 'Ah, Lord, great and awesome God, keeping covenant and steadfast love with those who love you and keep your commandments, we have sinned and done wrong, acted wickedly and rebelled, turning aside from your commandments and ordinances. We have not listened to your servants the prophets, who spoke in your name to our kings, our princes, and our ancestors, and to all the people of the land… Open shame, O LORD, falls on us, our kings, our officials, and our ancestors, because we have sinned against you. To the Lord our God belong mercy and forgiveness, for we have rebelled against him, and have not obeyed the voice of the LORD our God by following his laws, which he set before us by his servants the prophets.' (Dan 9:3-10)

Daniel personally identified with the sin of his people, even though he had not personally participated in it. God honored his humility and faithfulness. Several years later, after another time of prayer and fasting, Daniel looked up and saw "a man clothed in linen, with a belt of gold" (Dan 10:5, 6) who closely resembled a description of the risen Christ in Revelation 1:13-15.

Throughout Scripture, we see evidence that God's people perceived the effects of generational sin. The prophet Isaiah, upon seeing a vision of God on the throne, cried out, "Woe is me! I am lost, for I am a man of unclean lips, and I live among a people of unclean lips" (Is 6:5).

Jesus confronted the Pharisees saying, "You say, 'If we had lived in the days of our ancestors, we would not have taken part with them in shedding the blood of the prophets.' Thus you testify against yourselves that you are descendants of those who murdered the prophets" (Mt 23:30-31).

Stephen, one of the first deacons, identified with the sin of his people when he declared before the High Priest, "Our ancestors were unwilling to obey [God]; instead, they pushed him aside, and in their hearts they turned back to Egypt" (Acts 7:39).

The Apostle Paul put forth a careful argument in Romans that Jesus came to cancel the generational sin that reigned from the time of Adam. He concludes:

> Therefore just as one man's trespass led to condemnation for all, so one man's act of righteousness leads to justification and life for all. For just as by the one man's disobedience the many were made sinners, so by the one man's obedience the many will be made righteous.... so grace might also exercise dominion through justification leading to eternal life through Jesus Christ our Lord. (Rom 5:18-21)

Jesus continues to be our hope when we seek him to heal generational wounds. The author of Hebrews reminds us that although Jesus frees us from generational sin, we must invite him into our hearts and lives in order to receive the benefits of his grace (Heb 3:7-14). A distinct pattern becomes evident in the pages of Scripture. The consequences and patterns of sin pass from generation to generation unless the power of sin is broken through confession, repentance and seeking God for cleansing and forgiveness.

For Reflection

Read 2 Corinthians 5:17-19 (below) and meditate on what God is calling you to be and do as a "minister of reconciliation."

> So if anyone is in Christ, there is a new creation: everything old has passed away; see, everything has become new! All this is from God, who reconciled us to himself through Christ, and has given us the ministry of reconciliation; that is, in Christ God was

reconciling the world to himself, not counting their trespasses against them, and entrusting the message of reconciliation to us. (2 Cor 5:17-19)

Review the wounds you have traced through your generations at the end of Chapter 1. Look for one situation that strikes you and develop it into a case study by telling it as a story with as many details and you can remember.

1. Describe the situation and your involvement in it.
2. How did you first become aware of the problem?
3. What indications pointed to a generational wounding?
4. How did the recurring sin affect you personally?
5. How does the wounding affect your family or organizational system?
6. What strategies have you (or the group involved) used to deal with the issues?
7. How have these interventions affected you (and/or the system)?

Chapter 3

Spiritual Resources for Generational Healing

Although scripture provides us with deep insights into the process for healing the consequences of generational sin and wounding, it does not provide a specific formula. God may draw us into the process at different points; however, the basic elements in the healing process remain fairly constant. Drawing from Scripture, we will now look at four powerful resources and ten process steps for generational healing.

Resources for generational healing

We cannot practice generational healing in our own strength, abilities, or willpower. While counseling and psychotropic drugs may temporarily relieve symptoms of generational wounding, they do not get to the root of the problem. The wounds recur in the affected person, family, community, or organization and reappear in subsequent generations. When the wound-bearer is an organization or faith community, the generational sins may recur years after the original "problem people" are removed from the situation.

Four powerful resources lay the foundation for generational healing and provide wisdom and direction in the process. God's Word, the presence of the risen Christ, the Cross, and Holy Communion bring us into the presence of God and empower us through the Holy Spirit to minister in the authority that Jesus imparted to His followers.

God's Word

The Bible is an interactive book. Long before the printing press and now, electronic documents, email, and texting, God communicated directly with His people. Thankfully, over the centuries, those messages were recorded in what we now call the Holy Bible. Although the Canon of Scripture is officially closed, God continues to speak. Primarily, He speaks to us today through His living, incarnate, indwelling Word, brought to our awareness by the Holy Spirit, as we engage Scripture and attune to God's presence. Hebrews 4:12-13 explains:

> Indeed, the word of God is living and active, sharper than any two-edged sword, piercing until it divides soul from spirit, joints from marrow; it is able to judge the thoughts and intentions of the heart. And before him no creature is hidden, but all are naked and laid bare to the eyes of the one to whom we must render an account.

We see the power of the Word of God demonstrated throughout Scripture. When the people of Jerusalem gathered to hear Ezra read the law for the first time since it had been rediscovered in the ruins of the Temple, "All the people wept," and turned to God in repentance (Neh 8:9). The Psalmist wrote, "[The Lord] sent out his word and healed them and delivered them from destruction" (Ps 107:20). It is "a lamp to my feet and a light to my path" (Ps 119:105). Jeremiah prophesied, "'Is not my word like fire,' says the Lord, 'and like a hammer that breaks a rock in pieces?'" (Jer 23:29). Jesus Himself is the incarnate Word of God—God in the flesh (Jn 1:1).

In the process of generational healing, the Word of God often cuts through the mysteries buried with generations long ago to reveal sources of deep wounding and/or blessing. Certain words or phrases in Scripture will resonate with the person or group seeking healing as the Holy Spirit brings them alive in that person's or community's life and history.

■ For example, the words, "Do not be afraid," would jump out whenever Susanna read them in Scripture. At the same time, she would find herself trembling and feeling guilty about her lack of faith. Susanna sought healing prayer regarding a life-long struggle with depression. Both of her siblings also suffered from chronic depression, as did her grandparents, parents and nephews. She could not identify what made her feel so afraid, but she was constantly concerned about her own welfare and the security of her family. During a prayer session, the words of Isaiah 43:5 came to Susanna's mind, "Do not fear, *for I am with you.*" She then felt safe enough to revisit the family story of how her great-grandmother had been brutally raped and murdered when she was a young woman. At that point, generational healing could begin. ■

When a person has a rich heritage of biblical knowledge from childhood, the words stored in the heart will often come to the surface as living words from God in the midst of the healing process (Deut 6:6-9). Thus, parents convey a rich generational blessing when they teach their children the faith when they are young (2 Tim 1:3-7, Ps 78:5-8).

God also speaks by his Spirit through words, images or sensations that come to mind. A person may "hear" words such as *occult, adultery, abandoned* or *suicide* when viewing a picture or the name of an ancestor. They may see images of a violent death, or see scenes from an ancestor's life re-enacted in their imagination. Sometimes, the person seeking help will sense emotions such as fear, depression, anger or loneliness when recalling a particular ancestor. Often both the person seeking healing and the prayer minister will receive the same words or images. These apparent promptings from the Spirit are then tested by evaluating their consistency with Scripture and historical research.

The Risen Christ

In generational healing, most people encounter the Risen Christ in the healing process. Jesus appears in the person's imagination and conveys love, comfort, healing and sometimes gives specific information. Although this may seem surprising, it is merely the God of eternity breaking into time. In our world, we view the Cross and Resurrection as historical events. In eternity they are powerfully at work in what we experience as the present. Christ was present in creation and is present now.[11]

Paul wrote to the Colossians:

> He is the image of the invisible God, the firstborn
> of all creation; for in him all things in heaven and
> on earth were created, things visible and invisible,
> whether thrones or dominions or rulers or powers—
> all things have been created through him and for
> him. He himself is before all things, and in him all
> things hold together. He is the head of the body, the
> church; he is the beginning, the firstborn from the

dead, so that he might come to have first place in everything. For in him all the fullness of God was pleased to dwell, and through him God was pleased to reconcile to himself all things, whether on earth or in heaven, by making peace through the blood of his cross. And you who were once estranged and hostile in mind, doing evil deeds, he has now reconciled in his fleshly body through death, so as to present you holy and blameless and irreproachable before him. (Col 1:15-22)

The Risen Christ appeared in both the Old and New Testaments. He seems to appear to Abraham as Melchizedek, "King of Salem" (Gen 14:17-24; Heb 4:14-5:5). Daniel seems to have seen the Risen Christ as "a man clothed in linen, with a belt of gold...his body was like beryl, his face, like lightening, his eyes like flaming torches, his arms and legs like the gleam of burnished bronze, and the sound of his words like the roar of a multitude" (Dan 10:5, 6). The Apostle John saw him on the Isle of Patmos as

> ...one like the Son of Man, clothed in a long robe with a golden sash across his chest, his head and his hair were white...his eyes were like a flame of fire, his feet were burnished bronze...and his voice like the sound of many waters...his face was like the sun shining with full force. (Rev 1:13-16)

Other appearances in the New Testament occur both during and after the forty days before Christ's Ascension into heaven. As Stephen was being stoned, he saw Jesus at the right hand of God (Acts 7:55). Paul met Jesus on the Damascus Road as a "light from heaven" and heard him speak, "I am Jesus, whom you are persecuting" (Acts

9:3-5). After Paul's conversion, Jesus continued to appear to him in visions (2 Cor 12:1-4). When Jesus appeared as the Risen Christ to the disciples before his Ascension, he told them, "Remember, I am with you always, to the end of the age" (Mt 28:20). Should it surprise us, then, if he appears today?

The Cross

The Crucifixion of Jesus Christ poses the greatest mystery in God's plan. Jesus' disciples could not understand why Jesus had to die on the cross and the Crucifixion continues to baffle his critics, as well as his followers, today. Human logic does not expect the conquering King of the Universe to die a criminal's torturous death. Furthermore, the Crucifixion of Jesus is not only a historical event, but a continuous healing work that no one fully understands. On the one hand, Jesus' death on the cross was once and done. Hebrews 12:2 explains that Jesus "for the sake of the joy that was set before him endured the cross, disregarding its shame, and has taken his seat at the right hand of the throne of God." On the other hand, we continue to experience power of the cross today. Paul explained to the Corinthian church, "For the message about the cross is foolishness to those who are perishing, but to us who are being saved it is the power of God" (1 Cor 1:18).

Isaiah prophesied:

> Surely he has borne our infirmities and carried our diseases; yet we accounted him stricken, struck down by God, and afflicted. But he was wounded for our transgressions, crushed for our iniquities; upon him was the punishment that made us whole, and by his bruises we are healed. (Is 53:4, 5)

To the Church in Ephesus, Paul further explained how the cross reconciles Jews and gentiles:

> He has abolished the law with its commandments and ordinances, that he might create in himself one new humanity in place of the two, thus making peace, and might reconcile both groups to God in one body through the cross, thus putting to death that hostility through it. (Eph 2:15-16)

The work of the cross continues in our lives 2000 years later, bringing power for healing and reconciliation. Peter explained, "He himself bore our sins in his body on the cross, so that, free from sins, we might live for righteousness; by his wounds you have been healed" (1 Pet 2:24).

Often, in the process of healing and reconciliation, people will be drawn to the cross in a fresh way. Sometimes they will see visions of the cross, usually with Christ on it—even those from non-liturgical backgrounds. However, those visions are seldom of a sad, lifeless corpse. Christ is usually envisioned as alive and active—speaking and reaching out toward them and others. The cross is usually bathed in blinding light. These mystical experiences are consistent with visions described in the Scriptures.

Furthermore, the Crucifixion of Jesus Christ on the Cross was the final blow to the evil one's principalities and powers. As Paul explained in Colossians:

> And when you were dead in trespasses and the uncircumcision of your flesh, God made you alive together with him, when he forgave us all our trespasses, erasing the record that stood against us with its legal demands. He set this aside, nailing it to the cross.

He disarmed the rulers and authorities and made a
public example of them, triumphing over them in it.
(Col 2:13-15)

Keeping a cross visible in the room when engaging in generational healing provides a concrete reminder to everyone involved—
including any demonic presence—that we minister in the power and
authority of Jesus.

Holy Communion

Holy Communion is often called the "Eucharist." The term comes
from the Greek *eukharistia*, which means *thanksgiving* or *gratitude*.
The root words combine the concept *eu-* (well) with *kharis* (favor or
grace). Since the Early Church, Holy Communion has been associated with healing. Through the gift of Christ's Body and Blood he
makes us *well*, forgives our sins and brings us into *shalom*—reconciling us to God and neighbor.

Jesus instituted Holy Communion at the Last Supper in the
Upper Room:

> While they were eating, Jesus took a loaf of bread,
> and after blessing it he broke it, gave it to the disci-
> ples, and said, 'Take, eat; this is my body.' Then he
> took a cup, and after giving thanks he gave it to them,
> saying, 'Drink from it, all of you; for this is my blood
> of the covenant, which is poured out for many for the
> forgiveness of sins.' (Mt 26:26-29)

In Luke's account of the Last Supper he added Jesus' statement,
"Do this in remembrance of me" (Lk 22:19). The Greek word for
remembrance is *anamnesis*, which means to remember something

66

that happened in the past so that we can enter into the event in the present. It is more than merely recalling a historical event. For Plato, it was a recollection of information that a soul had known before birth.[12] In the Christian sense, we see the effect of eternity interfacing with time as Jesus comes to us in Holy Communion to forgive and to heal the wounds of the past, as well as the present and the future.

The Apostle Paul explained this phenomenon in First Corinthians: "The cup of blessing that we bless, is it not a sharing in the blood of Christ? The bread that we break, is it not a sharing in the body of Christ? Because there is one bread, we who are many are one body, for we all partake of the one bread" (1 Cor 10:16, 17).

Furthermore, Paul tied Baptism and the Eucharist with the Exodus, thus including previous generations:

> I do not want you to be unaware, brothers and sis-
> ters, that our ancestors were all under the cloud, and
> all passed through the sea and all were baptized into
> Moses in the cloud and in the sea, and all ate the same
> spiritual food, and all drank the same spiritual drink.
> For they drank from the spiritual rock that followed
> them, and the rock was Christ. (1 Cor 10:1-4)

Paul also chastised the Corinthian church for abuses at their Eucharistic meals, suggesting that their irreverence at the Communion table was causing many of them to become weak and ill. Some of them had died. He identified their sin as receiving the elements "without discerning the body" (1 Cor 11:29).

Holy Communion remains a mystery. In it we encounter the Risen Christ in a powerful way that no one can fully explain. Jesus the Healer is still healing and reconciling past, present and future generations to himself and to one another. Jesus assures us that "Those who eat my flesh and drink my blood have eternal life, and I will raise them up on the last day; for my flesh is true food and my blood is true drink. Those who eat my flesh and drink my blood abide in me, and I in them" (Jn 6:54-56).

Interventions for generational healing

As we turn to the actual generational healing process, Scripture provides a fairly consistent pattern of interventions in the accounts in Nehemiah and Daniel described earlier in chapter two. These same patterns also occur in the Law (first five books of the Bible), the Psalms, the Prophets and the New Testament. Generational healing is more like a journey than a set procedure. It can progress quickly, but more often, it takes years. It is complicated by a wide web of relationships developed over a long time span. As one strand of rela- tionships is reconciled, another may appear, needing healing. We weave in and out of the process as new information is uncovered, or new crises arise revealing the need for additional healing. God often protects us from delving too deeply until we are able to handle the new information.

Step 1: *Awakening to the present influences of the past and calling out to God*

The first step that Daniel and Nehemiah took when they became aware of the effects of generational sin among their people was to call out to God, seeking wisdom and direction. God told Jeremiah, "Call to me and I will answer you, and I will tell you great and hidden things that you have not known" (Jer 33:3). James assured his readers, "If any of you is lacking in wisdom, ask God, who gives to all gen- erously and ungrudgingly, and it will be given to you" (Jas 1:5). We even read of Jesus himself calling out to the Father in the Garden of

Gethsemane as he took on the generational sins of the whole world (Mt 26:36-46; Mk 14:32-42; Lk 22:39-46).

This initial step of calling out to God usually occurs when someone notices repeated patterns of sin or wounding that seem to have no obvious explanation. Patterns such as sexual sin, child abuse, substance abuse, occult involvement, excessive attachments, fear, depression, violence, bitterness, low self-esteem, failure or poverty over several generations may seem impervious to change, despite attempted interventions. This is the phase of crying out, "Why?" "How long?" and "Help!"

The Psalms provide vivid examples of this stage in the healing process:

"Why O Lord, do you stand far off? Why do the wicked renounce God, and say in their hearts,

'You will not call us to account?'" (Ps 10:1, 13)

"How long, O Lord? Will you forget me forever? How long will you hide your face from me?

How long must I bear pain in my soul, and have sorrow in my heart all day long? How long shall my enemy be exalted over me?" (Ps 13:1-2)

"Help us, O God of our salvation, for the glory of your name; Deliver us and forgive our sins for your name's sake" (Ps 79:9).

This is the point of initial awareness that the problem may be generational and systemic rather than merely personal. Such awareness often drives the person to reach out for solutions, but it may not immediately follow into the phase of seeking God's face, or listening to God. Instead, the person might seek counseling, attempt self-help strategies, read books, attend workshops, take courses, change jobs or churches, move to another location or try other methods to fix the situation. However, when we call upon God for help, he continues to pursue us, nudging us to the next phase in the healing process.

Step 2: *Seeking God's face (listening to God and community)*

Nehemiah "sat down and wept and mourned for days, fasting and praying before the God of heaven" (Neh 1:4). Daniel "turned to the Lord God, to seek an answer by prayer and supplication with fasting and sackcloth and ashes" (Dan 9:3). The Apostle Paul wrestled before God over the generational sin of Israel until he saw from Scripture that he could not change things by himself:

> I have great sorrow and unceasing anguish in my heart. For I could wish that I myself were accursed and cut off from Christ for the sake of my own people, my kindred according to the flesh... What then are we to say? Is there injustice on God's part? By no means! For he says to Moses, 'I will have mercy on whom I have mercy, and I will have compassion on whom I have compassion.' So it depends not on human will or exertion, but on God who shows mercy. (Rom 9:2-3, 14-16)

Seeking God's face requires us to give up our perceived sense of control, or striving for control and self-sufficiency, and to listen quietly to God.

We see the movement from calling out to God to seeking God's face in so many of the Psalms. The psalmist often begins by crying out in fury or despair but ends in praise after hearing God. For example, Psalm 13 begins, "How long, O Lord? Will you forget me forever? How long will you hide your face from me? How long must I bear pain in my soul, and have sorrow in my heart all day long?" After his rant, the Psalmist begins to seek God's face: "Consider and answer me, O Lord my God! Give light to my eyes, or I will sleep the sleep of death, and my enemy will say, 'I have prevailed'; my foes will rejoice because I am shaken." Apparently God spoke to him because the psalm concludes, "But I trusted in your steadfast love; my heart shall rejoice in your salvation. I will sing to the LORD, because he has dealt bountifully with me."

Listening to God—inwardly and through others—does not come easily. We much prefer being heard. However, the Apostle James wrote to the early church, saying: "You must understand this, my beloved: let everyone be quick to listen, slow to speak, slow to anger; for your anger does not produce God's righteousness" (Jas 1:19-21).

As we seek God's face, we allow his grace to sensitize us to hearing him speak. God may then begin to reveal roots of generational wounding and give reassurance of his love and forgiveness. Sometimes he speaks through Scripture, wise counsel from a friend, or words and pictures that he plants in our minds. At other times he speaks through dreams (Gen 37-41), visions (Acts 9:3-5), angels (Acts 12:7) or other surprising events. The key task in this phase involves giving up personal control and agendas so that God can use us to bring healing and reconciliation into apparently intransigent situations.

Throughout the generational healing process, the prayer minister listens carefully to the person(s) seeking healing while at the same time listening to God. Jesus demonstrates this kind of listening in his conversation with the Samaritan woman at the well in the Gospel of John, chapter four. In doing so, he saw through her sarcasm and defensiveness to uncover the pain in her soul. Samaritans had suffered generations of discrimination from the Jews. Women in Middle Eastern culture were generally regarded as the property of men and had no voice apart from their fathers or husbands. This woman had been rejected by five husbands and Jesus perceived that the man with whom she currently lived was not her husband; therefore, she had no voice. Her encounter with Jesus transformed her so radically that she not only gained a voice, she became an effective evangelist among the Samaritan people.

Careful listening involves hearing beyond the surface and honestly facing the sin that is festering within the wounds uncovered. Jeremiah prophesied against the leaders of Judah because "they have treated the wound of my people carelessly, saying 'Peace, peace,' when there is no peace" (Jer 6:14). Generational wounds grow deeper and more painful when they are not acknowledged or if they are handled superficially. Jeremiah continues, "Thus says the Lord: 'Stand at the crossroads, and look, and ask for the ancient paths, where the good way lies; and walk in it" (Jer 6:16).

The Transfiguration (Mt 17:1-13; Mk 9:2-8) gives us a glimpse into a generational healing session in which Peter, James and John saw Jesus conversing with Moses and Elijah. In their excitement, they jumped to conclusions and immediately began planning an inappropriate follow up strategy. At that point, they heard the voice of God saying, "This is my Son, the Beloved; listen to him" (Mk 9:7). Only then did the disciples stop and ask Jesus questions about what they had witnessed—and listen to him. In the same way, the prayer minister who is leading a generational healing session, as well as the person(s) seeking healing must carefully listen to what Jesus is really saying as he appears in the midst of recalling situations in which generational sin and wounding took place.

Step 3: *Researching the sins, wounds and blessings of the past*

George Santayana's famous quote, "Those who cannot remember the past are condemned to repeat it,"[13] describes the dynamics of generational wounding. We live in a culture with a shallow memory of roots. America has always been a refuge for people escaping oppression, famine, war and personal demons. Our nation has also perpetrated those sins on others, such as Native Americans and African slaves, as well as illegal immigrants and child sex slaves today. Our history predisposes us to handle conflict by moving on, hoping for a better place, job, marriage or relationship and burying the past. Those buried wounds then arise to haunt us long after the actual causes are forgotten.

The Bible takes a radically different approach to the past. Running throughout its pages we read the *Heilsgeschichte* (salvation story), or metanarrative of God's people. Over and over, we read the story of creation, fall and redemption. It formed the heart of Jewish worship—reciting for one another and the next generation how God had demonstrated steadfast love and faithfulness to his unfaithful people. The New Testament continues this tradition, opening with the genealogies of Jesus. The deacon Steven recited the story, beginning with Abraham all the way up to Jesus, before the high priest (Acts 7). Paul told the story beginning with Adam in his letter to the church at Rome (Rom 5). The letter to the Hebrews carefully relates the Jewish worship heritage to the work of Jesus Christ and then recalls the faith of ancestors going back to Abel (son of Adam and Eve). In the Ten Commandments the Sabbath day was set aside for remembering "that you were a slave in the land of Egypt, and the Lord your God brought you out from there with a mighty hand and an outstretched arm" (Deut 5:15). These are corporate histories into which we have been grafted through Christ (Rom 11:11-24).

However, our own history—largely forgotten (or rewritten)—may not carry that same sense of shared community or continuity. Many North Americans have tended to value autonomy, individualism and personal achievement over heritage, faithfulness and reconciliation. Generational healing delves into politically incorrect territory. It involves revealing the secret sins and wounds of the past to expose them to the light of Christ. It also gives us the opportunity to discover and celebrate the long strands of goodness and faithfulness in our heritage.

Step 4: *Searching the heart of God for our lineages*

Often, we do not know how to pray for our lineages. Much of what we think we know about these lineages may be mere speculation, based on incomplete information. We may also be making assumptions from what we read in the Scriptures that are informed more by our culture and traditions than by the revelation of the Holy Spirit.

The prophet Isaiah enjoined us to "Seek the Lord while he may be found, call upon him while he is near" (Isaiah 55:6). Jesus told us, "Ask, and it will be given you; search, and you will find; knock, and the door shall be opened for you" (Mt 7:7). The Apostle Paul further reminds us:

> Likewise the Spirit helps us in our weakness; for we do not know how to pray as we ought, but that very Spirit intercedes with sighs too deep for words. And God, who searches the heart, knows what is the mind of the Spirit, because the Spirit intercedes for the saints according to the will of God. (Rom 8:26)

When searching for God's heart, be prepared for surprises, though.

We see the prophet Daniel, grieved by Israel's sin, seeking God when he writes, "Then I turned to the Lord God, to seek an answer by prayer and supplication with fasting and sackcloth and ashes. I prayed to the LORD my God and made confession" (Dan 9:3-4). It seems that Jesus himself showed up (Dan 10:5-6) and gave him insight into the spiritual warfare in the heavens and the coming final victory over sin and death (Dan 10-12).

When the early disciples sought the Lord about how to deal with persecution from the Jews, the Holy Spirit came upon them and turned the Scripture they were quoting to God into a whole new way of living (Acts 4). Later, when the Apostle Paul sought the Lord for his own Jewish people, the Holy Spirit revealed a radically new understanding about the children of Abraham (Rom 9).

Often, when we pray generational healing prayers, the Lord will use our imagination to show us what our forebears experienced, thought and prayed. He may give visions, dreams or words of knowledge about long dead predecessors and their relationships with others. Frequently both the prayer ministers and the person receiving prayer ministry will "see" or "hear" the same thing. At other times, a prayer minister will receive a vision, dream or Scripture passage which, when shared with the person being prayed for, will resonate strongly with the person. All these apparent revelations must be tested, both by Scripture and by the confirmation of others to be sure that it is truly from God, and not merely conjecture or wishful thinking (see 2 Cor 13:5-9; 1 Thes 5:19-22; 1 Jn 4:1-3).

Step 5: *Humbly confessing, personally and representationally*

The first mention of confession in Scripture occurs in Leviticus 5:5, "When you realize your guilt in any of these [sins], you shall confess the sin that you have committed." The Lord then outlined the proper ways to atone for those sins. Previously, the response to sin had been to hide from God (Adam and Eve), lie and walk away from the Lord (Cain), spiral into evil and violence (Noah's contemporaries, residents of Sodom), blame God or Moses (the Israelites in the wilderness). However, the times of revival in Scripture—and in more recent history—were always preceded by a period of confession.

"While Ezra prayed and made confession, weeping and throwing himself down before the house of God, a very great assembly of men, women and children gathered to him out of Israel; the people wept bitterly," Ezra told the people, "Now make confession to the Lord the God of your ancestors, to do his will" (Ezr 10:1, 10). Their confession led to mass repentance and reordering of their lives according to God's law.

Confession is often the key that unlocks the secrets of the heart. Once the sins are out in the open, then forgiveness, repentance, healing and reconciliation can follow. The psalmist described this process. "Then I acknowledged my sin to you, and did not hide my iniquity; I said, 'I will confess my transgressions to the Lord,' and you forgave the guilt of my sin" (Ps 32:5). Proverbs explains, "No one who conceals transgressions will prosper, but one who confesses and forsakes them will obtain mercy" (Pr 28:13). Confession is the appropriate response to the holiness of God. When Isaiah saw God on the throne, he responded by crying out, "Woe is me! I am lost, for I am a man of unclean lips, and I live among a people of unclean lips; yet my eyes have seen the King, the Lord of Hosts!" (Is 6:5).

The New Testament reinforces the importance of confession. "Therefore confess your sins to one another, and pray for one another, so that you may be healed" (Jas 5:16). "If we confess our sins, he who is faithful and just will forgive our sins and cleanse us from all unrighteousness" (1 Jn 1:9). Both public and private confession was incorporated into the worship life of the early church and continues to this day.

Step 6: *Apologizing, asking forgiveness and forgiving*

Forgiveness begins with God forgiving us, but cannot stop there. To fully receive forgiveness, we will apologize and ask for forgiveness. Furthermore, when Jesus taught his followers to pray, he told them to say, "Forgive us our sins (debts, trespasses), as we also have forgiven those who sin against us" (Mt 6:12). He then explained, "For if you forgive others their trespasses, your heavenly Father will also forgive you; but if you do not forgive others, neither will your Father forgive your trespasses" (Mt 6:14-15). Forgiveness is not optional for the Christian. It is foundational for a life of faith.

Forgiving is not condoning. God repeatedly forgave the sins of his people as documented in the Scriptures; however, he also expected them to turn from their sinful ways and return to him. Furthermore, he allows us to experience the consequences of our sins. He allowed Israel to go into exile and suffer cruel oppression from their captors so that they could see their need for God. The prophet Hosea gives us a glimpse into God's tender mercy and forgiveness, even when his people go astray:

> When Israel was a child, I loved him, and out of Egypt I called my son. The more I called them, the more they went from me; they kept sacrificing to the Baals, and offering incense to idols. Yet it was I who taught Ephraim to walk, I took them up in my arms; but they did not know that I healed them. I led them with cords of human kindness, with bands of love. I was to them like those who lift infants to their cheeks. I bent down to them and fed them. (Hos 11:1-4)

In the same way, God expects us to forgive those who sin against us, even when the sin is heinous. However, that does not mean putting ourselves in harm's way by returning to an abusive relationship or rescuing a wayward child from the consequences of irresponsibility. It does not mean keeping family or community secrets when to do so might allow potential harm to others.

Unforgiveness becomes fertile soil for bitter roots to grow. We see the generational effects of the roots of bitterness explained in Hebrews: "Pursue peace with everyone, and the holiness without which no one will see the Lord. See to it that no one fails to obtain the grace of God; that no root of bitterness springs up and causes trouble, and through it many become defiled" (Heb 12:14-15).

Those bitter roots grow under the surface, but they affect everything that sprouts from them. When roots of a family tree, a church, an organization or a community were not planted in peace and holiness, the sins and their consequences pass on from generation to generation. Fear, distrust, prejudice, sexual unfaithfulness, abusive behavior, substance abuse, poor self-image, depression, idolatry and familiar spirits can mysteriously pass from parent to children over so many years that the original source of bitterness is long forgotten. They may skip some generations, but recur later—a pattern that is evident in the long list of kings in the Old Testament. Good kings had evil sons, and then the next generation would be faithful, but their children would fall into idolatry.

Generational healing gives us the opportunity to confess, repent, forgive and ask forgiveness for the sins of the past as representatives of our ancestors. Jesus gave his followers profound authority in this regard, saying, "Truly I tell you, whatever you bind on earth will be bound in heaven, and whatever you loose on earth will be loosed in heaven" (Mt 18:18). So that, even if a person is already dead, a descendant's forgiveness can release present generations and perhaps even the deceased ancestor from the bondage still carried from the ancestors' sins and wounds.

Step 7: *Repenting: renouncing the old and asserting the new*

Once sin has been confessed, and forgiveness has been given and received, the next step is repentance, which involves turning away from sin and doing good (Eze 14:6; 18:30; 33:11; Is 45:22; 55:7; Joel 2:12-13, Mt 3:8, Rev 2:5). Primarily it means returning to God in obedience and faithfulness (Is 30:15; 55:7; Joel 2:13; 1 Pet 2:24-25). Sin is essentially the actions and attitudes that separate us from God and his righteousness; hence, when we return to God, our behavior changes to reflect the character of God. Repentance is more than remorse or saying, "I'm sorry," although that may be the first step.

In Revelation, chapters two and three, the Risen Christ appeared to the Apostle John in a vision. He gave instructions for repentance to churches in Asia, including very specific directions for changing sinful attitudes and behaviors. Genuine repentance leads to transformation. The Apostle Paul wrote to the Church in Rome:

> I appeal to you therefore, brothers and sisters, by the mercies of God, to present your bodies as a living sacrifice, holy and acceptable to God, which is your spiritual worship. Do not be conformed to this world, but be transformed by the renewing of your minds, so that you may discern what is the will of God—what is good and acceptable and perfect. (Rom 12:1, 2)

Repentance begins with a personal transaction with God, but does not stop there. We also must acknowledge our sin to the person against whom we have sinned and commit to change. Jesus explained in the Sermon on the Mount:

> I say to you that if you are angry with a brother or sister, you will be liable to judgment; and if you insult a brother or sister, you will be liable to the council; and if you say, 'You fool,' you will be liable to the hell of fire. So when you are offering your gift at the altar, if you remember that your brother or sister has something against you, leave your gift there before the altar and go; first be reconciled to your brother or sister, and then come and offer your gift. (Mt 5:22-24)

Jesus illustrated repentance in the Parable of the Prodigal Son, who returned to his father and asked to be treated as a hired hand: "Then the son said to him, 'Father, I have sinned against heaven and before you; I am no longer worthy to be called your son'" (Lk 15:21).

In generational healing, we may also need to repent for the sins of our ancestors or predecessors in order to be free of the patterns that bind us. Jesus called the Pharisees to repent not only of their own sin, but also the sins of their ancestors:

> You testify against yourselves that you are descendants of those who murdered the prophets. Fill up, then, the measure of your ancestors... Therefore I send you prophets, sages, and scribes, some of whom you will kill and crucify, and some you will flog in your synagogues and pursue from town to town, so that upon you may come all the righteous blood shed on earth, from the blood of righteous Abel to the blood of Zechariah son of Barachiah, whom you murdered between the sanctuary and the altar. Truly I tell you, all this will come upon this generation. (Mt 23:31-32, 34-36)

Jesus clearly held them accountable for benefitting from and continuing the violence done by their predecessors, and accused them of maintaining the same attitudes that led those ancestors to murder and oppress the prophets, sages and scribes in former times. We see similar effects of generational sin in our own culture. For example, the dominant culture benefits because our ancestors cleared land of Native Americans so that a European concept of land ownership could be enacted. Descendants of slave owners tend to be in a higher economic class than those who descended from slaves. Generations of slavery in which families were routinely broken up and sold to different owners—as well as slaves who were physically and sexually abused by their owners—continue to struggle with those legacies of violation. Although laws have changed, racial discrimination against people of color continues today and the benefits that the dominant culture gained from the sins of their ancestors continue through access to power and money.

Step 8: *Rebuking evil, breaking curses and restoring blessings*

Rebuking evil—casting out demons—was a key component of Jesus' earthly ministry, which he passed on to his disciples (and those of us who follow). The incidents recorded in Scripture about Jesus and his followers casting out demons range from the ordinary to the spectacular, but always demonstrate radical transformation of the affected persons.

After Jesus sent out seventy new disciples to "cure the sick" and proclaim that "the Kingdom of God has come near to you" (Lk 10:8), they returned awestruck, commenting "Lord, in your name even the demons submit to us" (v. 17). However, Jesus replied, "See, I have given you authority to tread on snakes and scorpions, and over all the power of the enemy; and nothing will hurt you. Nevertheless, do not rejoice at this, that the spirits submit to you, but rejoice that your names are written in heaven" (vv. 19-20). In other words, casting out demons just goes with the territory of healing prayer. It is essential, but that is not the major focus. Our focus must remain clearly on God and his in-breaking kingdom.

Another aspect of the Kingdom of God breaking into the kingdom of this world plays out in cursing and blessing. Blessing is speaking good over another person, place or thing. Cursing is the opposite— speaking evil over another person, place or thing. God blessed all of creation in the first two chapters of Genesis by declaring everything *good*. By Genesis, chapter three, sin entered the world through Adam and Eve's collusion with the serpent resulting in a curse that could only be broken by Jesus' death on the cross (Gal 3:13-14). The curse extended to people, the serpent (Satan) and even the land (Gen 3:17).

The Old Testament gives explicit directions for making and blessing holy oil (see Ex 37:29; 30:22-24) which we read the disciples used in healing prayer (Mk 6:13; Jas 5:14). Perhaps one of the most unusual passages about blessed objects comes in Acts 19:11-13, "When the handkerchiefs or aprons that had touched his [Paul's] skin were brought to the sick, their diseases left them, and the evil spirits came out of them."

From the beginning, God gave humankind a choice between blessing and cursing.

> See, I am setting before you today a blessing and a curse: the blessing, if you obey the commandments of the LORD your God that I am commanding you today; and the curse, if you do not obey the commandments of the LORD your God, but turn from the way that I am commanding you today, to follow other gods that you have not known. (Deut 11:26-28)

Both blessings and curses have real power. Consider the difference between a child who receives love and encouragement from parents and significant adults, and one who is told, "You'll never amount to anything" or "You are really stupid." Even our language, using expletives unthinkingly, carries power. Paul describes the state of those under the power (curse) of sin, saying, "Their mouths are full of cursing and bitterness" (Rom 3:14).

■ I (Judy) experienced this power of cursing one day while walking into a grocery store. I followed a young couple in from the parking lot. It seemed that each of them punctuated every sentence with "s___."

82

By the time I reached the entrance to the store, I literally smelled human excrement. Only when I prayed blessing on that couple and consciously broke the curse of negativity did the odor go away. ■

Blessing, on the other hand has greater power. Henri Nouwen explains, "To give someone a blessing is the most significant affirmation we can offer. To give a blessing is to affirm, to say 'yes' to a person's Belovedness. To give a blessing creates the reality of which it speaks."[14]

Jesus taught, "But I say to you that listen, love your enemies, do good to those who hate you, bless those who curse you, pray for those who abuse you" (Lk 6:27-28). Our prayers carry the power of Jesus Christ to bless and to break curses.

Step 9: *Praying for healing: inviting Jesus into our ancestral past to heal and restore*

The goal of generational healing is to bring all those involved in wounded history into the *shalom* of God that surpasses all understanding (Php 4:5-7). Praying with another person or group about the deep wounds from their past and previous generations brings the words of James into a generational application: "Confess your sins to one another, and pray for one another, so that you may be healed" (Jas 5:16). Generational healing prayer follows seamlessly from the previous steps. It includes listening, inviting the Holy Spirit's presence, identifying/recalling the problem, inviting Jesus into the problem to heal, blessing and sending the healed person out to bless others. Jesus Christ is invited to address the wounds of the past and heal those affected by their negative results (see Is 53:4-12). More specific explanations and examples of this kind of prayer ministry will be given subsequent chapters.

Step 10: *Reconciling actions*

Inherent in *shalom* is reconciliation. Healing is not intended to be a personal gift that we keep to ourselves. "All this is from God, who reconciled us to himself through Christ, and has given us the ministry of reconciliation; that is, in Christ God was reconciling the world to himself, not counting their trespasses against them, and entrusting the message of reconciliation to us" (2 Cor 5:18-19). The reconciled become reconcilers.

Because God dwells in eternity, time is not a barrier to healing. The Epistle to the Church in Ephesus contains a significant parenthesis: "(When it says, 'He *[Jesus]* ascended,' what does it mean but that he had also descended into the lower parts of the earth? He who descended is the same one who ascended far above all the heavens, so that he might fill all things)" (Eph 4:9-10). Peter further elaborates: "He *[Jesus]* was put to death in the flesh, but made alive in the spirit, in which also he went and made a proclamation to the spirits in prison, who in former times did not obey" (1 Pet 3:18-20). Our actions have eternal consequences. What we do today can counteract the sins of our ancestors, as well as bring *shalom* to those who come after us.

Jesus could bring back Moses, Elijah, Lazarus (Jn 11:43-44) and a widow's son (Lk 7:14-15) from the dead. What happens on earth has eternal significance because the past is still the present in eternity. Jesus continues to reconcile all things to himself—past, present and future—and gives us the privilege of being ministers of reconciliation to one another.

No more sour grapes

Both Jeremiah and Ezekiel comment on the Hebrew proverb, "The parents have eaten sour grapes, and the children's teeth are set on edge" (Jer 31:29-34, Eze18:1-4). The Jews recognized that much of their present suffering stemmed from their ancestors' sin. However, the prophets both warned and encouraged the people saying that God was bringing in a new agreement, in which they would be account-able only for their *own* sin. The bondage to (but not the effects of) old patterns and buried bitterness is broken by the cleansing power of Jesus' blood. Through this cleansing, we come into a more inti-mate relationship with God that allows us to hear his voice clearly and personally experience his presence and forgiveness.

Just as land contaminated with toxic chemicals must be tested and treated, generational healing traces long-standing patterns of genera-tional sin in our family, church and organizational history, exposing them to the light of Christ for cleansing and forgiveness. Sometimes this requires a lot of digging. As pockets of toxicity are revealed, more sources and contaminants may become evident. The genera-tional healing process is like decontaminating toxic waste affecting good soil.

Although we are not held accountable for the sins of our ances-tors, we experience their effects in the same way property owners may become ill from the toxic chemicals contaminating their land left by past generations. God *does* hold us accountable when we perpet-uate those sins by our actions, or by cover up and deceit. The purpose of generational healing is to remove the toxic effects of generational sin so that we—and generations to come—may be free to experience the fullness of God's love and peace.

For Reflection

Take a few minutes to silently seek God's presence, and then meditate on the words of Psalm 42.

As a deer longs for flowing streams,
    so my soul longs for you, O God.
2 My soul thirsts for God,
    for the living God.
    When shall I come and behold
    the face of God?
3 My tears have been my food
    day and night,
    while people say to me continually,
    "Where is your God?"
4 These things I remember,
    as I pour out my soul:
    how I went with the throng,
    and led them in procession to the house of God,
    with glad shouts and songs of thanksgiving,
    a multitude keeping festival.
5 Why are you cast down, O my soul,
    and why are you disquieted within me?
    Hope in God; for I shall again praise him,
my help 6 and my God.
    My soul is cast down within me;
    therefore I remember you
    from the land of Jordan and of Hermon,
    from Mount Mizar.
7 Deep calls to deep
    at the thunder of your cataracts;
    all your waves and your billows
    have gone over me.
8 By day the LORD commands his steadfast love,
    and at night his song is with me,
    a prayer to the God of my life.
9 I say to God, my rock,

"Why have you forgotten me?
Why must I walk about mournfully
because the enemy oppresses me?"
[10] As with a deadly wound in my body,
my adversaries taunt me,
while they say to me continually,
"Where is your God?"
[11] Why are you cast down, O my soul,
and why are you disquieted within me?
Hope in God; for I shall again praise him,
my help and my God.

Review your case study from the previous chapter in the light of the interventions described in this chapter. How have, or could, you apply them to your situation?

1. awakening to the present influences of the past and calling out to God
2. seeking God's face (listening to God and community)
3. researching the sins, wounds, and blessings of the past
4. searching the heart of God for our lineages
5. humbly confessing, personally and representationally
6. apologizing, asking forgiveness and forgiving
7. repenting: renouncing the old and asserting the new
8. rebuking evil, breaking curses and restoring blessings
9. praying for healing: inviting Jesus into our ancestral past to heal and restore
10. reconciling actions

Chapter 4

Dynamics of Generational Healing

Having worked for years with families in psychotherapy and witnessed powerful generational influences operating through bloodlines, I (Doug) became intrigued with the irrefutable pull of blood, belonging and culture. Human beings identify themselves by their ties to others. For example, I am a Schoeninger and a Purvis, my parents' birth family surnames.

■ Recently my experience at a family reunion of Purvis cousins brought this home to me. I was prepared for the usual common interest in our ancestry. Each of the seven cousins present and some of their children began telling stories and exchanging information about our common ancestors. We displayed an energy I have observed over and over again in families, to know our forebears better and, in imagining them and their lives, to experience a deeper sense of knowing ourselves, "who we are." However, I was not prepared for our excitement as we asked each other what we were each doing with our lives, what was most important to each of us and the values we most care about.

In these exchanges I heard and felt the reverberations and themes of our parents' and grandparents' deepest concerns (as best we can know them). I was amazed, and captivated, by the wonder of our common values seemingly woven into us across the generations spanning at least a century and a half. We cousins identified ourselves religiously, some as Christian, some as agnostic or atheist. Yet when it came to social values, how we view the value of persons and their care, we are very similar. Somehow a family legacy of values has infiltrated all of us with the sacredness of human life and human persons. Imagine my happiness to hear my atheist cousin using the same language to talk about her students and their intrinsic worth (she is a special education teacher) as I use to talk about my clients (I am a psychologist and psychotherapist). My cousins challenged me, "How can there be a God when believers fight each other and fail to follow the Gospel?" In this I recognized my family's historic frustration with Christianity over the church's failure to consistently stand for the poor and disenfranchised. My cousins asked me, "How can you believe and yet share the same concerns that distress us?" They then listened willingly as I shared my experience of the presence of God in my life and relationships.

However, other aspects of our family dynamics proved injuring and silencing. Relationships tend to get stuck in destructive and silencing patterns as well. These are equally honed generation to generation. It took an outsider, an in-law, to point out that we Purvises were not easily welcoming newcomers into the family conversation. In our family culture, outsider introverts were having a hard time getting their voices heard.

What is culture and why is culture an important perspective for generational healing?

Culture is the embodiment of the ways particular peoples creatively and habitually engage their world. Culture includes shared patterns of relating, loyalties, attitudes, behaviors and motivations, values, beliefs, identities, relationship expectations, rituals, prejudices, symbols, forms of creative expression and celebration. Cultural patterns live in and through families and are shared by larger multi-family groups and lineages. Cultural patterns are alive, as well, in other forms of affiliation that persist across time and generations, in social, religious, educational, governmental and vocational institutions. Even sports teams generate their own culture. Beliefs and mindsets also permeate whole societies and develop across many centuries. We share national, regional, municipal and geographic cultures. There is also a shared human culture that is reflected in the concept of a "collective unconscious." Ultimately, those ways common to all human affiliations connect us to Adam and Eve.

In generational healing we are touching both injured and blessed aspects of culture. Sinful patterns and consequences of wounding, as well as the blessings of love and forgiveness, have become part of the patterns that persist from generation to generation. These have become imbedded in the culture of every particular group lineage and its legacies. For example, a mission agency may carry a glorious legacy of effective evangelism, while at the same time harboring ingrained patterns of emotional and/or sexual abuse among key leaders.

As groups merge, the cultural patterns from prior generations feed into the joint culture. These legacies shape each new generation's choices and patterns.[15] We all inherit the good and the bad. Every culture is a mixture of constructive and destructive tendencies, those that promote life and those that diminish life. Culture includes the truly remarkable variety of life-giving ways peoples have engaged their walk in this earth together. It also includes the variety of ways peoples rebel against God, injure each other and harbor wounds in silence, in protective exclusions, in resentments and prejudices, in self-justified pride and superiority. A generational healing approach seeks to see the health and the dis-ease in our cultural ways. Then we are able to credit life-giving contributions that continue to give and to confess unfinished business, generations of loss, injury, violence and alienation that continue to infect crippling attitudes and actions. These patterns may even crystallize into social identity. For example, a historically persecuted group may identify themselves as victims. Those belonging to the traditional ruling class may see themselves as intrinsically superior. When each group tells their generational stories as part of the generational healing process, both gratitude and repentance flow. Appreciative and merciful understandings can then lead to corrective action through confession, forgiveness, repentance, healing, reparation, reconciliation, re-engagement and restoration.

The Christian perspective espoused here sets generational healing in the context of redemption and reconciliation. All participants and their relationships come into union with God in Christ. Repentance and re-engagement lead to healing. Participants turn away from that which injures and destroys and toward that which heals and gives life. Then they may re-engage the good that has been lost or marred. Our strength as healthy persons and groups depends on healing the legacies in which we are rooted and that continue to strengthen and weaken us. Our ways of seeing, valuing and relating become transformed to express the beautiful, mutually beneficial diversity of life in God.

■ For example, St. Matthew Church carried a legacy of several generations of youth workers who sexually abused members of the youth group. For years these youth workers were simply asked to resign without informing the congregation about the grounds for dismissal. This led to simmering anger among those who thought the youth workers were doing excellent work, as well as deep wounding of the victims who were sworn to secrecy and never adequately supported. When the problem surfaced again, the church board decided to inform the congregation and to bring in counselors who could help them deal openly and compassionately with the grief and shame. As victims told their stories, others from previous generations began to surface to tell their own stories. Board members openly repented to the victims and carefully initiated safe-church policies. ∎

Repentance and reconciliation both personally and publicly lead to healing and freedom to change. They can also influence redemptive changes beyond the immediate victims. Healed survivors often become agents of healing in their extended families and other affiliations.

Entering the Cultural Healing Process

The cultural healing process begins whenever we recognize that our personal distress is deeper than what appears on the surface. The distress may include:

- Anxieties
- Depression
- Distrust
- Separation
- Alienation
- Hostilities
- War

Something does not feel right, mentally, emotionally, relationally, ethically, spiritually or physically. The generational contributions to the distress lead to an awareness that current experiences seem to replay or draw disturbing energy from unfinished, unhealed or unforgiven events generations past.

A person will say things like:

- "This grief is more than mine. I feel like I am carrying the grief of many," where there has been much death through war, disease and famine in the generations.
- "I can't understand the intensity of my anger and bitterness. It feels like it comes from another time," when ancestors have weathered much oppression and dispossession.
- "I feel like I've been physically assaulted, but to my knowledge no one has ever hit me," where there have been generations of child abuse, sexual assault or racial beatings.
- "I'm always expecting the other shoe to fall, yet my life experience does not seem to justify the intensity of this expectation. I know my father always says, 'Don't get comfortable,'" where many generations were uprooted just when they had begun to reestablish their lives.
- "This racial fear and hatred in me, where does it come from?" when a person's heritage is filled with ancestors denying others (or being denied) opportunities due to race, ethnicity, or class.

The injuring encounters generations past seem to grip us claiming a voice and an address. Redemptive changes sometimes require a healing dialogue with our ancestral past and between present carriers of generationally distant injuries and animosities.

Generational healing work is about persons engaging aspects of their own consciousness that are shared with others, therefore culturally and generationally rooted. This is done for the purpose of personal healing and reconciliation between persons, within groups, with other groups and with God. It also fosters the recovery and creative reengagement of fading and dormant cultural patterns, values, symbols, art forms, rituals and other life-giving practices that express the heart and will of God for today. It recognizes and appreciates the potential gifts present in alienated groups though mutual dialogue and creative action among those whose ancestors were estranged.

■ For example, Marge, a woman in her late forties felt disturbed by continuing expressions of racial superiority in her family. She had concluded that her own fear of black men was somehow connected to this prejudice. She also wondered if she was projecting the shame she felt for her family's bigotry or their fear of retaliation from the descendants of slaves. She began a generational healing process hoping to dissolve excessive fear and lighten the grip of racial prejudice on her siblings and children. She chose a liturgy of Holy Communion as the context for her healing prayers. A Presbyterian minister led the service. Several friends and colleagues attended.

The liturgy began with covering and binding prayers. These included seeking God's presence, guidance and gifts of discernment. They also bound evil, especially any generational spirits that may have been part of keeping racial prejudice alive and strong generation to generation. Marge had done considerable research, pulling together available family history and drawing a family tree with data itemized and located on her drawing. She had also read pertinent historical accounts of the periods and places that concerned her and had been praying to receive impressions and images of what may have been critical sins and wounds still festering in current attitudes.

After summarizing all of this data and subjective impressions, those gathered prayed for focus and for further awareness of sins and wounds needing attention. Afterward, they shared images and words that came to mind. Marge's attention was drawn to the era of slavery and her ancestors in Georgia who had been slaveholders. She possessed records documenting the slave holdings of certain ancestors. Family stories had told of good relationships between owners and slaves. Family members also helped former slaves at the time of emancipation. Marge sensed that both truth and denial were embedded in these tales. During the group's prayers both Marge and others in the group began to see images of cruelties committed and curses sent against her family members in retaliation.

Marge offered penitential prayers with the support and intercessions of group members. She confessed her ancestors' sins, as she imagined them, as well as contemporary family bigotry and fear-evoking projections. She asked God for forgiveness for racial cruelty and the usury of slaves and especially for sexual abuses of slave women, asking that she and her children's memories be cleansed of the weight of these sins and that racial prejudice be loosed from her siblings, herself and her children, to be replaced with true contrition and remorse. She also spoke forgiveness to her ancestors for their ethical blindness and self-serving use of slaves, seeing as well the cultural idolatries and political and economic insecurities that shaped their lives.

As Marge's grief surfaced in deep sobs for all the suffering and cruelty she felt and saw inwardly, prayers flowed to break the power of retaliative curses that may have been invoked against her people by those who had been abused by her ancestors, especially against women in her family. Such curses might have been influencing tendencies toward sexual victimization and problems with procreation within her family. She was moved also to forgive those who had cursed her ancestors, understanding their rage and plight, and to ask for God to heal the consequences of her ancestors' usury, cruelty, enslavement and bigotry in the descendants of those whom they had injured.

As praying continued, others augmented Marge's prayers with their own, according to what they were imagining and according to their growing awareness of similar sins and wounds in their own families. During this time of penitence, there were moments when praying was difficult for everyone present as if they were trying to push through molasses. These moments were met with additional attempts to discern and bind any evil presences trying to impede or divert progress. Binding prayers seemed to clear the air and free the formation and articulation of confessions.

The service then proceeded to the consecration of the elements of bread and wine and to receiving the Body and Blood of Christ for the healing of wounds inflicted and wounds received, and cleansing persons and bloodlines of bondage to the consequences of the sins confessed. As Marge sat silently after receiving the consecrated elements, she experienced a distinct lifting of heaviness, shame and fear. She could see in her mind's eye, as if a video were running, her ancestors and those who had been their slaves reconciling with each other and with Jesus. After a brief silence, participants shared their prayer experiences with one another and then a closed with a benediction.

In this type of generational prayer liturgy those present often "see" ancestors reconciling with each other and with Jesus during this period of silent meditation after receiving Communion. Is this "seeing" the manifestation of a deep healing of the memories carried in the blood-lines? Is this a glimpse into the reconciliation that has been accomplished among those who have died? Is this a window into reconciliation going on in Jesus' presence in the spirit world as a result of the prayers of repentance and forgiveness just prayed?[16] Of course we do not know. We can only say that at times all of these possible realities feel true.

Marge's story does not end at this point, for the day after this liturgy tragedy struck and the healing process took an unexpected turn. About two o'clock in the morning, 38 hours after the healing prayer, Marge was awakened to a man of African American descent plunging a knife toward her heart. She turned to the left as she awakened and the knife missed her heart and cut into her arm severing sensory nerves. She instantaneously rebuked the man in the name of Jesus and he drew back. He then threatened to rape her and she again bound the evil in him in the name of Jesus. He drew back from his sexual intentions. As her terror dissociated into a distant corner within her soul, she somehow gathered the strength to negotiate obtaining a towel to help stem the bleeding and to search for the little cash she had on hand which he insisted she find and give to him. Finally he left cash in hand and Marge was able to summon the police. The strength of the moment, of course, gave way to shock and terror. Years of healing were required before anniversary nightmares diminished. Yet, in the midst of post trauma shock Marge heard an inner voice speak, "It is finished." She recognized the voice as Jesus and she knew he meant that the particular curses to which she had been subject from her ancestors' sins and the slaves' retaliations had been put to rest. How the deep peace of healing and the terrors of recent trauma could live simultaneously in her human soul is almost beyond comprehension, yet this was her experience.

Then the unanticipated occurred. Marge was met by racial hatred spewing forth from friends who came to support her. She cried to the Lord, "Please do not let what has happened to me reinforce this sin." Inwardly, but silently, she was pleading with her friends, "Stop this. It is finished. No more!" And then she witnessed her daughter's racial fears re-intensified. Marge inwardly cried out, "Lord turn this around." Without the strength to address her world directly, she persisted in prayer insisting that the repentance enacted accomplish its goals. Gradually the negative feeding on her trauma subsided.

Major healing came two years later when one of Marge's daughters became engaged to a man of African American descent. He knew Marge's story and felt no bitterness. His presence was healing in itself to Marge. One Sunday afternoon Marge was walking with her daughter and future son-in-law on the sidewalk of a busy city street. Approaching them from the opposite direction were three black men walking briskly engaged in animated conversation with each other. Marge panicked, trembling with terror as a flashback triggered. Without hesitation her future son-in law stepped between her and these men shielding her with his body. Her terror melted and the mutual care, person to person, black to white and white to black, descendant of slaves to descendant of slaveholders, cemented in their souls. Later, mutual exploration of their family trees revealed that their slave and slaveholder ancestors were from the same county in Georgia.

Our contemporary context

In our present North American culture, and in the world as a whole, powerful values draw people toward controlling, acquiring, image-making, power and greed. These values threaten ethical engagement between persons and the generational continuities of traditional cultures. At the same time we see many people moved to remember their ancestors and to value their heritages. In some cases people seek to recover lost values and ways of relating. We see this reflected in genealogical investigation and in the rise of ethnic studies, associations, celebrations and festivals.

Some people groups are tapping old generational injuries to exact justice through revenge against the descendants of those who violated their ancestors, rekindling distrust long submerged. On the other hand, significant movements of remembering are developing to help put historical wounds to rest through acts of repentance and forgiveness. The public generational confessions of Pope John Paul II on behalf of the Roman Catholic Church and its leaders and members, reflect this direction of accounting for past wrongs. The prayer work called "representational repentance" for the sins of one's ancestors/predecessors through voicing apologies to God and to the descendants of those injured, has been growing also in Protestant circles.[17]

Core concepts and convictions

Commonly accepted spiritual and psychological concepts, as well as clear Christian convictions undergird generational healing.

Often surprisingly, we see biblical concepts demonstrated in empirical evidence.

Intrinsic value of each human being: Generational healing work is rooted in the premise that each human being, from the first appearing on earth to the most recently born into the human family, is created in the image of God *(imago Dei)*, essential to the human family and deserving of consideration and mercy. All are equally pursued by God for eternal fellowship.

Historical consciousness: Generational healing work requires developing a historical consciousness. We realize that we are part of continuities, generation to generation. We inherit energized, invested ways of believing, seeing and relating and we pass on what we do with these to the next generations. The consequences of actions and attitudes of generations past persist into the present as active forces for good or ill. Each generation's necessary dependence on the older generations means that the senior generations' cares and ways, as well as their genes, shape and nurture the young. Historical consciousness also includes awareness that each moment is a history-making moment. Just as past actions have consequences that become the context to which we now respond, actions in this moment are immediate history to the next.

The movie *Pay it Forward* illustrated historical consciousness well. The movie shows people giving to someone, passing forward benefits received from another. Conversely, untended emotional wounds will also be passed forward by inflicting similar wounds on others. Earlier today I (Doug) was stood up by a friend who did not show up for a lunch meeting. I felt hurt and angry and inflicted this anger on my wife through undeserved irritability. On a broader scale, we see this pattern every time we read or view the daily news. Acts of terrorism, domestic violence and school shootings usually stem from emotional wounds harbored by the perpetrators.

Relationship between present and past: Our ancestors are a part of us. Their lives speak through ours in myriad ways. Their loves infect our joys. Every time I cook, especially with my children or grandchildren, I tap my mother's pleasure in my cooking with her and grandmother's pleasure in my mother being in the kitchen working side by side with her. Also, transgressions not turned from or forgiven are repeated generations hence. Unheard voices, pain unacknowledged, grief not faced or guilt not confessed cry out in blood lines, in locations and in institutions. They continue to speak, just as God told Cain in Genesis, "Listen, your brother's blood is crying out to me from the ground" (Gen 4:10; *New Jerusalem Bible*).

Generational healing breaks the power of this pattern through the cross of Jesus Christ. This redemptive action of Jesus through his death and resurrection, appropriated by faith and through confession, repentance and forgiveness, ends the cycle of evil and destruction.

Memory: Memory is the means by which past experience continues to influence present consciousness and behavior. We commonly use the word memory to refer to conscious awareness of past events—being able to picture, feel, or in some way recover the sensations of previous experience. This is *explicit memory*. Scientifically, memory has a broader meaning. It includes *implicit memory*, which refers to a set of past events that affect present events or persistent modifications of behavior resulting from an organism's past experience.[18] Culture depends on both kinds of memory. There can be no culture without memory because there could be no repetition of ways of thinking, believing or relating without referencing prior experience. Without memory there could be no habits or learning, no awareness of change because there would be nothing to change.

Generational healing begins with the assumption that everyone, past and present is a valued person, created in the image of God. The individual and collective stories of every human being and people group matter and continue to influence the present. By entering into the stories—told and untold—of those who have gone before us in a spirit of repentance and reconciliation, we honor not only the past but future generations as well. Ultimately, generational healing is the gospel in a nutshell, "All this is from God, who reconciled us to himself through Christ, and has given us the ministry of reconciliation; that is, in Christ God was reconciling the world to himself" (2 Cor 5:18-19).

For Reflection

Take a few minutes to simply listen to God, and then meditate on the longing of the psalmist in Psalm 43.

Vindicate me, O God, and defend my cause
    against an ungodly people;
from those who are deceitful and unjust
    deliver me!
²For you are the God in whom I take refuge;
    why have you cast me off?
Why must I walk about mournfully
    because of the oppression of the enemy?
³O send out your light and your truth;
    let them lead me;
let them bring me to your holy hill
    and to your dwelling.
⁴Then I will go to the altar of God,
    to God my exceeding joy;
and I will praise you with the harp,

O God, my God.
⁵ Why are you cast down, O my soul,
    and why are you disquieted within me?
Hope in God; for I shall again praise him,
    my help and my God.

Return to your personal or group case study. What cultural issues appear in it? Consider the ethnic, geographic, family and institutional cultures involved.

1. How have people been valued or devalued (now and in the past)?

2. How much do you know about your family or group history?

3. How were the group stories preserved (e.g., oral legends, written stories, songs, genealogy, official documents, audio/video recordings)?

4. Who could you interview to learn more about your family or group history?

5. If your case study is of a group to which you belong, why was your group/institution founded? What founding principles continue to influence present values and decisions? To what extent have founding principles been rejected?

6. In what ways have you sensed the presence of implicit memory influencing current behavior?

Chapter 5

How Generational Memories Develop

The day my husband and I (Judy) moved into our new home, my mother died. We traveled to Virginia for the funeral and then, with my sister, cleaned out her apartment. We returned to Pennsylvania with a trailer loaded with family heirlooms and incorporated them into our home. After everything was in place, my husband looked around and commented, "This feels like your mother's living room — but that's good, it feels comfortable."

The following year we traveled to Yorkshire, England, to explore my maternal roots (my grandmother emigrated from Yorkshire to Virginia in 1872). The first morning, as we passed the television in the living room of the Bed and Breakfast, we saw news reports about a bombing of the London Underground and several buses. However, despite the horror portrayed on the TV, I felt strangely comforted. Looking around the room, I saw the same pink roses on the walls and furniture as in our own living room, my mother's living room, and probably in my grandmother's as well (she died before I was born). This is where my ancestors came from — Yorkshire. I felt strangely connected to my forebears, and also calmed in knowing that they, too, had survived difficult times while leaning on the faithfulness of God. ■

The continuing influence of past experiences across generations implies some sort of inheritance of memories passing from generation to generation. If we use the broader definition of implicit memory—continuing influence or persistent modifications—we see how one generation instructs the next. Our ancestors pass on generational memories through their ways of seeing, valuing and living. Past experiences, both positive and negative, continue to influence future generations.

Children "feed" from their parents' and other caretakers' perceptions, attitudes, emotions, motivations, beliefs and patterns of relating. These become normative reality for the child. Children absorb and invest in their parents' and caretakers' ways of thinking and acting while creating their own ways of perceiving and living, and then pass these patterns to the next generation.

■ My (Doug's) daughter's and son's experiences as children with me continue to shape the ways they relate to their own children. They give their children experiences similar to ones they valued as children, recreating these experiences in their own way. I learned to cook from my mother. My father took up cooking when my mother became ill. I really enjoy cooking and follow their example. I became household cook when my wife became ill. My son is the chief cook in his family and teaches his sons.

My children also attempt to give their children experiences they wish they had been given as children, converting wish into practice. Thus they build from what they felt was missing in their childhoods. My daughter supervises her children's activities and friendships more intently than I ever did with her or my son. She felt that she was given too much leeway and seeks to address this concern in how she parents. ■

Each generation relates to the next one in ways that draw from memories of their parents' relating with them, as their parents and grandparents did. This constant drawing from memory is accomplished without thinking. It proceeds creatively and spontaneously, usually without conscious reflection.

Memory serves to transmit, recreate and pass on culture. In other words, humans create from what they have taken in. In this sense events long past, many generations ago, continue to influence present culture through the sequential enculturation of each generation. The meaning of any "way" is partly tied to events in distant generations, in that it partly evolved as a response to those events.

In addition to enculturation, ancestral memories (events in generations past) may also persist in their influence through genetic and epigenetic inheritance, group and place memories, the inheritance of justice dynamics, the presence of the departed, the action of the Holy Spirit, the spiritual dynamics of blessing or curse, or the action of evil spirits.

Genetic and epigenetic inheritance: Briefly, we can see that the action of human genes are responsive to human experience through *epigenetics,* the study of inheritable changes in the gene function that have an external origin but do not affect the underlying DNA sequence. The encoding that regulates gene expression is adapted to facilitate certain responses under certain conditions.[19] This encoding is passed from generation-to-generation and its presence manifests in propensities to respond in certain ways under certain conditions. If ancestors were repeatedly attacked, their homes invaded by hostile intruders again and again, a descendant might respond with fear and interior images of imminent intrusion upon hearing rustling noises outside her house at night. These tendencies to project danger could have some epigenetic basis.

Group and place memories: Numerous attempts have been made to explain the resonance between contemporary experience and past people, places and events. British biologist Rupert Sheldrake proposes a hypothesis of *morphic resonance.*[20] Through *morphic fields,*[21] persons not only draw their behavior patterns, thinking and believing, they may sometimes even access the actual subjective experience of certain ancestors.[22] The existence of such fields could explain the phenomenon of seeming to enter into and relive ancestors' experiences during generational healing prayers, during times of personal trauma and when in places where ancestors lived.

The existence and action of fields or some similar reality is also reinforced by recent reports that some heart transplant recipients experience the memories and behavioral tendencies of their deceased donors.[23] There have also been reports of children dreaming about their parents' traumatic experiences of which they had no direct knowledge.[24]

■ While no one knows for certain how these ancestral memories resonate within us, empirical evidence remains strong that such resonance is real and powerful. For example, last summer I (Judy) visited a museum where I came upon the breviary of a distant direct ancestor (16th century). I stood, transfixed and weeping, sensing the need to repent for the sins of her husband (my distant grandfather). In his greed, he had her declared "mad" and banished her to a convent, so he could claim her property and remarry. This event occurred 500 years ago, yet I felt her presence with me in that room. ■

The Scriptures speak of blood crying out from the ground (Gen 4:10), stones shouting out (Hab 2:11, Lk 19:40), of land hearing the word (Jer 22:29) and of God healing the land in response to a nation's repentance. When Isaiah proclaims, "Your ancient ruins shall be rebuilt; you shall raise up the foundations of many generations; you shall be called the repairer of the breach, the restorer of streets to live in" (Is 58:12), he is referring to more than physical rebuilding. He is calling up ancestral memories of community, of wholeness and brokenness. He is describing the restoration of the historical covenant between God and his people.

The inheritance of justice dynamics: In 1984, in the book *Invisible Loyalties,* psychiatrist Ivan Boszormenyi-Nagy brought to light justice dynamics in human relationships. He explains how trust and loyalty are grounded in justice dynamics between persons and the person and group to which they belong. Trust and loyalty grow between persons through direct address, seeking to heal wounds, rebalance inequities, and reconcile injustices; also through honoring those who have given to us by giving back to them and passing forward their blessings. As Boszormenyi-Nagy explains, "We regard justice as a multi-personal… principle with equitable reciprocity as its ideal goal."[25]

■ My grown children are eager to give back to me. Recently when I (Doug) became ill and hospitalized, needing surgery, my son rushed to be at my bedside, traveling across country. My daughters who live within an hour's drive were right there, within the hour. I could see their concern and pleasure in giving to me. Likewise my friends and psychotherapy clients seemed to be elevated by expressing concern for me, praying for me and writing kind notes to me. ■

Having received much moves us to give back to balance the scale in a relationship. This is an inherent justice dynamic. Appreciation, honoring what one has received, is such a motive born of value received in a relationship. Grown children, so deeply indebted to those who cared for them when they were young and helpless, often give back by giving forward to their children and grandchildren. There is often joy in a parent's or grandparent's heart when they see their children and grandchildren giving forward. They feel affirmed when they see their progeny investing what they have received in the next generations.

On the other hand, failure to honor and appreciate life received can stagnate a person in guilt that is hard to identify, depressing the person's spirit. This can burden life for subsequent generations as appreciation is left stagnant and unfulfilled, never taught and called forth.

In generational healing work, this is why we include appreciating life received alongside forgiving and repairing injuries. No matter how injured we are and our ancestors have been, we each have received the benefits of life given through the generations. My maternal grandfather's ingenuity and creativity, grown from his father's penchant for learning and forging new paths, continues to feed me and build me up, especially as I honor their giving.

This inherent drive for justice in any close relationship also manifests in attitudes and actions to repair or avenge injustices. Blame and revenge are attempts to repay another for injuries sustained. Usually revenge leads to further retaliation rather than reconciliation and then is passed forward down the generations of a family or organization. Ivan Nagy called this the "revolving slate" as children become parents and inflict harm onto their spouse and children similar to that which they received as children (e.g., domestic violence), or persons injured in an organization perpetrate similar injuries on those who subsequently join the organization (e.g., hazing or denying insider information to new members).

■ I (Doug) identify with this understanding. As a child I felt the expectation to father my father, to somehow make up for his father's suicide when my father was seven. I invited my siblings and father into a family therapy session, after which the therapist reflected to me, "Your father and siblings clearly look to you to lead, to be the parent." ■

The motive to repair and rebalance inequities in close relationships seamlessly passes from generation-to-generation. That which is unfinished or not reconciled between a parent and their parents, often becomes the task assigned to those most obligated and vulnerable to the parents, their own children. That which remains unrequited continues to pass from generation to generation. Early on, as a young parent, I looked to my children to lead me.

■ Bill also experienced justice dynamics passed down in his family. Bill's German cousins held his father (an American living in the US) accountable for the injustices their great-uncle subjected them to during World War II. The anger continued to fester. Why? Their great-uncle, upon his death, had left his entire estate to Bill's father, and had cut out those in Germany who had suffered his cruelties. In fact there were even more generations involved in this. Previously, Bill's great-uncle had convinced his father to will his entire estate to him, cutting out his siblings. ■

Such passing forward of injury and injustice can only be stopped through identifying the generational roots and reconciling with those who have gone before: appreciating the life and struggles of those who did harm and passed it forward. In most situations they were injured themselves. The cycle stops when the present generation forgives and then cares for themselves and their progeny.

Further, Jesus teaches the relationship between forgiving others' and taking in God's forgiveness. He told his disciples, "In prayer there is a connection between what God does and what you do. You can't get forgiveness from God, for instance, without also forgiving others. If you refuse to do your part, you cut yourself off from God's part" (Matthew 6 14-15, MSG).

Thus, refusing to forgive keeps us from taking in the forgiveness God offers to us and guilt stagnates in us, cutting off life.

Also, Jesus tells us to keep short accounts, to act on reconciling a relationship at the moment we become aware that someone is holding something against us and, I would add, when I become aware I am holding something against another. Jesus said,

> This is how I want you to conduct yourselves in these matters. If you enter your place of worship and, about to make an offering, you suddenly remember a grudge a friend has against you, abandon your offering, leave immediately, go to this friend and make things right. Then and only then, come back and work things out with God. (Mt 5: 23-14, MSG)

Injustices must be addressed and reconciliation attempted. Of course we cannot predict how another will respond, but admitting our wrongs and reaching out to "make things right" has merit, is Godly, and enhances our wellbeing.

The presence of the departed: Almost every culture recognizes the presence of departed spirits. Even our post-Enlightenment culture maintains a nagging suspicion that departed family or community members may be lurking in the shadows. We still fear "ghoulies and ghosties … and things that go bump in the night,"[26] even if we hesitate to discuss them in public.

The late British psychiatrist Kenneth McAll, discovered that some of his clients seemed to be "haunted" by spirits of those who died suddenly and traumatically, in drugged states or during acts of violence and hatred. These spirits seem bound compulsively to their earth-life, perhaps hanging onto unfinished business. They appear to cling to the living, infusing them with their subjective state and behavioral propensities.[27] Are these spirits trying to continue to "live" through the living, or calling attention to their plight and appealing for help from the living in order to move on? Sometimes they give the impression of trying to get the attention of the living in order to reveal something or reconcile certain relationships. In a sense their culture, their perspectives, habits and thought patterns persist in the living through the living person's vulnerability to their possessive, clinging presence. The presence and influence of departed human spirits, or *familial* spirits, is to be distinguished from *familiar* spirits— evil spirits masquerading as departed human spirits and intensifying "old" patterns formed in one's ancestral past in order to maintain Satan's grip.

Biblical examples of the intervention of departed spirits include Israel's King Saul seeking out the spirit of Samuel through a medium. Both were shocked when Samuel showed up in a foul mood (1 Sam 28:3ff). New Testament examples include Moses and Elijah appearing at the Transfiguration (Mt 17:2; Mk 9:2) and the story of the rich man and Lazarus (Lk 16:19ff). Jesus himself appeared to the disciples after his death and Resurrection.

The action of the Holy Spirit: Theologically, we say that God is all-knowing and all-present. We speak of the "eternal now." [28] All times, all events, all experiences, all moments of every person's life are present to God. In eternity, there is no past, present or future. God is completely present to every moment of every existence from the beginning of creation. God's complete knowledge and presence means that in God we are connected to any ancestral event and experience. The experience of entering into an ancestor's subjectivity might be the action of the Holy Spirit drawing us into the ancestor's world so that we might take action in prayer to right a wrong that needs human consciousness and prayer action in order to be made right.

Romans 8:26-27 assures us,

> The Spirit helps us in our weakness; for we do not know how to pray as we ought, but that very Spirit intercedes with sighs too deep for words. And God, who searches the heart, knows what is the mind of the Spirit, because the Spirit intercedes for the saints according to the will of God.

Furthermore, James 1:5 instructs us, "If any of you is lacking in wisdom, ask God, who gives to all generously and ungrudgingly, and it will be given to you."

The spiritual dynamics of curse and blessing: Past events may also persist in their influence through spiritual forces of curse and blessing. In a sense ancestral memory is contained in the blessed or cursed condition of present generations. Derrick Prince in his book, *Blessing or Curse, You Can Choose* (1990)[29] interprets the punishment to the third and fourth generation described in Exodus and Deuteronomy as a propensity to repeat the same sins and as blocks to flourishing. We certainly see both exhibited in families and cultures. Where sin goes unrepented we see a tendency toward repetition in subsequent generations—in addictions, prejudice, violence, war and sexual promiscuity. We also witness failures to flourish in repeated financial crises, early death, persistent despair, inability to fulfill goals and breakdown of relationships.

Generational cursing can also occur through sayings such as, "We're just dumb Dutch" or "We'll never get out of the ghetto." Sometimes it comes in the form of a physical ailment, "My father and grandfather both died of heart attacks in their forties; so will I."

The words become a self-fulfilling prophecy, with destructive effects, that are passed from one generation to another.

On the other hand, generational blessing can provide a wall of protection and predilection toward peace and/or success for subsequent generations. A parents' blessing frees their offspring to flourish. The faithfulness of a long line of ancestors in trusting God, manifested in Christian ministry and lived Christian lives, may yield further generations of faithful Christian leaders and protected fruitful lives. Blessings spoken and blessings received through trusting God can break the effects of cursing.

The action of evil spirits: Evil spirits, permitted access through generational sin, may strengthen inherited sinful tendencies in present culture—revenge, prejudice, greed, addictive attachments and fears of all kinds. Generationally rooted sinful cultural *strongholds,*[30] such as witchcraft, power-based spiritualities, attraction to violence, addictions to lust and greed, beliefs in racial or ethnic superiority and demonizing of enemies become places of evil habitation. Evil familiar spirits, masquerading as departed human spirits, strengthen such strongholds in families and organizations. Evil habitation intensifies compulsivity and resistance to repentance and change.

Discerning ancestral memories

A prayer minister or therapist, or the person seeking generational healing, may discern any or all of these means by which ancestral memories impact present lives and culture as significantly active in a particular generational healing work. Ancestral memories may uncover roots and meanings for present action, providing a reservoir of experience to explore. They also illuminate ways of seeing and valuing that shape interpretation and provide understanding and options for responding. Memory enables stability, belonging, continuity and identity in the midst of constant change. On the other hand, each moment is new and unique, each human encounter fresh and original. However, orientation to the moment depends on memory, which reveals the experienced continuity of self and others within it, as well as the meanings attached to it.

Memory carries the energies of unfinished business and lost ways as well as residuals from past wounds, shaming transgressions and former spiritualities. All of these seek voice, visibility, restitution, restoration, reconciliation and healing. We find these energies and their memories hidden in racial and ethnic prejudice, in gender expectations, in historical distortions, denial and idealizations.

Memory is the means of continuity in family, community and place, the faculty through which family and group culture exists and persists. Therefore, *remembering* is our primary focal point for the generational healing of family, community and place. Remembering refers to bringing something back to mind by an effort. It involves recalling and becoming conscious of the past. Healing often, but not always, requires remembering.

Of course generational healing can occur without conscious remembering. When our children provide an experience for their children that they themselves longed for as children, healing may occur in the adult children without conscious awareness of their own original injuring deprivation. They receive through giving. Memories are healed. In fact, deep ancestral memories may be touched with healing as cumulative deprivations passed from generation to generation, are finally addressed.

■ For example, I (Doug) witness my children working to provide their children with more father-presence and greater parental involvement in all facets of their lives. This is healing the impact of generations of fathers captive to work, parents lost through death and distance created through emigration and divorce. Their actions, in turn, bring healing for the culture they carry and are part of healing the culture that surrounds them. They address the realities of the culture common to many—the loss of father-presence in industrial society, as well as parental distance through divorce and separation from family members through emigration. ∎

Usually, however, healing requires conscious remembering. Past events, personal and ancestral, must be brought to mind, viewed from new perspectives and addressed in a redemptive, healing way. Such conscious remembering seems necessary when past experience and its interpretations continue to impact our present responding to the point of binding and imprisoning us.

For example, if I am bound by hate because my ancestors have been violated, I continue to hold the descendants of my ancestors' enemies in contempt. I determine that they must pay for my ancestors' injuries. I fear that if I see the descendants of my ancestors' enemies as persons like myself with the same longings and similar wounds and forgive them, I will be disloyal and expect accusations of disloyalty, even be disowned by my own people. Thus anger, prejudice and resentment continue. I may continue to revere my ancestors, extol their deeds and justify their violence. My sense of worth seems to depend on it. If I allow my ancestors' limited vision, their greed, their demonizing and dehumanizing of others to be seen alongside their bravery, creativity and industriousness, I fear that shame may overtake me and I may be lose credibility and standing with myself and within my family and community.

However, if I confess and repent of (turn from) my ancestors' sin, justifications that hold the superiority of certain ways in place will begin to dissolve. I can begin to question whether the culture I adhere to is really "advanced" and therefore entitled to dominate. Freeing present family, community and place from such captivities often requires active and deliberate remembering.

■ For example, I (Judy) grew up in a fairly "color-blind" environment as a military dependent. I lived on three continents and in four states before graduating from high school in New York. When I arrived at college in Virginia during the early 1960s, I was appalled at the racial prejudice and injustice that prevailed. I quickly became involved in the Civil Rights Movement. In doing so I risked everything from my credit rating to my academic standing, and at one point even my life. However, several years later, as a counselor at a Christian camp, some of the African American counselors (whom I viewed as my good friends) began accusing all the Caucasian counselors at the camp of being racist and demanding that we repent. I felt hurt and betrayed; however, several of us finally apologized to the African American staff for the sins of our race and repented for our ancestors, and of our own unrecognized prejudice. After doing so, the whole climate changed. The African American staff began to trust us with their stories of suffering and rage. We began to better understand their wounds and healing occurred among us.

Historical inquiry as a healing endeavor

Historical research can be a means of healing. Historical inquiry may provide a means that allows our ancestors to speak about their experience, their horizons, their philosophies and understandings, the substance of their lives, the events that shaped their life experiences, opportunities and limitations, hopes and dreams, losses and injuries. Historical research is an exercise in imagination. By envisioning the events, context and experiences of those who preceded us, we begin to view and interpret past events according to the values, perspectives and understandings of the times in which they occurred. Understanding the perspectives and experiences of our ancestors/predecessors in a healing way involves imagining events from each participant's side with their mindset, their way of experiencing consequences and the impact of events on their lives. We see their gains and losses as experienced and their views of appropriate, faithful and/or loyal action. In doing this for our ancestors/predecessors and their contemporaries we try our best to shed our contemporary perspectives in order to view the situations and mindsets of the times, and thus to honor the created personhood and the human struggle of all persons involved.

A good historical novel is an example of using imagination to reconstruct the impact of historical events on everyday life. Just as the novelist attempts to place characters in their historical setting, envisioning what it would be like to live through events of the time with the values and knowledge of the time, we can imagine our ancestors living through the events that shaped their lives. Reading novels about the events and places your ancestors/predecessors experienced, such as immigration, slavery, war, famine, persecution, wealth, leadership roles and life in their countries of origin may give insight into values, fears and emotional struggles.

Several criteria for approaching historical evaluation in a healing way are spelled out in the study by the International Theological Commission of the Catholic Church, *Memory and Reconciliation: The Church and the Faults of the Past*. Speaking of historical and theological judgment the document states:[31]

> The determination of the wrongs of the past, for which amends are to be made, implies, first of all, a correct historical judgment, which is also the foundation of the theological evaluation. One must ask: What precisely occurred? What exactly was said and done? Only when these questions are adequately answered through rigorous historical analysis can one then ask whether what happened, what was said or done, can

been understood as consistent with the Gospel, and,
if it cannot, whether the Church's sons and daughters
who acted in such a way could have recognized this,
given the context in which they acted.

What are the conditions for a correct interpretation of the past from the point of view of historical knowledge? Essentially, we must take account of the complexity of the relationship between the subject who interprets and the object from the past which is interpreted.

First, their *mutual extraneousness* (coming from outside of one another's culture) must be emphasized. Events or words of the past are, above all, *past*. As such they are not completely reducible to the framework of the present. Their density and complexity prevent them from being ordered in a solely functional way for present interests. It is necessary, therefore, to approach them by means of a historical-critical investigation that aims at using all of the information available, with a view to a reconstruction of the environment, of the ways of thinking, of the conditions and the living dynamic in which those events and those words are placed, in order to ascertain the contents and the challenges that they propose to our present time.

Secondly, a critical aspect of mutual extraneousness is the recognition that those persons whose actions are being examined in the historical events in focus are different from us. They had no knowledge of the impact or outcomes of their actions. As historian Karen Kupperman emphasizes in the preface to her book, *Indians and English: Facing Off in Early America,*

The key to understanding this early tentative period
is, as far as possible, to sweep away our knowledge
of the eventual outcome of the train of events set in
motion during it...to recover the uncertainty and
fear in which all sides lived, as well as the genuine

curiosity and sense of unimagined possibilities with
which groups of people approached each other.[32]

Thirdly, the concerns of persons in the times under consideration in any generational inquiry are unique to their moment, place, legacies, resources and social-political environment. Fairness requires that present regrets for actions taken by generations past include attempts to appreciatively imagine the circumstances, pressures, mindsets and worries of those times. To illustrate, according to Kupperman, the early modern English interfaced with Native Americans for the first time during a period when there was great concern in England with the blurring of social boundaries and their demarcations. Foreign influences were increasingly felt as pressing at the foundations of "good order." Traditional gender distinctions were threatened. In this context, the beginning and fragile dialogue with Native Americans was both a source for demonstrating the inherent nature of gender demarcations (through finding these in 'unspoiled' Native culture) and a threat to traditional social hierarchies and distinctions should too much merging with Native culture take place. Grasping the motives and actions of our early American ancestors requires imagining their horizons and concerns.

Fourthly, granting otherness to the subjects of historical inquiry is further enhanced by self-scrutiny, a look at how our own concerns and mindsets shape what we see. Dialogue with other interpreters, especially with descendants of other peoples equally involved in the historical events being explored, helps to reveal biases and to evolve the multisided representations which truth demands and reconciliation requires.[33]

This way of "doing" history, honoring each person's side, imagined in their time and context, is inherently healing. People whose voices have never been heard beyond their immediate kin, if at all, are finally given value in a public forum. Someone in the human community is honoring their lives or the lives of persons like themselves. Such historical voicing brings healing through finding the lost and enlarging the human record. Faulty justifications of past actions can be exposed, understood, appreciated and justly undermined. Tendencies to demonize or idolize our ancestors/predecessors may be put to rest.

Exposing the roots of inherited beliefs and motives deepens self-understanding. Dialogue between the various inheritors of the histories being imagined can open the possibility of richer and deeper understandings of self and others. Through such multisided historical imagination, still-active cultural influences—energies set in motion long ago still seeking resolution and rest—are exposed in a way that a freeing confession and repentance can be engaged compassionately.

For Reflection

Open yourself to God in prayer, meditating on the Psalm 90:1-12.

Lord, you have been our dwelling place
    in all generations.
2 Before the mountains were brought forth,
    or ever you had formed the earth and the world,
    from everlasting to everlasting you are God.
3 You turn us back to dust,
    and say, "Turn back, you mortals."
4 For a thousand years in your sight
    are like yesterday when it is past,
    or like a watch in the night.
5 You sweep them away; they are like a dream,
    like grass that is renewed in the morning;
6 in the morning it flourishes and is renewed;
    in the evening it fades and withers.

[7] For we are consumed by your anger;
  by your wrath we are overwhelmed.
[8] You have set our iniquities before you,
  our secret sins in the light of your countenance.
[9] For all our days pass away under your wrath;
  our years come to an end like a sigh.
[10] The days of our life are seventy years,
  or perhaps eighty, if we are strong;
  even then their span is only toil and trouble;
  they are soon gone, and we fly away.
[11] Who considers the power of your anger?
  Your wrath is as great as the fear that is due you.
[12] So teach us to count our days
  that we may gain a wise heart.
  Now go back to your case study.

If your case study is a family:

1. How far back can you trace your ancestors? What do you know about their social status?
2. What occupational pursuits seemed to recur over the generations?
3. What characterized the relationships among the family members over the years? Which of these characteristics (both positive and negative) seem to be passed down from generation to generation?
4. In what ways was the family system affected (or not) by the values, beliefs and practices of their internal culture?
5. What major crises did your ancestors face? How did each crisis affect the family system?
6. Identify the generational sins/wounds of the family system.

7. Identify the generational blessings/accomplishments of the family system.

If your case study is a church, organization or community:

1. Why was this church/organization/community founded?
2. What was the original mission? How has it changed (or not)? If it changed, what seemed to precipitate the changes?
3. What characterized the relationships among the members over the years? Which of these characteristics (both positive and negative) seem to be passed down from generation to generation?
4. What characterized the leadership over the history of the group—both lay and clergy or paid and volunteer?
5. In what ways was the organizational system affected (or not) by the values, beliefs and practices of their culture?
6. What major crises did this church/organization/community face? How did each crisis affect the corporate system?
7. Identify the generational sins/wounds of the corporate system.
8. Identify the generational blessings/accomplishments of the corporate system.

Chapter 6

Accepting Responsibility in Generational Healing

Over a five year span Jane watched her 96-year-old mother Anna become forgetful and frail. She could no longer live in her own home alone, so Jane and her husband Steven decided to care for Anna in their home. As Jane expected, her mother's presence in their home soon tested their somewhat healed relationship. A jumble of sympathy and rage rose up in Jane's heart whenever her mother tried to impose her will on Jane by saying things like, "You don't want that," when she really meant, "I don't want that."

"I thought I was beyond these reactions," Jane reflected. "All the years of learning to claim my own voice seemed to evaporate. I feel like a child again under Mom's constant attempts to impose her will on me."

Jane began to probe the roots of her mother's unrelenting impositions more deeply, asking the Holy Spirit to reveal the basis of her mother's behavior. She then began to see her mother, Anna, as a child, afraid that she would be abandoned by her parents and grandparents if she departed from their rule in any way. She had few opportunities to find and express her own voice. Anna had been left in Europe with her grandparents when her parents and siblings emigrated to the USA. She became terrified that she might do something to displease her elders and permanently separate herself from her closest kin. This new awareness helped Jane. She found herself more compassionate and understanding, even as her mother continued to tell her how to feel and what to want. Her mother's motive began to make sense. Consequently, Jane felt freed to be herself, to express her own desires and perspectives, even as her mother continued to try to impose her will on Jane.

More complete freedom waited, however, until after her mother's death. Grieving, Jane became increasingly critical of her husband. The logical pattern of his thoughts, his cool analytic style and his reticence to trust or express emotion constantly annoyed her. She also tore at herself with crippling doubts, magnifying perceived inadequacies as she embarked on a new career. "Is this Mom's voice, with her grandparents' intolerance, coming out in me?" she wondered. "I hate finding these attitudes in me. I vowed never to be like my mother." Then Jane realized that she was treating her husband as her mother treated her and as her grandparents treated her mother.

Jane spent a day working with her husband on his job. Appreciating his abilities and all that his skill had meant to her and their children further tempered the hold of judgment. Eventually, Jane could say,

> There is nothing final about Mom's stuck place, or my grandparent's judgments, or the legacy they inherited and passed on to me. They had their context and reasons and I have mine. I can be loyal to them by living my life. I can give my husband room to be himself. Free to be me, perhaps I can enjoy him. I have been holding onto my ancestors prejudice and inflicting it onto myself and onto him. I have new choices to make.

As Jane sought the heart of God for herself, her husband, her mother and her grandparents, she grew free to accept responsibility for her complicity, for continuing her mother's and grandparents' and more distant ancestors' judgmental intolerance of difference. As she accepted responsibility for continuing these ways, she was free to respond in new ways, to make new choices. As she owned her ties to her mother's and grandparents' judgmental attitudes, she was able to hand them their responsibility. She reflected, "They passed this to me. I picked it up from them. I modeled myself after them." And then seeing their narrow, ethnic-centered, attitudes about right and wrong, about *the only way*, she began to forgive them, saying, "Father forgive them for they did not know what they were doing."

What does it mean to accept responsibility?

Responsibility requires that we recognize and own our responses. Jane *owned* that she harbored a judgmental attitude and a narrow right-and-wrong assessment of others. Her mother and grandparents demonstrated similar attitudes.

Ownership does not necessarily mean that you freely or consciously willed the offending thought, word or deed. You may not have known whether it was right or wrong, or if it would help or injure. Jane realized that she had not been aware that she was acting judgmentally. She did not consciously *want* to be judgmental. Taking responsibility for an action retrospectively does not necessarily mean confessing that you willed it and are therefore culpable—or praise-worthy—for what took place in your past. As others make us aware of the consequences of our actions, we are in the position to confess faults we did not realize, or only faintly recognized, as faults at the time of the action. In a similar way, we may not be aware of the positive effects of our unintentional actions in the past; therefore cannot take undue credit for our benevolence when the effects are revealed.

Accepting responsibility includes *accountability*. We are accountable for our own attitudes and behavior. We have the social obligation to account for why we responded the way we did and to attend the consequences of our attitudes and actions toward others. Furthermore, we can seek to mend or amend any damaging consequences. Jane sought to understand the generational roots of her attitudes and own the impact of her attitudes on her husband, herself, her mother and her children and committed herself to change. She *repented* (turned in a new direction). In repenting she began to enjoy her husband as he is, to respond anew and to see him in his context, just as she saw her mother and grandparents in theirs. So *owning, understanding, addressing consequences, amending, changing (repenting)*, these are elements of accepting responsibility.

Why should we engage in generational inquiry and healing prayers?

When individuals or groups recognize that a present destructive attitude or pattern of relating seems intractable, they may begin to explore some of the generational wounds that occurred in the past. On further reflection, they may discover attitudes and relational patterns of prior generations of family, or predecessors of a community, reappearing in the present.

In families this may manifest as attitudes, behaviors or ways of relating that repeatedly surface in multiple generations, even when members no longer remember their precipitating cause. For instance, these patterns may include a tendency toward hoarding, depression, low self-esteem, unhealthy parenting styles, unsuccessful marriages, failure, prejudice or fears.

Communities, including churches and organizations, may recognize patterns such as a succession of weak or abusive leaders, a hostile work environment that does not change after apparent perpetrators are removed, ongoing sexual harassment, internal conflict, distrust, dishonesty or corruption.

In generational healing, we often pray about patterns of behavior that began long ago with persons we never knew. What is our responsibility for something someone else did? How can we respond to the event or person in a healing way that frees current and future generations? And how do we view the responsibility of those who preceded us and contributed benefits and burdens? The questions we must ask in generational healing include what are we *able* to do, *obligated* to do, *justified* in doing and *authorized* to do? Furthermore, what can we own as *ours* to do?

What are we able to do?

To gain freedom to change, we must enter into fair historical imagination. What was believed, said and done in prior generations? What attitudes were carried and enacted? What wounds and benefits accrued, and who among the living and deceased bears responsibility? Who were the actors? We do this *with compassionate awareness.*

Although we view our ancestor's actions and attitudes from the position of our present awareness as destructive or constructive, at the time those actions and attitudes may have been socially and religiously loyal, even thought to be in God's will. We bring to light, to the best of our ability, our ancestors' harmful or helpful behavior and express sorrow for the injuries caused and gratitude for consequent blessings. At the same time we acknowledge that these ancestors may not have understood their actions as unjustly injuring others or as blessing others. They may even have seen the injuries caused as justified, or necessary, or brought upon themselves by those injured. They may not have viewed their actions as violating God's will or following God's will. We must apply the concept of *mutual extraneousness.*[34] That is, we proceed with the understanding that we cannot interpret the attitudes and actions of generations past in terms of today's awareness and beliefs. We must attempt to imagine the mindset, the limitations and horizons of the periods we are investigating. We gain freedom only as we imagine the context, motivations and understandings of those who laid down the patterns from which we are seeking freedom. One thing for certain, no one acts with certain knowledge of what the consequences of their actions will be. You can anticipate consequences but one can never know what the actual consequences and ramifications will be.[35]

Consider the following beliefs held in prior periods of history in Western cultures that changed over time:

- The innate roles and natures of men and women and the rights and responsibilities that go with these roles;
- Assuming racial superiority, which justified the subjugation of one race to another, genocide, slavery and prejudice used to maintain economic advantages;[36]
- Presuming membership in a "superior" culture made one's goals righteous and entitled to use power to dispossess those whose ways interfered with progress;[37]
- Determining that children "should be seen but not heard," that children are inherently misguided, even evil, and therefore must be broken and made to conform.

Our experiences during generational healing prayers often confirm the Holy Spirit's activity in our understanding the context of our ancestors or predecessors. Frequently views of our ancestors' lives change dramatically during prayer. We are helped to see their actions compassionately, with insight into their concerns and struggles as persons in a historical context, as well as with insight into the concerns and struggles of those who injured them or whom they injured.

Experience reveals many degrees of responsibility.

- People of the era under examination may have been capable of knowing the wrong of the actions being examined. However, our ancestors/predecessors, or those who injured them, may have been blinded by their grieving and wounded hearts, and therefore felt justified in retaliating.

- Our ancestors/predecessors, and/or those who injured them, may have truly believed they were fulfilling God's will, especially in maintaining an order believed to be inherent in God's creation.

- Our ancestors/predecessors may have felt that something was wrong but had no ability to accurately understand what was wrong. Their guilt may have been misplaced, even assigned to the ones injured.

- Those preceding us may have been sensitive to the transgressions committed but overwhelmed with doubt or confused by the social pressures or perceived economic vulnerabilities of the times.

- The relative restraint of their actions in comparison with injustices they had undergone may have muted their sensitivity to harm done. For example in the United States, violence and genocide committed in the name of freedom and "manifest destiny" may have drawn powerful energies from the injustices and dispossessions that had driven the aggressing pioneers from their own homelands.

- Our ancestors/predecessors, and those who injured them, may have been silenced by real and perceived threats to their persons, their families, or their cherished institutions.

- Our ancestors/predecessors may not have been silent but rather overwhelmed in their protestations by powerful minorities who threatened others into silence. Perhaps they were killed or socially ostracized or severely sanctioned for their visible attempts at halting continued harm and unrighteousness committed against their own or by their own against others.

On the other hand, at times, when reading historical accounts, we are surprised by an unexpected degree of awareness of responsibility at the time of the injuring actions, a degree we had not expected from someone in that time and context. Thus we must be careful not to morally infantilize our ancestors/predecessors even as we grant them otherness, or to dilute the destructiveness of their actions even as we attempt to imagine the limitations of their horizons. For example Mansio Serra, a Spanish conquistador, and a conqueror of the Incas in Peru, wrote in his will and to his King Phillip II:

> For we have destroyed by our evil behaviour (sic) such a government as was enjoyed by these natives.... When they saw that we have thieves amongst us, and men who sought to force their wives and daughters to commit sin with them, they despised us. But now they have come to such a pass in offence of God, owing to the bad example we have set them in all things, that these natives from doing no evil have changed into people who now do no good, or very little... I beg God to pardon me, for I am the last to die of the conquistadors and discoverers.[38]

Too often historical analysis has been the servant of justification for present political and social objectives rather than a courageous search for the most accurate representation of multisided realities truly extraneous to us. Imagining the nature of your ancestors' responsibility for harmful attitudes and actions or their part in their own wounding is similar to considering your own past responsibility for the actions you have taken. *A healing approach always requires imagining the position, mindset, resources and limitations of the persons being considered, including yourself.* A person's awareness of wrong at the time of action has many degrees, as does the ability to have made any other choice under the circumstances. To be fair, compassion and awareness of limitations must temper ethical scrutiny. Whatever degree of awareness of wrong and options for action can be attributed to our ancestors, or to those who injured them, objective harm may have occurred.

Thus *we can distinguish objective and subjective responsibility* and make our generational confessions accordingly. *Objective responsibility* refers to the moral value evil done—the consequences of the act in itself insofar as it is good or evil, constructive or destructive. The evil done often outlives the one who did it through the consequences of historical actions that can become heavy influence and burden on the consciences and memories of the descendants.[39] *Subjective responsibility* refers to a person's conscious perception of the goodness or evil of the act performed.

What are we obligated to do?

The way in which the consequences of our forebears' actions weigh upon us can help us to determine our responsibility for taking action. This may be in the form of a burdened conscience, or feeling compromised, bound by fear, failure to thrive, anger and bitterness, revenge or guilt as a consequence of injustices suffered or inflicted by our predecessors,

The revelations called forth by the Holy Spirit in generational healing must be confessed, yet may not be easy to admit and articulate. They can be frightening and disorienting, even though just, truthful and ultimately reconciling. A view that sheds new light, reshapes the historical record, and breaks down old stereotypes so that others are seen more fairly, can feel disloyal and unsettling.

While the intellectual assent to a changed and righteous value may be wholehearted, implementing that value in a social context can be stressful and unnerving and bring tension and conflict with group loyalties.

Revealing my (or my ancestors) weaknesses to my children and grandchildren, or the failings of formerly adored leaders in my organization or community, feels like failing my children or co-workers. They may actively discount what I am revealing. They may resist believing what I say, not wanting to disturb their images of parents, ancestors or former leaders. Felt shame can manifest in swift exoneration, either excusing what was done or harshly blaming and disowning ties. The healing and freeing effect of such revelations may take time to appear. I (Doug) never like confessing that my ancestors were slave holders, or that my church taught me to judge and condemn those of other denominations and religions, or that my grandfather committed suicide.

■ On a corporate level, this hesitancy to take responsibility could be seen when the National Park Service (NPS) worried that George Washington's reputation would be tarnished by the revelation that he held slaves while serving as President of the United States in Philadelphia. Officials were concerned that this information would disturb the loyalty and patriotism of present generations. Organized protesters demonstrated in the streets, demanding that the NPS honor the enslaved who labored for George Washington and the first United States administration. In fact, much healing has resulted as the enslaved have been honored and Washington has come into clearer view. Exposing reality leads to the possibility of real embrace. ■

Religious loyalties in particular, with the identities and the belonging that they provide, make clear vision of cultural and religious transgressions and departures from the gospel of Jesus difficult to see. Christians tend to fear that facing and owning their faith traditions' historical dark sides and the hurtful consequences of ancestors' attitudes and actions will bring dishonor and disgrace to formerly revered historical leaders and debilitating shame to the present generations.

Extreme denial leads to reconstructing history to exclude the attitudes and actions that are pressing upon our awareness. A contemporary movement denies that the holocaust of Jews ever occurred during World War Two. A counter-movement has led a public outcry against booksellers carrying *The Protocols of the Elders of Zion*, a book used by Holocaust deniers which appeared in Europe in the early 20th century and was used then to stir violence against Jews in Czarist Russia and Eastern Europe.[40]

Pressure for denial is understandable among those who are children and grandchildren of those who participated in or were in proximity to those atrocities. These descendants say, "My ancestors could never have done that or tolerated that. These accounts must be contrived or at the least greatly exaggerated. It is a political lie by Jews to manipulate the world to succumb to their control. The father (or grandfather) I knew would never have participated in such violations." Because the facts of genocide are so clear, minimization is the most this movement can sustain. Yet such minimization serves denial of wrong by recasting the context in a way to nullify undeniable facts. In their arguments the greater fault ends up being the responsibility of the Jewish people. And the greater fault ends up justifying the actions of the actual perpetrators of evil. Any breakthrough in embracing truth, revealed by the Holy Spirit inwardly and through historical evidence, will necessitate addressing powerful forces of shame and the compensating idealizations that have held cultural self-worth together.

There is no question that honest appraisal of our ancestors' and our own attitudes and actions will bring moments of shame and infect ambivalence into our identifications and belongings. Those who have been idealized will at least temporarily fall from favor. The culture and history we have trusted may lose its luster. As destructive attitudes and actions are revealed and our conscience is struck, we will each, at least momentarily, want to deny or minimize what is being revealed or in anger seek to dissociate ourselves from our traditions and their legacies. We have witnessed these reactions again and again among Christians as the historical role of our churches in the genocide of peoples and cultures is exposed to our contemporary consciousness. On the other hand, if terrible abuses to our familial and religious ancestors are made more explicit for us, we may find ourselves filled with deep outrage and a fierce resistance to seeing the offending others as real struggling human beings as well.

Loyalties run deep. They have a way of surprising us, of suddenly showing up. That to which we are loyal resists critique and tends to be felt as *right* or *wrong*, *superior* or *inferior*. The generational repentance needed takes courage because it makes us vulnerable, both relationally and spiritually. The process requires social support and collaboration. However, it leads to healing past injustices and wounds, freeing present and future generations.

Owning our responsibility

Having attempted to fairly assess our ancestors' subjectively understood and objectively consequential responsibility, we then must ask what claim these responsibilities make on us. What are our obligations, our responsibilities, in relation to their responsibility?

Our obligation is partly revealed in our experienced connections with the history under consideration. Deeply into the investigation of our ancestral past, *we remember that we would not have been engaging this inquiry at all were we not already burdened by the impact of the past being searched.* We have become aware of destructive attitudes, prejudice, unworthiness, hopelessness, bitterness and resentment, unforgiveness, shame, guilt feelings and remorse, through which the unconfessed and unhealed ancestral sins and wounds continue their expression. Our obligation partly rests in our desire to change, be healed, to be freed and to reconcile with others. Generational prayers are at times essential to these goals for ourselves and those close to us. We can consider the burdens, the stuck attitudes and patterns, a nudge from the Holy Spirit to take action, to research our generational histories and to bring our discoveries to God for healing and transformation.

In addition, *our obligation rests in our indebtedness to those who have preceded us.* Without their survival, we would not be here at all. Their investments in life, nurturing the young, securing a livelihood, developing talents and gifts, acting with integrity and seeking God, however imperfect and lacking, undergird our inheritance, the foundations on which we stand. In some sense our ancestors cry out to us, within the experience of their continuing impact, to acknowledge with gratitude and rekindle their gifts to us, to see them fairly and to bring to rest the impact of their transgressions and wounds. Through consequences their lives continue to speak to us and in us, as in, "Listen, your brother's blood is crying out to me from the ground" (Gen 4:10 *New Jerusalem Bible*).

We may also be subject to the longings of our predecessors, given to us through the Holy Spirit, as they have come close to God in their life beyond death and now yearn to have us and all the earth released from the negative effects of their lives. And at times we may sense their cry revealing the bound state from which they are seeking release by appealing for our prayers.

Our obligation may proceed as well from our responsibilities in the body of Christ. Communion in the one Holy Spirit also establishes a *communion of saints* in a historical sense, by virtue of which the baptized of today feel connected to the baptized of yesterday and as they benefit from their merits and are nourished by their witness of holiness, so likewise they feel the obligation to assume any current burden from their faults.

The baptized of today may also feel obligated to assume any current burden from the faults of ancestors not baptized, as well. Through appreciation of their ancestors' contributions and their plights, forgiving their failures and transgressions, the current generation may plead with God for their ancestors' forgiveness, for their healing and for their eternal life. These prayers are not presumed sufficient for salvation, but they are moved in the hearts of those who have been humbled by their own limitations and God's forgiveness and are filled with the mercy of God. We desire that no one be lost, knowing that, "but by the grace of God there go I."

What are we justified in doing?

We have affirmed that as Christians God has given us the *ministry of reconciliation* and God has made us *ambassadors for Christ* (1 Cor 6:18-20). However, just as ambassadors in the secular world have limited powers in the country to which they are assigned, Christians are also bound by the rules of engagement of the world in which we live. We are not justified in commanding anyone to receive the grace of God. We can only communicate the good news and make ourselves available to serve.

The Apostle Paul reminds us,

> My friends, if anyone is detected in a transgression, you who have received the Spirit should restore such a one in a spirit of gentleness. Take care that you yourselves are not tempted. Bear one another's burdens, and in this way you will fulfill the law of Christ. For if those who are nothing think they are something, they

deceive themselves. All must test their own work; then that work, rather than their neighbor's work, will become a cause for pride. For all must carry their own loads. (Gal 6:1-5)

So, what *are* we justified in doing in the meantime? *First, we begin our own work of confession, forgiveness and reconciliation without judging or seeking revenge on those who continue perpetuate the communal sins of our forbearers* (Mt 6:14; 7:1-5). This is a time for examining ourselves and our motives before God in prayer. It is helpful to work with a spiritual director, counselor or trusted friend who can honestly help us to recognize our own contributions to the problem and support us as we work through the conditions of our heart.

Secondly, we are justified in exposing injustice, but without hypocrisy or self-righteousness (Mt 7:21-23). We can research and document the wounding that has occurred in the past and trace the effects from one generation to another. The data need to be accurate and objective. Reading accounts of the family or community history from various perspectives, interviewing those who appear wounded and seeking the discernment of the Holy Spirit will build our case in appealing to leaders for a hearing and for their cooperation in the healing process.

Thirdly, we are justified in caring for the "sheep," those within the fold who have been wounded (Jn 10:1-30; 21:15-19). This includes providing prayer for deep level healing and deliverance with family members, and in organizations, for the individuals and small groups involved as they seek help. Seminars on healing prayer and generational healing may open doors for further ministry in a church or Christian organization. It may take years before the whole family or group, or even the leaders, are really open to corporate healing. This crucial stage also prepares the way so that the generational healing

work can be done with a critical mass of healed people who are prepared to care for others.

*Fourthly, as a member of a family lineage or organization, we
are justified in doing generational intercession as called forth and
led by the Holy Spirit.*

*Fifthly, we are justified in accepting "no" as an answer from
other family members and organizational leaders who we ask to join
us in a generational healing process.* Jesus did not press when faced
with rejection or unbelief. He moved on to more receptive areas (Mt
6:5-6; 10:5; 13:57-58; 22:1-14; Jn 12:36-43). We can always continue to intercede and plant seeds of hope as the Holy Spirit leads.

What are we authorized to do?

When Jesus commissioned his first disciples, he empowered them
with an astounding charge, "Then Jesus called the twelve together
and gave them power and authority over all demons and to cure diseases, and he sent them out to proclaim the kingdom of God and to
heal." That commission is extended to us in Jesus final words to his
followers,

> All authority in heaven and on earth has been given
> to me. Go therefore and make disciples of all nations,
> baptizing them in the name of the Father and of the
> Son and of the Holy Spirit, and teaching them to
> obey everything that I have commanded you. And
> remember, I am with you always, to the end of the
> age. (Mt 28:18-20)

As members of a community we are authorized to pray and fast,
representationally repent and claim the power of Jesus' name. For
Daniel, that occurred as an exile in a foreign country (Persia) and

separated from his people. Ezra, a priest, returned to Israel with a group of exiles. There he led them in rebuilding the Temple and in corporate repentance for the sins that had forced them into exile. Nehemiah later heard the call of God in Persia and returned to Jerusalem appointed as governor to rebuild the city wall and continue the process of healing the nation. Daniel's prayer appears to have paved the way for the later work of Ezra and Nehemiah. In the same way, our prayers may open doors in our own communities, even when the leadership is not currently open to repentance or change.

We are not authorized to meddle in communities with whom we are not associated unless invited. Although we may speak prophetically about sins such as racism, sexism, ageism or abuse by informing leaders and supporting victims, we cannot impose change from without. For instance, if a history of systematic abuse is uncovered through historical research in a church or organization with which you are not affiliated, the facts can be reported and shared with members, but they cannot be forced to repent by an outsider. However, humbly laying a foundation in prayer for that church or organization may eventually lead to their openness to repentance and change.

So what can we do?

Important interventions include:

- awakening to the present influences of the past and calling out to God
- seeking God's face (listening to God and community)
- researching the sins, wounds, and blessings of the past
- searching the heart of God for our lineages
- humbly confessing, personally and representationally
- apologizing, asking forgiveness and forgiving

- repenting: renouncing the old and asserting the new
- rebuking evil, breaking curses and restoring blessings
- praying for healing: inviting Jesus into our ancestral past to heal and restore
- reconciling actions

We will enlarge on the interventions above in the next chapters.

For Reflection

After spending a few minutes in silence before God, read Daniel's prayer below.

> Ah, Lord, great and awesome God, keeping covenant and steadfast love with those who love you and keep your commandments, [5] we have sinned and done wrong, acted wickedly and rebelled, turning aside from your commandments and ordinances. [6] We have not listened to your servants the prophets, who spoke in your name to our kings, our princes, and our ancestors, and to all the people of the land.
>
> [7] Righteousness is on your side, O Lord, but open shame, as at this day, falls on us, the people of Judah, the inhabitants of Jerusalem, and all Israel, those who are near and those who are far away, in all the lands to which you have driven them, because of the treachery that they have committed against you. [8] Open shame, O LORD, falls on us, our kings, our officials, and our ancestors, because we have sinned against you. [9] To the Lord our God belong mercy and forgiveness, for we have rebelled against him, [10] and have not obeyed

the voice of the Lᴏʀᴅ our God by following his laws, which he set before us by his servants the prophets.

[11] All Israel has transgressed your law and turned aside, refusing to obey your voice. So the curse and the oath written in the law of Moses, the servant of God, have been poured out upon us, because we have sinned against you. [12] He has confirmed his words, which he spoke against us and against our rulers, by bringing upon us a calamity so great that what has been done against Jerusalem has never before been done under the whole heaven. [13] Just as it is written in the law of Moses, all this calamity has come upon us. We did not entreat the favor of the Lᴏʀᴅ our God, turning from our iniquities and reflecting on his fidelity. [14] So the Lᴏʀᴅ kept watch over this calamity until he brought it upon us. Indeed, the Lᴏʀᴅ our God is right in all that he has done; for we have disobeyed his voice.

[15] And now, O Lord our God, who brought your people out of the land of Egypt with a mighty hand and made your name renowned even to this day—we have sinned, we have done wickedly. [16] O Lord, in view of all your righteous acts, let your anger and wrath, we pray, turn away from your city Jerusalem, your holy mountain; because of our sins and the iniquities of our ancestors, Jerusalem and your people have become a disgrace among all our neighbors. [17] Now therefore, O our God, listen to the prayer of your servant and to his supplication, and for your own sake, Lord, let your face shine upon your desolated sanctuary. [18] Incline your ear, O my God, and hear. Open

your eyes and look at our desolation and the city that bears your name. We do not present our supplication before you on the ground of our righteousness, but on the ground of your great mercies. [19] O Lord, hear; O Lord, forgive; O Lord, listen and act and do not delay! For your own sake, O my God, because your city and your people bear your name!" ~Dan 9:4-19

Revisit your case situation. Ask yourself the following questions:
1. In what ways am I responsible for this situation?
2. Why am I interested in pursuing healing in this situation?
3. What am I able to do right now?
4. What am I obligated to do?
5. What am I justified in doing at this time?
6. What am I authorized to do (and for what reasons)?

Now go back to Daniel's prayer and substitute your own names and situations for Jerusalem, Israel and Egypt.

Chapter 7

A Process for Generational Healing

Generational healing is more of a journey than a set procedure. It can progress quickly, but more often, it takes years. It is complicated by a wide web of relationships developed over a long time span. As one strand of relationships is reconciled, another may appear. We weave in and out of the process as new information is uncovered, or when new crises arise revealing the need for additional healing. God often protects us from delving too deeply until we are able to handle the new information.

Steps for Generational Healing

1. Awakening to the present influences of the past and calling out to God
2. Seeking God's face (listening to God and community)
3. Researching the sins, wounds, and blessings of the past
4. Searching the heart of God for our lineages
5. Humbly confessing, personally and representationally
6. Apologizing, asking forgiveness and forgiving
7. Repenting: renouncing the old and asserting the new
8. Rebuking evil, breaking curses and restoring blessings

9. Praying for healing: inviting Jesus into our ancestral past to heal and restore
10. Reconciling actions

Step 1: *Awakening to the present influences of the past and calling out to God.*

Within each person who has felt drawn to this kind of prayer, is some awareness of influences that persist from the past in our various lineages, such as family, church, community, organization, ethnicity, land or nation. These influences may be both life-giving and life- diminishing. A nagging sense may arise that a difficult situation has developed from a deeper root than current circumstances warrant. An eerie feeling of *déjà vu* may linger. At other times, a crisis with strong emotional attachments may seem to erupt out of nowhere.

We have already established that anxiety, depression, distrust, separation, alienation, hostility, broken relationships and failure to thrive, may begin to reveal that something has not been right generationally. Injuring encounters from generations past, and the way they have been handled and remembered, seem to grip us, claiming a voice and a new and healing response. Releasing these binding influences usually requires engaging our ancestral past and on occasion dialogue between present carriers of generationally distant injuries and animosities. When current experiences seem to draw energy from unhealed and unforgiven events and relationships of generations past it is time to begin calling out to God for discernment and direction.

☐ *Take a moment to name and write down the negative behaviors,* emotions, attitudes, physical conditions, and relationship patterns that most burden or trouble you (physically, emotionally, spiritually, relationally) at this time, or that you feel especially sensitive to or concerned about, and that you suspect have generational roots.

☐ As you become aware of these troubles, concerns and/or burdens and of the possibility of historical or generational influences, *call to God for help*. Choose to trust that the Holy Spirit has already been leading you on this path of generational healing, or you would not have been attracted to this work.

☐ After naming the concerns that you are bringing to God for healing, *note the various lineages to which you belong*—family, culture, religion, church, organizations, community, work, location, nation, ethnicity or race. Which ones significantly shaped you and command your loyalty? List the lineages you are aware of at this time.

☐ Then, asking the Holy Spirit's help, *note which of these lineages seem to embody, or seem especially connected to the concerns*, troubles and burdens, you are bringing for healing at this time. Choose to trust what comes to mind as you seek the Holy Spirit's help. For now, limit your pursuit to the lineages that the Holy Spirit brings to mind.

☐ *List positive, life-giving, influences* that are part of these lineages and the consequent strengths and gifts that seem to have been passed from generation-to-generation. Expressions of gratitude for strengths and gifts received will be an important balancing perspective as destructive influences are addressed and healed.

☐ Next, *list the negative, life diminishing influences* or patterns that are part of these lineages and their consequent injuries and destructive impact. These can be brought for healing as the Holy Spirit leads.

☐ Now among the lineages that seem connected to or embody the concerns you are bringing for healing, *notice to which lineages you are most sensitive*, affected by, or burdened by at this time. Write down these lineages and the specific destructive patterns or realities that most burden or concern you. Then note and record the specific strengths and gifts that you appreciate in these lineages.

☐ After naming the lineages most related to your current burdens and concerns and the significant life-diminishing and life-giving patterns that came to mind for each, *invite the Holy Spirit to lead you* in attending to healing these patterns with their related transgressions and wounds.

Step 2: *Seeking God's face (listening to God and community)*

As you yield control and open yourself to listening to God for knowledge and direction, center and protect yourself spiritually. Intentionally open yourself to the Holy Spirit using the following exercises.

☐ *Focus on Jesus and his redemptive work.* Through Jesus' yielding to death, a completely faithful response to God, he released power that broke the curse of all generational sin back to Adam and Eve and touched all of humankind's wounds with healing (Gal 3:13-14; Rom 5:18-19). Our generational healing prayers draw on this power through confession, repentance, forgiveness and opening our wounds and the wounds in our generations to his love. Thus we begin listening by focusing on Jesus and what he accomplished. Each of us will have our unique way of focusing on Jesus. As a centering meditation, read Colossians 1:18-20.

> He is the beginning, the first-born from the dead, so that he should be supreme in every way; because God wanted all fullness to be found in him and through him to reconcile all things to him, everything in heaven and everything on earth, by making peace

through his death on the cross. (Col 1:18-20, *New Jerusalem Bible*)

God the Father reconciling all things to himself, through Jesus, everything in heaven and everything on earth, sets the tone and inclusivity for the listening to God that is essential for generational healing.

☐ *Protect yourself by binding the evil one in the name of Jesus Christ and seeking God's protection.* Ask for the protection of the blood of Jesus and his holy angels over yourself and all those present (if gathered as a group), as well as all who may be touched by these prayers. We find that anointing those present with oil blessed for healing and deliverance enhances our listening and sense of protection.

The following prayer is a common one for protection from evil. It is found in many forms and wordings, frequently with more detailed and complex wordings, but usually with the basic elements included here.

Binding and Covering Prayer

In the name of Jesus Christ and with the authority given me as a Christian, I bind all evil spirits in this place. I bind all communication, knowledge and interactions between evil spirits and send them to Jesus, for him to deal with them as he will.

In the name of Jesus Christ I seal this room in the blood of Jesus Christ. Lord send the protection of your Holy Spirit to everyone here and to their families and all associated with them. Surround us with your holy angels. Amen

---

☐ *Consciously orient and open yourself to the Holy Spirit, seeking God's guidance and revelations of truth.* Ask for a continuing focus among the concerns and lineages that you have noted, so that the particular concerns receiving attention at this time are those being called forth by God. Continue to accept, with the Holy Spirit's guidance, the focus or emphasis that comes to mind. Such a trusting step does not guarantee that your discernment will be perfect, but God will work through the choices you make. If your choice is not the best, you will be able to discern this as you move along in the process. In this way you can avoid being overwhelmed by the shear multiplicity of issues and the inexhaustible lines of inheritance that could be investigated, or by the struggle to know God's mind perfectly.

☐ Review those lineages and concerns that you have recorded as prominent and/or urgent in your mind. Then *ask the Holy Spirit to lead you in choosing one particular lineage to focus on for healing at this time.* If you have no such sense of emphasis or focus, then simply choose the lineage that seems most important to you now. Entrust your choice to God believing that the Holy Spirit is leading you as you proceed. Later you can return to seek healing for the other lineages that also embody and connect to the concerns that are currently troubling you.

Step 3: *Researching the sins, wounds and blessings of the past*

At this point you have chosen, according to your sense of the Holy Spirit's leading, a specific lineage and the concerns for which you feel moved to seek healing.

☐ In the light of these concerns, *proceed now to search in this particular lineage for*

- the historical roots and influences and their consequences passed from generation-to-generation;
- life diminishing patterns and burdens;
- gifts and blessings passed from generation-to-generation.

Research and listen to the facts of the past, subjective and objective, as well as the events and responses to events that seem to continue to influence these present conditions and patterns.

☐ As you do this, *attempt to see your ancestors or predecessors in this particular lineage from the perspective of their concerns,* perceptions, pressures and horizons, that is, their otherness. *Memory and Reconciliation* reminds us,

> Events or words of the past are, above all, 'past.' As such they are not completely reducible to the framework of the present... It is necessary, therefore, to approach them by means of an investigation that aims at using all of the information available, with a view to a reconstruction of the environment, of the ways of thinking, of the conditions and the living dynamic in which those events and those words are placed.[41]

☐ *Gather information from a variety of sources.* Explore genealogical data and historical perspectives in records such as old correspondence, diaries of deceased members, written reports, military records, church or organizational records and minutes, plus any paper trail a person may have left. Often you will be able to gain further information by searching online. Just entering a name in a search engine may reveal large amounts of useful information. Also look for written and audio recorded stories told by family or group members. Interview living members, including those who carry the generational stories from different perspectives, and who experienced different consequences. Reading relevant historical accounts and interpretations, such as historical novels or historical studies of the times and lineages being investigated may provide a deeper understanding of the attitudes and behavior of the times in which your ancestors or predecessors lived.

☐ *Seek the strength and guidance of the Holy Spirit for illumination of the collected data* and to engage in imagining the experiences of participants in each generation, creating generational story lines. In addition, seek the Holy Spirit for the generational hints in one's subjective experience or the subjective experience of other living members of the particular lineage, such as fears, resentments, prejudicial attitudes, failed entitlement, experiences of failure, talents and blessings. Such inner work may evoke images of ancestors' lives, images that fit what has been researched and add subjective substance to the historical skeleton.

☐ *From objective and subjective information, generational story lines begin to be delineated.* They will reveal objectively grounded and imagined sequential generational transmission of the particular emotions, vulnerabilities, attitudes, identities, beliefs, resentments, idolatries, addictions, interpersonal alienations and relationship patterns. These comprise the concerns for which you seek healing. As the stories take shape in our minds, we can ask the following questions.

- What truths (and whose truths) have been silenced, denied, mystified, not sufficiently voiced or admitted in this lineage (family/organization/community/ethnicity), currently and historically?
- What harm done or endured needs to be seen, heard, understood and admitted currently and historically?

- What and whose injuries need to be voiced and stood for currently and historically?
- Whose injuring actions need to be confessed, admitted, accounted for, voiced and apologized for?
- What and whose strengths and contributions need to be owned and voiced, credited and appreciated in this lineage?
- What strengths and contributions need to be owned and voiced, credited and appreciated in those who inflicted wounds on members of this lineage? In what ways were they wounded by members of this lineage?

List the strengths and contributions of persons/groups across the generations. Integrate these strengths and contributions with the injuries and harm done. Injuries often foster creative recovery and the development of gifts and talents. For example responses to harm done by one generation may lead to remorse and concerns for justice in the next or future generations.

☐ *Own your belonging to this history*, to this lineage: family, group, community, organization, or people group that this history concerns.
- Identify your complicity with harm done, such as your own part in continuing the attitudes and patterns that are the subject of this inquiry. How have you continued to participate in such harm or failed to name the harm and challenge it? Also identify how you have passed forward the blessings you received from the generations.
- Detail the consequences you have experienced from injuries suffered or transgressions committed in the generations of this lineage as well as the blessings passed forward to you.
- Tell the history you have constructed, and what you suspect but are still unsure about, to yourself and to others you trust

to hear you. Dialogue with others eliciting their feedback and reflections.

Step 4: *Searching the heart of God for our lineages*

Next give the facts you have collected and the assumptions you have made to God.

☐ *Ask the Holy Spirit to show you God's heart for this lineage* and to awaken love for your people.[42] Identify your love for your people in this lineage and your solidarity with the wounds, shortcomings, longings and desires that you have identified. Your belonging to this history may be experienced as a kind of impassioned solidarity with the past.[43] Where there is hurt or resentment, ask God to give you compassion and understanding.

☐ *Identify your authority to represent this lineage.* This is based in your belonging, role or position in the group (as a citizen, member, owner, official, parent, descendant) and/or in your special call by God to intercede for this lineage.

☐ *Name the good done,* that which has been especially gifting to past and present generations of this lineage. Seek God's perspective on the good done.

☐ *Identify wrongs done,* wounds created and degrees of culpability. Seek God's perspective. How does God see the wrongs done, the wounds created and the persons responsible?

☐ *Establish the leading of the Holy Spirit to do this representational work at this time.* Ask the Holy Spirit to lead and confirm the work that is to be done now.

☐ *Determine to whom and with whom to confess and where this is to be done.*

☐ *Remember God's call, kindness and covenant.*

Step 5: *Humbly confessing, personally and representationally*

Having become conscious your own sins and injuries, contributions and gifts, as well as those of your ancestors/predecessors in this lineage,

☐ *Confess to God the generational sins and wounds and your personal complicity* with continuing family/group transgressions. The sins and wounds may be both contemporary and ancestral. Simply express them to God, silently or aloud as you feel led, in as much detail as needed to fully confess. Speaking aloud to others is not always necessary but is usually helpful, because speaking aloud often gives a sense of having opened your heart to God and completed an action. Also when speaking aloud, hesitancies to own material are more evident to yourself and to those listening and receiving the confession. If you feel led to speak aloud to others, determine to whom, where and when God is leading you to speak this confession.

☐ As you are moved by the Holy Spirit, *express gratitude for the good* from which generations have benefited and *express remorse and sorrow for wrong doing* and destructive consequences.

Step 6: *Apologizing, asking forgiveness and forgiving*

☐ *Make apologies to God and others* (where appropriate and led by God) on behalf of yourself and your lineage expressing remorse and awareness of hurts caused.

☐ *Ask God's forgiveness for both personal and group/lineage trans-gressions, against persons in the lineage and against those of other lineages and then ask the forgiveness of others* (where appropriate and led by God). You can ask forgiveness from those standing in for or representing the persons in your lineage and in other lineages that have been injured by your people, asking God's intervention, release and blessing for all those affected.

☐ *Offer forgiveness to your ancestors/predecessors and others* (where appropriate).

☐ *Express gratitude for God's faithfulness and for the additional blessings of the generations* that have come to light, naming the strengths and values that have become evident.

Representational lineage apologies to God, to the generations of your lineage, and to those injured by you and your lineage proceed naturally from opening your lineage history to God. You can representationally express remorse for these injuries, trying to be as accurate as possible regarding the predecessors'/ancestors' awareness of wrong and their understanding of the injurious impact of their actions. As much as our predecessors/ancestors may have imagined the consequences of their actions for future generations, they did not actually know what those consequences would be. Therefore we cannot impute intent to harm through hindsight.

Step 7: *Repenting: renouncing the old and asserting the new*

Repentance means turning from one way to another way. Having confessed, apologized, forgiven and asked forgiveness, you are ready to change.

☐ *Renounce old patterns of thought, action, belief and alienation,* as specifically as possible, on behalf of yourself and your ancestors.

☐ *Commit to changing destructive attitudes and behavior patterns.*

☐ *Ask God to break the compulsive hold of destructive attitudes and behavior patterns* upon your existence, on your relationships and on this lineage. A helpful image to facilitate the action of such bondage-breaking is to visualize the cross of Jesus placed between the generations and between all persons in the lineage, absorbing and transforming all generation-to-generation influence. Likewise, visualizing the blood of Jesus flowing throughout the family tree or group lineage, healing all wounds and cleansing the stain and bondage of sin, can help you effectively articulate of this prayer intention.

☐ *Commit yourself and your lineage to replacing old destructive attitudes and patterns of thought, action and belief, with life-giving attitudes and patterns. Name the old and new attitudes and patterns.*

Step 8: *Rebuking evil, breaking curses and restoring blessings*

When taking a stand for change, it is a particularly fruitful time to *bind, rebuke and cast out any evil* that has found a dwelling place in the now renounced destructive attitudes, beliefs, identities, patterns and alienations and to break any curses. The doors of welcome have been closed to evil. *Prayer, at this time, may be devoted to discerning any evil influence* that can now be brought to light along with any curses that may still be binding. Of course, prayers for discernment and binding of evil may come into play at any point in the healing process when progress is spiritually disrupted or impeded.

☐ Curses to "the third and fourth generation" resulting from pre-decessors'/ancestors' violations, idolatries and other sins, or from words spoken against them, or by them against others are broken through repentance, forgiveness and the power of the cross. *Break any curses and renounce any vows related to old destructive personal and lineage patterns.* Curses are negative spiritual effects set in motion against persons and lineages and their members by disobedience to God, transgressions against others, words spoken by members of the lineage against others in the lineage, words spoken by members of the lineage against themselves, or against the lineage, or words spoken or invoked against members of the lineage or the lineage itself by those of other lineages. Ask God to release these curses, to break their hold. Accept the release and commit to walking in freedom. Forgive yourself, your lineage, your ancestors and others who have set curses in motion and sustained them.

Curses placed on lineage members and their generations by yourself and others can be *"broken into small pieces never ever to be assembled again"* as forgiveness and repentance frees the ground to which they held. In this regard it is especially important to ask forgiveness for your ancestors/predecessors whose injuring actions provoked cursing in retaliation. Follow-up reparative dialogue with descendants/successors of those injured and who injured your lineage in response may be required to fully put these legacies to rest. The consequences of curses may appear as failure to thrive—mentally, spiritually, physically—vulnerability to mental and physical disease, broken relationships, and felt alienation from God.

Especially lethal are curses set in place and motion by false worship, commitments made, knowingly and unknowingly, to spiritual powers or practices in conflict with God, or opposed to God's ways. The extreme is explicit satanic worship, also forms of witchcraft, especially those that idolize accumulations of personal power, group power or the power of one's family over others. Prayers to break

156

these curses should be prayed three times because many of these curses were invoked using a three-fold formula. Also subtler forms of idolatry and false worship, that can set curse effects in motion, may be imbedded in one's family or group culture and in the wider cultures of which one's family or group is a part, such as worship of power and money, commitments to revenge, commitment to domination, sexually, economically, etc.

Curses alight for two reasons:

1. Because you and/or those of your lineage have chosen a path apart from God's will and ways, opening you and your family or group lineage to the evil one and evil powers.

2. Because, words and intentions have been spoken or invoked against you and/or your family, organization, community, imparting their damaging authority and effect through vulnerabilities created by unhealed wounds and un-repented sin. Unhealed wounds create vulnerabilities to the impact of curses because of beliefs that take hold while processing painful experiences (e.g., *I am rejected, I am worthless, I am inferior*, etc.). Such negative beliefs have their own cursing effect and open us to curses sent by others. We may unwittingly and unconsciously agree with the curses sent.

Curses have power to destroy because our relationships are subject to forces opposing God's love, God's will and God's protection. Prayers for breaking curses are really a continuation of repentance, in that they are a further breaking of the hold of all that wounds and destroys in order to create space for God's love, God's protection and God's ways to be chosen, to take hold, and to be lived.

A prayer for breaking curses may be spoken aloud or silently. For example:

Lord Jesus, in your name, I break the power and authority of any curses against myself, my family/group members and my family/group lineages resulting from our disobedience to you, our transgressions against others, words spoken against others, words we have spoken against ourselves and/or our own lineage, or words spoken or invoked against us and/or our lineage by others. Specifically, in Jesus name, I break the power and authority of _____ (name the curses and consequences you sense may be present). Further, in Jesus name, I break the power and authority of curses invoked or spoken against others and other family/group lineages or communities by us, by members of my family/group lineage. Lord, forgive us and heal the consequences of curses we have wrought against others. I command, in Jesus name, that all of these curses be broken into small pieces never ever to be reassembled.

Accept the release and commit to walking in freedom. Forgive yourself, your ancestors and others who have set curses in motion and sustained them.

☐ Breaking the power and authority of curses can be followed by *prayers to bind and cast out any remaining influence of evil spirits.* This is a particularly fruitful time to bind, rebuke and cast out any evil that has found a dwelling place in the now renounced destructive attitudes, beliefs, identities and patterns, and in the curses whose power and authority have been broken. For example:

In the name of Jesus I bind any evil spirits that have indwelled and empowered the destructive patterns and curses that have now been broken. I bind you in your network of communication, interaction and interplay. I specifically bind _____ (name any specific evil spirits which you have discerned to have been involved). I cast you each out immediately, completely and permanently. I send you directly to Jesus Christ for Him to do with you according to his will.

☐ Free of the grip of destructive patterns and their evil spirit partners, *the participant is now increasingly liberated to embrace transformed attitudes and new beliefs, identities, behaviors and ways of relating.* Real changes are effected by conscious and articulated goals for change. Emptied out and freed one must "put in" by replacing the negative with a positive commitments and blessings.

Step 9: *Praying for healing: inviting Jesus into our ancestral past to heal and restore*

Prayers for healing personal and ancestral memories can flow freely after repentance and deliverance. These healing prayers may be engaged while participants are meditating after receiving Holy Communion (if Holy Communion has been the context for generational prayers) or while sitting before the Blessed Sacrament (in Roman Catholic tradition) or in a quiet place at the end of a generational prayer session.

☐ *Ancestors/predecessors can be imagined with Jesus who is actively touching their wounds with healing,* with understanding, with protection, or, at times, righteous indignation at the wounding that occurred. Persons may think of Jesus healing, picture him healing or hear him speak healing depending on the dimension of imagination that is flowing best at the time. At times healing thoughts and imaginings occur spontaneously after a repentance and deliverance period. And remember, there is no strict order to these steps. Healing words and imagery may be given or occur spontaneously before repentance and deliverance as a strengthening prelude.

☐ *Prayers for those in the lineage who have died, may also flow in this period* after repentance and deliverance intentions. You may sense that the living would benefit from expressing their love in this way or that those who have died need family/group love expressed in the form of prayer in order to progress on into a peaceful rest. You may also want to pray for someone who has died to express forgiveness and love. Prayers may feel incomplete, even selfish, if not concluded with intercessions for the departed. This movement of prayer is a natural extension of felt ties, love, loyalty and a growing faith in God's mercy. Of course, we do not control anyone's eternal destiny. However, we can express to God our love for and forgiveness of those who have died and our desire that they find their way home to God.

Kenneth McAll, the British psychiatrist and pioneer of generational healing prayer, has developed a useful protocol for these prayers. The prayer below paraphrases his prayer sequence.[44] McAll believed that prayers for the departed are most efficacious when prayed in the context of a liturgy of Holy Communion. Thus his prayer protocol is set in that context.

A. Dear Lord God, I am/we are _____ and want to praise and thank you for all you did through your Son. I/we ask your mercy on _____. There were _____ (e.g. stressors, loyalties, group pressures, ignorance, prejudices, etc.) that predisposed_____ to disobey your laws by _____ (e.g. taking his own life; throwing away the baby, hurting other family/group members, performing acts of cruelty in war, committing racial violence, etc.)

B. We ask your forgiveness for _____ for his/her/their sins.

C. We extend our forgiveness to _____.

D. We ask your forgiveness if we have failed to heed your call to do this before.

E. Please may _____ now know family/group love and reconciliation and your love.

F. Here I/we wish to show forth to _____ and his/her/their angels all you have achieved,

   1) that in the bread I receive is your life and teaching, brokenness and healing through your stripes,
   2) that in your shed blood is the free gift of freedom from the guilt, bondage and stain of sin,
   3) the fact that through the torn veil we have direct access to God,
   4) that in rising you defeated Satan and his minions, and
   5) that you became available to the departed.

G. Now we ask that the angels and the departed see that you ascended and opened heaven. Now we ask that they be gathered together and go on toward heaven and be united there with each other and with you.

H. Now Lord, because we have forgiven and released the departed into your care, may we be healed and become the people you intended, to live to your praise and glory.

☐ *Prayers of gratitude and reengaging positive legacy* often flow spontaneously during healing prayers. A deep appreciation of ancestors'/predecessors' gifts, investments in justice and developed talents, along with the benefits received from these by current generations, tend to gather as repentance and healing cleanse and transform the impact of negative legacy. Also, forgiving ancestors/predecessors and those who injured them frequently awakens a desire to reconnect with lost or muted gifts and values.

☐ *At times generational healing is experienced as reengaging lost culture.* For example, Richard, a man of Welsh ancestry, found himself strongly attracted to the events of contemporary Welsh societies. Singing Welsh songs and joining in Christian Welsh-Celtic celebrations seemed to satisfy a hunger in his soul and to bring portions of him alive. He would say, "I feel more myself when I actively engage these roots."

☐ *It is not uncommon for sessions of generational healing prayers to end with thanksgiving* to God and to one's ancestors/predecessors for gifts of life given and received and with the explicit request that the blessings God intended to flow through these lineages now be released.

Step 10: *Reconciling actions*

☐ *Allow the Holy Spirit to form next steps* within your mind and imagination.

☐ In dialogue with others, *explore and identify healing, reparative and reconciling actions* which can be taken, for example, to spread the truth(s) identified.

☐ *Create safe forums for listening and dialogue* among others around the legacies revealed and their consequences today.

☐ *Change personal attitudes and ways.*

☐ *Describe to others what you have learned* about your lineage's guilt and your own sorrow, and complicity, as well as the lineage's wounds. Choose your audience carefully so that others in your lineage are not unfairly implicated.

☐ *Seek to dialogue with those from the lineages who injured your lineage, or who were injured by your lineage.*

☐ *Find ways to honor the life-giving contributions* made by members of your lineage and of the other lineages who have touched you and your lineage.

We are only beginning to understand generational healing work. One thing seems sure. God has opened a window of understanding and a way to increased freedom. We have moved beyond our individualistic focus and been given a vision of our connectedness. We have become partners with our generations in the redemptive work of God for the healing of his world. We are becoming privileged intercessors.

For Reflection

You have done a great deal of emotionally draining work if you have put these principles into practice with your own situation. Lift up the notes you have taken to the Lord. Listen quietly for his voice. After a few minutes, meditate on Psalm 78:1-8.

Give ear, O my people, to my teaching;

incline your ears to the words of my mouth.
²I will open my mouth in a parable;
    I will utter dark sayings from of old,
³things that we have heard and known,
    that our ancestors have told us.
⁴We will not hide them from their children;
    we will tell to the coming generation
the glorious deeds of the LORD, and his might,
    and the wonders that he has done.
⁵He established a decree in Jacob,
    and appointed a law in Israel,
which he commanded our ancestors
    to teach to their children;
⁶that the next generation might know them,
    the children yet unborn,
and rise up and tell them to their children,
    ⁷so that they should set their hope in God,
and not forget the works of God,
    but keep his commandments;
⁸and that they should not be like their ancestors,
    a stubborn and rebellious generation,
a generation whose heart was not steadfast,
    whose spirit was not faithful to God.

Review your personal case study and the work you have done so far in the chapter reflections. Use the steps in this chapter to organize your material and walk through the generational healing process. At this point, you may find it helpful to work with a trained prayer minister.

Part II
Applying the Process

Chapter 8

Healing a Family Lineage

We are each a unique creation and rooted in a genetic lineage.
Being alive in this world depends on God and our biological parents
and all those who preceded our parents on whom their existence
depended. Our genetic blueprint manifests this dependence on parents, grandparents, great grandparents ("she has her grandmother's
eyes," "he's an introvert like his father"). Each person's nature, while
certainly unique and "one of a kind," none-the-less reflects ancestors'
natures, biologically, psychologically and spiritually. This rootedness
is certainly part of God's plan, as it is anchored in human conception, early dependence on caretakers and lifelong interdependence
with others.

Non-biological lineages also shape us. Certainly those who have
been adopted, fostered, raised by step-parents or by extended family
(and those who issue from a sperm bank, or who came into life
in a surrogate mother's womb) are strongly shaped and influenced
by non-biological lineages. Actually, we all are, even as genetically
rooted influences persist.

Consider the people who greatly influenced your life in childhood or as a young adult, those not biologically related to you (a

close family friend, a teacher, coach, parents of a close friend). Each influence represents additional lineages. What you received from them was shaped by the biological and non-biological lineages on which they have depended.

Furthermore, we are born weak and in need of nurturing in order to survive. Each generation must continually draw life through bonded, trustworthy, intimate exchange with parents, grandparents, siblings and other caretakers. Food, shelter, clothing, touch and affection must be provided by others. No human can survive, let alone thrive, without these fundamentals. Self-sufficiency is not a human possibility at any age but most obviously from conception through early childhood.

Given human dependence on care-giving and receiving with parents, grandparents, siblings and other caretakers, how can we strengthen these relationships and the life-giving resources that they transmit? How can we heal and transform the deprivations and injuries that have crippled persons from generation-to-generation? These are our tasks in the generational healing of families.

Change comes through family members deciding to behave and relate differently. Generational healing provides resources to help them do it. Inquiring into influences that persist from the past can lead to a way of praying for healing that releases and strengthens blessings for present and future generations.

Remembering and imagining the care given to us as children and young adults connects us to a positive root and enables us to act justly by giving credit. We can even express gratitude for distant care coming through our ancestral past. The ancestors who cared for each generation, down to the care given to those who cared for us, benefits us and those in our care. Being thankful for that care enhances our sense of worth and well-being and enlivens gifts passed forward.

We are also indebted to the damaging things that have impeded our lives. As healing occurs, these experiences may give structure and meaning to our lives.

■ For example, Jack's family struggles with depression. A sense of unworthiness has passed through the generations. Jack sees this in his grandmother's negative attitudes, his father's depression, his own depression and his children's struggles with work and relationships. Through a healing process he can become a person who experiences the power of God's love and understands the wounds that feed depression. And he can convey this understanding and compassion to his father, his children and his friends. He then begins to see that through healing his wounds yield great gifts and deep meaning.

Working through the ten steps

Applying the ten steps for generational healing to families provides a way to heal the wounds and celebrate the blessings that family lineages hold. As you read this chapter, keep Chapter 7 marked in your book. Review the basics of each step as you work your way through the following application of the process to family lineages.

First, we will illustrate the use of the ten steps for generational healing in two cases where persons used these steps. In these examples we proceed through the steps in the order we have given. These persons were coached through the process. Recognize, however, that these steps often flow one to the other in a seamless way. As you confess you may find yourself flowing into forgiveness and repentance in one piece without any sense of moving to another step. You may enter the process at any point. For example, you might find yourself moved to forgive particular ancestors before you have consciously pinned down exactly what the individuals did that you are forgiving. You simply realize that resentment has been carried against them and passed down the generations and you are moved to forgive. When we are doing generational healing, the list of steps serves as guidance, a check list to use to call to awareness important actions to be taken.

Illustration: Lisa

Step 1: *Awakening to present influences of the past in your family lineages and calling out to God.*

Lisa felt *wrong* and unworthy. She tended to isolate herself socially, feeling that she did not belong anywhere. When she engaged in genealogical research, which she thoroughly enjoyed, she noticed that certain ancestors had not been included in the family records she had obtained from her cousins. She mused, "Other family members must have felt excluded as well. They were not even recorded as existing." Lisa was moved to research the generational roots of her feeling excluded from her family, and subsequently feeling unable to belong anywhere. She decided to investigate her mother's family lineages, where she observed these exclusions and specifically her Jewish ancestry.

Step 2: *Seeking God's face for your family lineages (listening to God and community)*

Lisa weekly received Holy Communion in her Episcopal parish. After receiving she would sit quietly in a pew and meditate on Jesus and his love for her and invite Jesus to heal her wounds. She began to grow in awareness of the wounds in previous generations that seemed to repeat generation-to-generation. So she invited Jesus to heal these wounds as well. As she did this, Lisa became aware of the condemnation her mother and grandfather probably would have experienced from other family members if they had acknowledged their Jewish ancestry.

Step 3: *Researching the sins, wounds and blessings of the past in your family lineages*

Lisa persisted in genealogical research and pursued conversations with cousins, who shared their own family experiences and family stories told to them by their parents and grandparents. She was able to trace her mothers' lineage to rejected Jewish roots and relatives and to second sons losing their inheritance, forcing them to leave the family land and search out a life elsewhere. She also became aware through several of her cousins that certain alienated ancestors had become very angry with God and sought empowerment through witchcraft practices.

Lisa was hesitant to own her belonging to her family. She experienced herself as unwanted. Her mother had told her on several occasions that she was unexpected and not wanted at the time she was born. She felt that her existence was resented. Her siblings followed suit seeming to resent her and treat her as if she were not part of the family. She felt a certain bond with her father but he rarely openly opposed her mother's attitudes. Saying the words, "my family," did not come easily. However as she prayed and sought the guidance of the Holy Spirit, she realized that God had placed her where she was and that she did indeed belong in her family. The authority for belonging in her family came from God.

Step 4: *Searching the heart of God for your family lineages*

Lisa, unwanted by her mother at the time of her birth, none-the-less slowly developed a love for and devotion to her family. Researching her mother's family and upbringing gave her compassion for her mother's childhood emotional wounding and for the attitudes she was taught. While not excusing her mother's choices, she began to comprehend the influences that made an early pregnancy difficult for her mother to handle. A career was the way to achieve value with her parents who apparently had little time for the softness and nurture required for successful maternity. Also, as she researched her family tree, she began to connect with the interests and experiences of her cousins and ancestors. Her love of history connected her with cousins who also love history and were interested in helping with her genealogical research. She documented that she did descend from Jewish ancestors, explaining her affinity with the Hebrew roots of Christianity. In her wounds and those of her ancestors and in the strengths and gifts passed from generation-to-generation she began to feel a solidarity and belonging.

As Lisa sought God's direction and leading in searching her family roots she began to absorb God's love for her family and appreciate the goodness and giftedness God had planted in them to be named, unearthed and lived among them. Lisa felt moved to thank God for those in her lineage who had continued to honor their Jewish ancestors and to include Jewish symbols and celebrations within their Christian prayer and lifestyle. She expressed gratitude that she had been motivated and encouraged to continue these practices.

Lisa sensed in her prayer, as she listened to God, that God was shining his light on the exclusions that she uncovered in her family research—persons excluded in family discussions, ancestors never mentioned, those treated as if they did not exist or as if they were not part of the family. She also saw clearly her part in treating herself as not a member of the family. She had bought into the exclusions she had experienced, especially from her mother and sisters. These exclusions, enacted by others and by herself, were transgressions to be confessed to God. In her prayer she was also sensitized to the wounds of those who had turned to witchcraft and to the destructive impact of curses they had placed upon the family lineage.

As Lisa considered these foci, she asked again for the leading and confirming of the Holy Spirit. She felt confirmed and emboldened to proceed. She was impressed by how deep and far back this pattern of exclusion seemed to go and by her own and others' anger at exclusion. She saw additional expressions of this pattern in her ancestry. Lisa chose to confess these transgressions to God privately in the context of a Holy Communion service.

Step 5: *Humbly confessing, personally and representationally*

Lisa spoke her family confessions out loud alone, whispering quietly while sitting in a church pew after receiving Holy Communion.

> Lord, I bring to you our family pattern of exclusion, of judging each other as good or bad, as worthy of belonging or not worthy of belonging. We have valued certain members more than others, even to the point of refusing to recognize some as family members and denying their rights of inheritance. We have failed to accept all whom you have placed in our family with us. I also confess that some of those excluded retaliated against the family by send curses through witchcraft.

Step 6: *Apologizing, asking forgiveness and forgiving*

Lisa continued:

> For these transgressions against each other and against you, I am deeply sorry. I am sorry for all of the pain caused by our excluding and refusing family

belonging and love to some. I am sorry for excluding myself. I apologize for myself and for my ancestors. We have failed to accept and embrace those you sent to be part of our family. And I apologize on behalf of those who sought to retaliate through witchcraft. I am sorry for their pain but sad for their turning against you. However, we have also been blessed through our generations. Even as we wounded you and each other, some of my ancestors maintained our connection to our Jewish roots and they passed this desire on to me. For this I am grateful. I love this connection with my Jewish roots. Thank you Jesus!

After this, Lisa prayed:

Lord forgive us, forgive me and my family, those living and those departed. We refused to provide belonging to certain family members. We disowned them, tried to disinherit them. Especially forgive me for disowning myself. Forgive my mother, grandfather and great-grandmother for excluding children born at inconvenient times or with unwanted personalities. We failed to welcome the gifts you had given us and to enjoy and grow from these relationships as you had intended. Also, Lord, forgive me for the anger and resentment I have built up against my parents, siblings and ancestors for excluding me and others of their children, grandchildren, nieces and nephews from family belonging. And please forgive those of us who turned to witchcraft in our anger and to cursing other family members.

Later, having done her family research, Lisa imagined her parents and ancestors lives and experiences and the wounds she had discerned that her mother, father and grandfather had suffered. Knowing God's forgiveness of herself, her siblings and her ancestors, Lisa was ready to express her forgiveness to both living and deceased family members. She forgave them aloud before God in the privacy of her home, saying:

> Mom and Dad, Judy and Susan (her siblings), and grandfather, I forgive you for excluding me, for telling me that I did not belong, was not wanted, and did not deserve to be part of the family. I forgive you for treating me as if I had to earn my belonging and for making even earning a place difficult, really impossible. Distant ancestors and cousins, I appreciate your pain and forgive you for turning to empowerment through witchcraft and for cursing our family lineage.

At this point Lisa was surprised at the deepening awareness of all that she had received from God through her family research and prayers. She had come to genuinely feel a part of her family, an important part, with a mission to facilitate healing of her family lineages. "For this I am so grateful," she privately said to herself and to God.

Step 7: *Repenting: renouncing the old and asserting the new*

Lisa was ready to repent. She wrote down *exclusion* as the pattern to break and *inclusion* as the attitude and behavior to embrace. She wanted to simply and privately speak aloud to God and to herself. She prayed:

Lord, I lay down this pattern of exclusion of certain family members from family belonging. I ask you to break the hold of this pattern in me and in us, my family. Infuse us with the will and desire to include everyone born to us, accepting and welcoming those you place into our family. Also grant us the will and desire to include anyone adopted into the family. I commit to including myself. I am included, regardless of how other family members treat me, because you chose this family for me and me for this family. Thank you! I also renounce the use of witchcraft as a means of empowerment and inclusion. I commit to the knowledge that I belong, we all belong to each other, because you placed us here in this family lineage. I commit us all to this knowledge.

Step 8: *Rebuking evil, breaking curses and restoring blessings*

Lisa found it helpful to break the curse effect of words spoken against her and other family members, living and departed. She spoke aloud privately to God and to herself.

In the name of Jesus, I break the power and authority of words spoken against me and against other family members, living and departed, by our parents and grandparents, siblings, cousins and other family members, disowning us and pronouncing us unworthy to belong and excluded from belonging to the family. I accept my belonging to my family lineages and welcome all who have been excluded. In the name of Jesus, I break the effect of all curses sent against family members and the family lineage through witchcraft practices. I declare them null and void.

I bind all evil spirits that have preyed upon our family though these destructive patterns and curses, especially the spirit of exclusion and destruction of blessings. I bind all evil spirits who have oppressed my family lineages through their networks of communication, interaction, and interplay. I cast you out of me and my family lineages and relationships, immediately, completely, and permanently. I send you directly to Jesus for him to do with you as he wills.

Step 9: *Praying for healing: inviting Jesus into our ancestral past to heal and restore and praying for the departed*

Lisa prays for generational healing in her family whenever she feels the Lord's nudge to do so and when deep feelings surface that seem to be generationally connected, such as grief and fear of poverty, as well as exclusion. When she has confessed, forgiven, asked forgiveness, repented, broken curses and cast out evil, she sits quietly asking the Lord to heal her and her family. She rarely sees pictures in her mind's eye. She does hear words and feel intuitions. Recently, regarding the wound of exclusion, she sensed Jesus bringing all of those in her family lineages who had felt excluded, due to gender, religion, birth order, timing of conception or personality into his presence. She described this experience, saying, "I felt Jesus bestowing the gift of knowing they belonged, that he had chosen and placed them where he wanted them to be. I felt their joy and the angels' joy in heaven. What a celebration!"

Lisa belongs to a liturgical tradition where prayers for the departed are a part of every Holy Communion liturgy. So she found

Kenneth McAll's prayer form (see Chapter 7) useful and wanted to pray especially for specific Jewish ancestors who had been excluded from the family, for those who had turned to witchcraft in anger, and for her parents and grandparents who had excluded others from family belonging. She sat quietly after receiving Holy Communion one Sunday and prayed for her deceased ancestors to be united with Jesus using a printout of McAll's prayer form.

Lisa was thrilled to feel joined with her long-denied Jewish ancestors and their faith. She spoke aloud to God, "Thank you! I am blessed. I commit to nourishing my connection to these Jewish roots. Bring this desire alive in my siblings and cousins."

Step 10: *Reconciling actions*

Lisa then chose to disclose her generational healing process and experience more completely to certain of her cousins. This has led to additional joint genealogical research with these cousins and to a deeper bonding with these family members, who now include each other in the family.

Also Lisa has found that her commitment to treat herself as a valued family member has taken vigilance and ongoing attention. The habits of feeling excluded and not worthy were strong. So she has persisted in practicing the language of belonging when speaking of herself in her family.

Illustration: Tom

Step 1: *Awakening to the present influences of the past in your family lineages and calling out to God.*

Tom was adopted as an infant by parents of German ancestry. By the time he engaged generational healing prayers, his adoptive parents had both died. He had a brother, also adopted, two years his senior who was still living. Their adoptive father loved playing sports, especially baseball, and taught his boys well. They excelled. He felt loved by his adoptive parents, although they were not given to tactile affection. His adoptive mother could be harsh at times. His adoptive father was more accepting but also could be stern and demanding. So while Tom knew that he was wanted and loved, he also hungered for warmth and affection. Hunger for human warmth and acceptance was a healing concern he identified from his adoptive roots. With his biological roots he had no idea of specific healing concerns or benefits received, but would say, "I want to be connected to the persons who share with me this quality of being that I know. There are needs within me and passions I sense that are hard to pin down. What are they and where do they come from?"

Step 2: *Seeking God's face for your family lineages (listening to God and community)*

Tom tended to pray on the fly. He was an action guy. At times he was conscious of God's presence and he attended daily Catholic Mass. Mass provided him with a time of quiet, although his mind remained pretty active with his concerns of the day. It was during daily Mass that he became most aware of a growing desire to search for his biological parents.

In the quiet of daily Mass his deeply felt family concerns tended to awaken. Tom wanted to better understand his adoptive parents' reticence and lack of physically expressed warmth. He wanted to express affection toward his wife and to hug friends, but would pull back. He wanted to overcome his own reticence and coolness. He felt these tendencies in both of his adoptive parents' families. And he was increasingly determined to find a way to locate his biological parents.

Step 3: *Researching the sins, wounds and blessings of the past in your family lineages*

Tom talked with cousins who had done genealogical research and who had talked to their parents about the roots of these reticent tendencies. And he pursued information about his biological parents from the agency through which he had been adopted.

Tom began to understand that withholding of affection in his adoptive family was related to loss.

The early death of young children back several generations had set in motion a fear of attachment translating into withholding of touch. His cousins revealed to him several abortions that they knew about in their grandparents' generation, perhaps another indication of the fear of attachment. He also became aware that cancer was a prevalent cause of death. Understanding his biological family lineages awaited finding family members. A hope was growing.

Tom had to work through an inner barrier to saying, "I belong to my adoptive parents' lineages." His cousins and his brother helped him do this. His cousins, being biological kin to his adoptive parents, were key to helping him. They were clear, "You are one of us." On the other hand owning his belonging to his biological parents presented a different barrier. Yes, he was related, but did they *want* him? Could he own his belonging if they did not? This remained to be seen, if he could find them.

Tom was aware that the qualities in his adoptive family combined in him with those from his biological family. He had absorbed his adoptive father's interest in athletics, which his father had inherited from his father and uncles. He sensed that his longing for and enjoyment of affection was not only from the lack in his adoptive family but also in him naturally, inherited somehow thorough his biological lineages.

Step 4: *Searching the heart of God for your family lineages.*

Tom felt a growing love for his biological parents that he could only attribute to God. He didn't even know them. He also felt increasing urgency to try to find his biological family. Further, he sensed that God wanted him to bring for healing the losses, grief and guilt his adoptive grandparents, great aunts and uncles and great-grandparents felt from the early death of children and from several abortions. These wounds had never been healed and were imbedded in their emotional distancing and possibly compromising immune functions and enhancing vulnerability to cancer.

As Tom submitted his thoughts to the Holy Spirit's guidance, he sensed a growing authority to represent his adoptive family to God. This amazed him. Tom chose to discuss this awareness with his adopted brother. They had a common experience and he trusted him to listen. He asked his brother to meet him in a chapel where they could talk quietly and pray together.

Step 5: *Humbly confessing, personally and representationally*

Tom met his brother at a Catholic chapel, near his home. He liked to pray there. He had previously talked to his brother about the healing process he was engaging. He and his brother were rarely talkative with anyone about interior thoughts and feelings, so this was a new adventure for them. Tom's desire for healing and hunger to find his biological family gave him impetus to enter this new relational territory. Tom confessed aloud, but softly.

> Father I have harbored anger against my adoptive parents for their emotional distancing. No hugs. No affection. I now understand that this comes in part from their parents and grandparents who lost young

children through disease and abortion. Perhaps they withdrew from getting close to their other children as they were afraid of further losses and feeling guilt. So I bring to you their fear of loss, my parents' fear of loss, my fear of loss and our reaction of withdrawal. I bring to you their depriving their other offspring of affection and touch. I bring to you my parents and my need for warmth and touch. I bring to you this family's compromised immunity and susceptibility to cancer. I bring to you my desire to find my biological family.

His brother added, "Yes. I have the same need for affection. Searching for my biological family, I don't know. It scares me to think about it."

Step 6: *Apologizing, asking forgiveness and forgiving*

Tom asked God's forgiveness for himself, his parents, grandparents, great aunts and uncles, and great-grandparents.

Father, please forgive us. Forgive me for harboring anger against my parents for withholding affection from me. They were lacking affection from their parents. Forgive my parents, grandparents, great aunts and uncles and great-grandparents for withholding touch and affection from their children. Forgive those who aborted their children from fear of attachment and responsibility. I can see their hurt and grief and need. We are all in need. I forgive them, even though I am still hungry for touch and affection. I also feel confused as to why my biological parents gave me away. Somehow I know that my mother loved me. I still feel abandoned. I forgive her. Father, forgive her. I don't want to hold anything against her. I just want to find her.

His brother added. "I forgive my adoptive parents also. But I am not ready to forgive my biological parents. I can't even think about them without feeling enraged."

Tom had already forgiven his parents in the process of asking God's forgiveness. He was surprised, though, at his sudden gratitude toward his adoptive parents. "Thank you, Mom and Dad, for choosing me and keeping me. Thank you Father for finding me a home. I realize that your choice for me has helped me to love my wife's children (from her previous marriage) as my own. I never thought of that before."

Step 7: *Repenting: renouncing the old and asserting the new*

Tom wrote down *withdrawal of affection*. He then spoke out loud,

> I break the hold of this pattern on us, this withholding
> of affection from our children, this fear of loss. Father,
> break its hold. I commit to providing affection for my
> wife's children. I renounce the act of ending a life to
> avoid attachment. I break the hold of this pattern on
> all in these family lineages and commit us to embrace
> new life. I commit to my brother here that I will give
> him hugs the way I want to, if he will let me.

His brother smiled, "You can try."

Tom continued, "I repent of my hesitance to take further action in finding my biological family. I am going to act. Father, break the hold of any resistance in me."

Step 8: *Rebuking evil, breaking curses and restoring blessings*

Tom was again amazed at the prayer that came from his mouth.

> Father, in the name of Jesus, I cancel any curse upon my adoptive family's lineage that blocks conceiving children. If the fear of loss and the act of abortion opened the way to such a curse, I break the curse effect of that fear. I claim for this family the power and grace of conceiving children and raising them to adulthood. I wish this even though I am grateful for my parents' choice to adopt me when they could not conceive. Lord, have mercy. And I break any curse of cancer that has taken hold of grief, guilt and the fear of loss.

These prayers released in Tom a sense of being loved beyond what he could have imagined. Fear seemed to melt away.

> In the name of Jesus, I bind any evil spirits that promote fear of life, fear of conception, fear of loss, vulnerability to cancer. I bind these spirits from any hold they have had upon my adoptive family lineages. I command these spirits loosed and dismissed and send them immediately, completely and permanently to Jesus for him to do with them as he wills.

Step 9: *Praying for healing: inviting Jesus into our ancestral past to heal and restore and praying for the departed*

Tom and his brother sat before the Blessed Sacrament in the chapel after their prayers and conversation. Tom asked simply, "Father heal all the relationships between parents and children in my adoptive parents' lineages. Bring the children who died young and those aborted to their parents for healing and blessing." In his imagination he saw many hugs and kisses being shared in the next life and his adoptive parents smiling at him. "Father, I ask that you convey my love to my adoptive parents and bring them and all of their lineages into their home with you."

As Tom prayed this way, he visualized Jesus blessing his departed family. Suddenly, and without request, in his imagination he saw Jesus and Mary holding three babies, a little girl in Mary's arms and two little boys in Jesus arms. They seemed to be bringing the babies to him. One at a time each child was placed in Tom's arms and he was asked to bless and name each one. These seemed to be the babies who were aborted generations back. Tom was in tears. He blessed each child and named each child, Mary, Edward, and Samuel. These were names that came to him as he held each child in his imagination. Then he welcomed each child to the family saying, "You are part of us. You belong." Jesus and Mary then received each child back from Tom, thanked him and carried the children with them into the light. Tom sobbed, feeling deep joy. As he described to his brother what had happened, he felt so honored that Jesus and Mary would entrust this welcoming to him. "How amazing!" he exclaimed.

As this image faded and his tears abated, he then turned his attention to his biological parents. "Father, connect us. Help me find them now." All he could see was a faint image of his biological mother longing for him. He resolved to recommence a search for his biological parents.

Step 10: *Reconciling actions*

Tom repeated to his brother his determination to try to find his biological family. And he asked him, "Will you support me in my search?" His brother agreed,

Yes, I support you. Please keep me informed. Maybe I will get more comfortable with searching for my biological family. Right now, thinking about them makes me angry. I don't want to find them. I would like to keep praying together like this though. I feel so much better about myself and our childhood.

Walking through the generational healing steps for your family lineages

Having read Lisa's and Tom's journeys through generational healing prayers, we will now walk you through these generational healing steps in your own family lineages. You might be helped in doing this to mark the pages in Chapter Seven that correspond to each of the 10 generational healing steps. While we will name the steps here, the full discussion of each step appears in Chapter Seven. As you work on each step, review that step in Chapter Seven.

Step 1: *Awakening to the present influences of the past in your family lineages and calling out to God.*

You may become aware of attitudes or behaviors that your parents or ancestors exhibited recurring in yourself such as anxiety, depression, distrust, separation, alienation, hostility, broken relationships, struggles with faith, or failures to thrive. Even physical diseases may reveal that something has not been right generationally. Notice any current relationships and/or conditions that seem to draw influence from transgressions, unhealed wounds, unforgiven events and broken relationships of generations past. Also note thriving talents, loving relationships, generous forgiveness and/or sturdy faith, which may have been nourished, encouraged and appreciated from generation-to-generation, providing beneficial resources.

Benefits received and hurts suffered often have roots that extend to our parents' childhoods and to their parents' childhoods, and even further back. At some point, something triggers a nagging sense that you are reliving old history.

Think prayerfully about your own family lineages. Where do you see relationship patterns, unforgiveness, resentments or negative attitudes? Explore any mental, emotional or physical conditions, diseases, occult spiritual practices, distrust of God. Where do you see love, encouragement, forgiveness, faith, or other positive traits in prior generations repeated in or clearly affecting your life today? What has been passed from generation-to-generation that strengthens and weakens you and your relationships?

Now among the family lineages that seem connected to or to embody the concerns you are bringing for healing, notice which family lineages you are most sensitive to, affected by, or burdened by at this time.

☐ *Write down these lineages and the specific destructive patterns or realities that most burden or concern you.*

☐ *Then note and record the specific strengths and gifts* that you appreciate in these lineages.

☐ *Review your notes and look for patterns* that seem to be present. Then speak your awareness to God.

Step 2: *Seeking God's face for your family lineages (listening to God and community)*

As you awaken to generational influences in your family lineages, begin to center on faith in God's presence and leading. We respond to God's work in us. God acts, we follow. As Romans 4:3 describes,

187

"Abraham entered into what God was doing for him, and that was the turning point" (MSG).

☐ At this point *give to God everything you have become aware of in your family lineages*. Lay it all down and say,

> God, I give to you all I now know about my family.
> Take these thoughts and concerns. Sort them for me.
> Illumine and expand my awareness. Then lead me
> in this generational healing of my family lineages.
> Take me by the hand into the work you have pre-
> pared for me.

We each have our ways of seeking God's face, of reaching to God and entering God's presence. In Chapter 7 we detailed several spiritual actions which can now be applied in your own family context.

☐ *Focus on Jesus and his redemptive work* within your family lineage.

☐ *Protect yourself by binding the evil one in the name of Jesus Christ* and seeking God's protection.

☐ *Consciously orient and open yourself to the Holy Spirit*, seeking God's guidance and revelations of truth, of all that you need to be aware of in your family lineages.

☐ *Now review those family lineages and healing concerns* that you have recorded as prominent in your awareness thus far. Ask the Holy Spirit to lead you in choosing a particular family lineage and concerns to focus on for healing at this time.

Step 3: *Researching the sins, wounds and blessings of the past in your family lineages*

For each healing concern you identified, search your family lineage for the historical roots, influences and consequences that may have passed from generation-to-generation. Look for life diminishing injuries, patterns, burdens, and life giving gifts and blessings that passed from generation-to-generation. Research and ponder the stories of the past, subjective and objective, the events and responses to events which seem to continue to influence present conditions and patterns.

☐ As you do this, *attempt to see your ancestors from the perspective of their concerns*, perceptions, pressures and horizons, that is, their otherness.

☐ *Gather information from a variety of sources.*

Appendices A, B and C may help your search for roots of your present healing concerns. In Appendix A are instructions for drawing a genogram (family tree) which can be a helpful method for recording family data and keeping the generations clearly pictured. We have included a list of types of significant information in Appendix B that can help stimulate awareness and research inquiry. Also the chart in Appendix C can be used to record your findings generation-by-generation showing patterns and inter-relationships.

Explore specific ancestors' contributions in your lineage by talking to family members—with siblings, parents, grandparents, aunts and uncles, cousins and close family friends. You will find as many points of view as there are individuals. Each perspective can help you enlarge your range of viewpoints and help to differentiate between those held in common and those that are unique to specific family members.

We need multiple perspectives to enlarge our awareness of what has been given, by whom and to whom, in each generation. What others see and appreciate helps you to understand the contributions to your own life. The process of dialogue itself can yield deepened connections among those speaking to each other, as well as with those not present and those deceased whose cares, contributions and impact are being searched.

Seek to be fair, to give credit where it is due, as well as account for deprivations and injuries, by searching the context and resources of each family member so you can, in turn, seek to realistically honor your ancestors in light of their legacies.

Children can never fairly evaluate how and what their parents gave (and how they deprived and injured) without seeing into the contexts of their parents own births, growth and struggles as adults. Thus an evaluation of anyone's contributions to posterity involves understanding at least three generations: the child, parent and grandparent generations of the person being considered. An ancestor's actions may actually appear heroic in the light of the tragic life context and minimal resources of the ancestor. Validation of debilitating factors (genetic, economic, cultural), relational deprivations and injuries in their lives, as well as the benefits they received, can recast the meaning of our parents' or grandparents' apparent failures, making positive attempts at caring plain. For example, a parent or grandparent who was abused as a child may believe that withholding himself would prevent his child or grandchild from being more seriously wounded by his own deficiencies. He may view himself as inadequate and *bad* for others.

This is not to romanticize ordinary human deeds or to deny the destructive effects of real injury. Nevertheless, it is to see and honor the heroic in the ordinary. Even the choice to live can be heroic when the pressures to give up, to yield, to submit to death are great enough. A person's actions must be understood in context.

☐ *Seek the strength and guidance of the Holy Spirit for illumination of the collected data.* Ask the Holy Spirit to engage your imagination so that you can envision each person's experience in each generation, creating generational story lines. This searching process can unite with prayer for strength and insight as you recognize the indwelling healing, catalytic and reconciling action of the Holy Spirit on behalf of each person, living and deceased. The inquiry process can be healing in itself, as persons are better understood in their time and context with their strengths and limitations.

☐ *From objective and subjective information, you can begin to outline your generational story lines.* You can begin to imagine sequential generational transmission of the particular emotions, vulnerabilities, attitudes, identities, beliefs, resentments, idolatries, faithfulness and unfaithfulness, addictions, interpersonal alienations or relationship patterns for which you seek healing.

Stop reading now to record your present view of the generational passage of injuries, deprivations, broken relationships, emotional conditions, and strengths and blessings that have been taking shape for you so far as you have investigated the family roots of the concerns that you have identified.

☐ *Own your belonging to this history, to this family lineage.* "This is *my* history. These are *my* people." Speak this in a way that is meaningful to you. Note any resistances to owning your belonging.

☐ *Identify your complicity with harm done,* your own part in continuing the attitudes and patterns that are the subject of your inquiry. Identify your part in continuing the blessings that have passed generation to generation. *Detail the consequences to your life of injuries suffered or transgressions committed* in the generations of this lineage and the consequences in your life of blessings passed forward. *Tell the history you have constructed* and what you suspect but are still unsure about, to yourself and to others whom you trust to hear you.

As you continue your research, reflect on the relationships you are forming with your family history; and therefore, with your family ancestors. Your relationship to your family history (and your ancestors), can be viewed as an ongoing conversation, a give and take, extending over long sweeps of time. Through research and imagination ancestors speak their experience, and we respond from our current predicament, state of health, stage of life, and so on.[45]

Step 4: *Searching the heart of God for your family lineages.*

☐ *Give to God the facts you have collected about your family, and the suppositions and imaginings you have about them.* Ask the Holy Spirit to show you God's heart for this lineage and to awaken in you love for your people, for your family.[46] Your belonging to this history may be experienced as a kind of impassioned solidarity with the past.[47]

As you explore your family roots, for whom is compassion growing in you? What are you finding that you have in common with your ancestors, your parents, your siblings, your cousins?

☐ *Identify your authority to represent this lineage.* As you seek God's heart for your family, see yourself as a fellow transgressor bringing the family to God for forgiveness, healing and transformation. Belonging and love entitle you to confess representationally, standing before God on behalf of your family lineage. Being a family member entitles you to confess representationally. God's nudge and call entitles you to bring your family lineage to him for forgiveness, healing and blessing. Note your sense of what God is urging and encouraging you to bring to him for healing and for strengthening.

☐ *Name the good done*, that which has been especially gifting to past and present generations of this lineage.

☐ *Identify wrongs done, wounds created and degrees of culpability.* As you have placed before God all you have become aware of, now ask God to reveal his heart and mind to you. How does God see the wrongs done, the wounds created and the persons responsible? Listen within your prayer for God's perspective. What is God urging you to bring in confession? From God's point of view what seem to be the significant transgressions, wounds and culpabilities that God is moving you to own and speak. Remember the Holy Spirit is active within you shaping God's perspective. Be at ease. Simply record what God seems to be underlining. List those wrongs, such a refusal to forgive, resentment carried, abandonment, cruelty, scapegoating, unfair blame or rejection. Write what was done generation-to-generation to whom, by whom, between whom, that you sense God moving you to bring into confession at this time.

☐ *Establish the leading of the Holy Spirit* to do this representational work at this time. Ask the Holy Spirit to lead and confirm the work that is to be done now. Write down your sense of the Holy Spirit's leading as to the specific focus of confession, forgiveness, repentance and healing now.

☐ *Determine to whom and with whom you are speak your generational confession* and where this is to be done. Look for someone who will understand the process and with whom to share what you have written as important to confess at this time. A trained prayer minister, a trusted friend, a family member who shares your struggle and is open to doing this with you could be appropriate. Or you may be moved to speak to God in private at this time.

☐ *Remember God's call, kindness and covenant.* Remember this is God's work through you. You are being led by One who is forgiving and merciful, who is making all things new, all things whole.

Step 5: *Humbly confessing, personally and representationally*

Remember that generational healing is a process. You are confessing what is salient *at this time* and what you sense the Holy Spirit is nudging you to bring into the light of confession now. As you go on, further research and increased imagination will probably reveal more understanding of the generational roots of the issues you are currently bringing into confession. Additional issues will gradually come to your awareness. Do not worry about being complete or comprehensive. Simply work with what you have at this time.

Make your family confession to God, silently or aloud, alone or with others, as you have been led, in as much detail as needed so as to fully confess. Speaking aloud, even to yourself (and to God) can be helpful. Hearing yourself may bring deeply felt emotions surprisingly alive, freeing a felt connection with ancestral roots. If you are working together with other family members on this healing project and pooling research and insights, remember to encourage each other to make your own confessions each from your own perspectives. In this way each exercises freedom of conscience, speaking of realities as they appear and are led by the Spirit at work in each of you. Take care with questions to each other. Refrain from judging. Respect and protect each other's sense of truth and the Spirit. Avoid strong-arming each other, shaming or manipulating others into feeling guilt. We call these family confessions representational in that they are spoken on behalf of yourself and your family lineage.

☐ *Now speak your family confession to God as the Holy Spirit is leading you*, using the notes you have accumulated and the particular perspectives God has shaped in you. If you are moved to speak these to others as well, make plans to do so. Experiment and search out what works best for you, what feels most meaningful and effective. You can always reengage this confession at another time, take a different step, or alter course as your experience with this grows. Remember this is God's work in and through you and is for you and your family. This work proceeds from God's love, forgiveness and mercy.

☐ *As you are moved by the Holy Spirit, express gratitude to God* for the good passed down to you and *remorse for wrong-doing* and its destructive consequences.

Step 6: *Apologizing, asking forgiveness and forgiving*

☐ *First, make apologies to God and others* (where appropriate and led by God) on behalf of yourself and your lineage, aware of hurts caused and sorrow (remorse, sadness) for wrong-doing and destructive consequences. Here you are saying that you are truly sorry. You are remorseful for your transgressions and for those of your siblings, parents, grandparents, extended family and ancestors. Name the transgressions, the hurt you see that has been suffered, the injuries and deprivations you truly grieve, and express your remorse.

☐ *Next, ask God's forgiveness for personal transgressions and transgressions in the family lineage* (a representational action)—things done and left undone that one has become aware of and confessed and for which one has been moved to seek God's forgiveness. These may include not only transgressions within the family, sins of omission and commission, but also injuries inflicted by family members on those of other families, organizations, or communities. Having asked God's forgiveness, you may be moved to ask forgiveness of others as well (where appropriate and led by God).

☐ *You may ask forgiveness from those in the living generations* of your family who have suffered the transgressions you have identified. This includes *asking forgiveness for your own transgressions* and complicities as they have affected others. You can also *stand in for ancestors asking those living for forgiveness on their behalf.* This *standing in for* may extend beyond your family. You may be moved by the Holy Spirit to seek out others who have been wounded by members of your family (through prejudice, unkindness, financial harm, etc.) or whose ancestors have been injured by your ancestors and to ask their forgiveness.

However, never expect or demand forgiveness. Simply and freely ask. Those addressed may not be ready or even see the need. Apologies given, and forgiveness asked, pave the way for God's intervention, release and blessing for all those affected and afflicted.

☐ *Offer forgiveness to your ancestors and to others* who have wounded members of your lineage (where appropriate). Forgiving proceeds from knowing God's forgiveness personally and becoming aware of your parents' and ancestors' and others' struggles, context and wounding.

☐ *Express gratitude for God's faithfulness* and for the additional blessings of the generations that have come to light in the process of confessing, asking forgiveness and forgiving. Name any additional strengths, gifts and values that have become evident to you.

Step 7: *Repenting: renouncing the old and asserting the new*

☐ *Commit yourself and your family lineage* (as a representative of the lineage) *to replacing old destructives patterns* of thought, attitude, action and belief with life-giving patterns.

☐ *Ask God to break the compulsive hold of the destructive patterns* upon your life, your relationships and on this family lineage.

☐ A simple way to do this is to *identify and write down the destructive patterns.* Then beside each pattern, *list the attitudes and actions that you commit to implement* in order to replace the destructive attitudes and actions.

Step 8: *Rebuking evil, breaking curses and restoring blessings*

☐ *Use the prayers in Chapter Seven to break the power of curses:*

> Lord Jesus, in your name, I break the power and authority of any curses against myself, my family members, and my family lineages, resulting from our disobedience to you, our transgressions against others, words spoken against others, words we have spoken against ourselves and/or our own lineage, or words spoken or invoked against us and/or our lineage by others... (Continue with this prayer in Chapter 7 applied to your family lineages.)

☐ *Pray to bind and send away any evil spirits:* "In the name of Jesus I bind any evil spirits that have indwelled and empowered the destructive patterns and curses that have now been broken..." (Continue with the prayer in Chapter 7 applied to your family lineages.)

Free of the constraining influence of destructive patterns, curses and their evil spirit partners, you and members of your family lineage are now increasingly liberated to embrace transformed attitudes and new beliefs, identities, behaviors and ways of relating. Emptied out and freed, you must now replace the negative with a positive commitment and blessing, inviting the Holy Spirit to fill the spaces left by the departure of evil spirits.

Step 9: *Praying for healing: inviting Jesus into your ancestral past to heal and restore and praying for the departed*

Using the prayer guidance in Chapter Seven, pray for the healing of your family lineages and the individual members of it. In our experience, prayers for healing ancestral memories, injuries and deprivations tend to occur while sitting in a quiet place in meditation after confessing, forgiving, repenting, breaking curses and binding and casting out of evil spirits. And they may continue to flow in following days and weeks as new awareness grows.

☐ *You can imagine family members, living and departed, including yourself, with Jesus,* who is actively mending family relationships and wounds with healing. Amazing experiences often occur during these generational healing prayers, especially when the work of confession, forgiveness, repentance and deliverance has been done for the healing concerns in focus.

☐ *Prayers for those who have died,* may also flow in this period after repentance and deliverance intentions. See McAll's prayer form in Chapter Seven as a way of praying for the departed. Pray for departed ancestors as you feel led by the Holy Spirit and according to your spiritual comfort with this practice. Specific prayers for aborted and miscarried babies can be especially needed and powerful at this point. These can include blessing the babies, naming them and receiving them into the family.[48]

☐ *Expressing gratitude and reengaging your positive legacy* often flow spontaneously from healing prayers.

☐ *Explicitly pray that the blessings God intended* to flow through these lineages now be released.

Step 10: *Reconciling actions*

Review the suggestions for Step 10 in Chapter Seven. Use those that you feel led to implement in relation to your family lineages. God's movement through generational healing always keeps on going. Next steps may be to engage another set of healing concerns in your family lineages. Also, further steps of reconciliation often flow from our generational healing prayers.

Allow the Holy Spirit to form next steps within your mind and imagination.

Generational healing can require considerable spiritual and emotional energy. Deep emotions often surface. Working through the process with a trained therapist, spiritual director or prayer minister, or simply a trusted friend or family member will ease the burden and provide perspective as you walk through the process.

For Reflection

Meditate on the following portion of Psalm 107, asking God to show you both the blessings and the desert places in your own family lineages:

[33] He turns rivers into a desert,
  springs of water into thirsty ground,
[34] a fruitful land into a salty waste,
  because of the wickedness of its inhabitants.
[35] He turns a desert into pools of water,
  a parched land into springs of water.
[36] And there he lets the hungry live,

and they establish a town to live in;
37 they sow fields, and plant vineyards,
   and get a fruitful yield.
38 By his blessing they multiply greatly,
   and he does not let their cattle decrease.
39 When they are diminished and brought low
   through oppression, trouble, and sorrow,
40 he pours contempt on princes
   and makes them wander in trackless wastes;
41 but he raises up the needy out of distress,
   and makes their families like flocks.
42 The upright see it and are glad;
   and all wickedness stops its mouth.
43 Let those who are wise give heed to these things,
   and consider the steadfast love of the LORD.

1. Make note of any additional issues that concern you that have not yet been addressed, including physical diseases, mental and emotional conditions, attitudes, behavior patterns, relationship struggles, or spiritual unease that seem to be passed generation to generation in your family lineages and for which you desire healing. Pick one issue and work through the Ten Steps in this chapter in regard to your particular concerns.

2. Take time to ponder your reflections, making notes of any further awareness and or insight that these reflections bring to mind regarding your family lineages.

3. Prayerfully consider whom God may be calling to walk with you through this process.

Chapter 9

Healing the Lineages of Churches and Organizations

Generational wounds occur in almost every church and organization. We are all sinful people who have been sinned against; therefore, when we gather as a community we bring our personal histories with us and compound them with the group histories. These wounds may be buried deep in our personal and corporate past. The initial wounding incident may be long-forgotten, or only communicated surreptitiously. "Stuffing it," what psychology calls *suppression*, is one of the most common ways of dealing with painful memories. However, even as the memories fade, powerful attitudes and behaviors continue to pass from generation-to-generation and shape the character of the community.

A classic example is a story told by Russ Parker of two dwindling parishes in England that refused to merge and work together as the bishop requested. After much probing, one older member of the smaller church finally admitted the real reason, "They didn't tell us that the Vikings were coming!" The congregation was still holding a grudge against the larger church because over 1000 years ago the neighboring church had spotted an incoming Viking invasion from their tower. However, they only warned their own members—not the other church or the wider community, which suffered greatly. Although few people knew about that incident, the attitudes of resentment and distrust still persisted.[49]

Deep wounds can occur through abuse of power, major trauma, broken trust, betrayal or even a theological controversy that resulted in castigating one another. Some form of sexual abuse usually shows up in the history of most wounded Christian communities, as does the abuse of power. Abuses of power include assigning responsibilities without giving commensurate authority or appropriate preparation, undermining the work of subordinates or volunteers, unfair or harsh evaluations, manipulating relationships to create conflict (often through spreading untruths or half-truths), lack of support, blaming, shaming and failure to follow through on promises. Abusive leaders are often charming and talented. They may garner respect, trust and loyalty from followers, only to humiliate them later. Therefore, those who have not experienced the abuse will have difficulty believing victims.

Community wounding is complex and usually involves a huge web of transgressions, often with varying degrees of healing in some parts of the web. Some victims will move on to victimize others in other settings. Others will find partial healing. However, it is only when the current body recognizes the corporate sins of the past, identifies with them, confesses and repents, that deep healing begins to flow.

We will follow two corporate stories of generational wounding through the healing process. As you read these examples and walk through the steps for healing, look at your own church or organization and bring it into this healing journey.

■ Saint Ambrose Church always seemed on the cusp of growth. Enthusiastic lay leaders showed a heart for evangelism and caring for the surrounding community. New people seemed drawn to the church. However, pastors stayed only about two to five years, and then moved on. Attendance would surge to about 150 as each new pastor began, and then gradually fall back to under 100. With strong adult leadership the active youth program would grow, become active and visible in the life of the congregation, and then suddenly fall apart. Youth advisors would start out deeply committed and passionate, but resign after a few years feeling disillusioned, often leaving the church as well. Youth group members would begin united and hopeful, only to slowly divide into rival cliques. A similar pattern seemed to occur among committees and the church council. Despite a positive veneer, an underlying spirit of negativity and distrust seemed to pervade the congregation's outlook. Church leaders puzzled over how, even though the people involved would change, the patterns remained the same. Why couldn't they get beyond these discouraging trends?

■ The Agape Community Food Bank tried desperately to live up to its name. Founded by an ecumenical group of churches deeply committed to the needs of the poor in their area, they established a nonprofit organization to provide food and other services for those in need. However, from the start there seemed to be a latent spirit of competition and an undermining of one another that reared up on a regular basis. Each church seemed eager to receive public recognition of their efforts without fully acknowledging the contributions of the other churches. Some of the churches seemed to have connections with the press, so they would often be featured in newspaper articles or the TV news, but no mention would be made of the other cooperating churches. The ignored churches would then feel slighted. Lack of communication caused services to be duplicated, or not carried through. Volunteers at the food bank would sometimes reorganize the inventory without consulting volunteers from the other churches, so that it became difficult to find needed items. Disparaging remarks would then be dropped around other volunteers and even to those who came for help. Monthly board meetings usually degenerated into shouting matches. Volunteers often became disillusioned and quit, but they were usually replaced quickly by eager new volunteers; however the patterns of competition and disparagement continued. Why couldn't they get along? ■

When churches or organizations experience unhealthy relationships and breakdowns in communication, the underlying systems can become both abusive and addictive. These dysfunctional behaviors and interactions can hook those involved, leading to dependency and "process addiction." For instance, when the shelves of the food pantry were constantly being rearranged, one volunteer, Sharon, took on the role of organizer and guard to ensure that all items remained in their proper places. Sharon came in whenever a new group began serving and made sure no one rearranged the shelves. She became so focused on that role that she spoke rudely and refused to budge when anyone challenged the arrangement. Eventually, it became an unwritten rule that nothing would ever change in the way the pantry was organized— even when the current arrangement became impractical.

Process addictions—addictions to specific way of doing things or thinking about things—may develop regarding work, sex, money, gambling, religion, relationships and certain types of thinking, such as self-deprecation or scarcity mentality.[50] These patterns often form as a result of generational wounding. The people of St. Ambrose and the churches who organized the food bank were both suffering from process additions. Think about your own church or organizational dynamics. How might the following characteristics of addiction for both individuals and systems be at work?

1. Denial—this is not really happening because we are nice people;
2. Confusion—why do things always end up in conflict?

3. Self-centeredness—everything that happens is "for" or "against" us;
4. Dishonesty—to self, people around us and world at large, including "putting up a good front," or rationalizing that everything is being done for the other's benefit;
5. Perfectionism—anything less is not good enough;
6. Scarcity model—feeling that there is not enough time, attention, or money go around;
7. Illusion of control—it won't be done right unless I do it;
8. Frozen feelings—emotions viewed as weaknesses;
9. Ethical deterioration leading to spiritual bankruptcy—the addictive process attacks the group's morality and deep spiritual values.[51]

An overall denial of dysfunction—an abnormal or impaired functioning within the system or social group—allows unhealthy situations to fester and grow. Church or organization members and leaders may feel confused. They may leave the church/organization without reporting the problems, allowing the patterns to continue unchallenged. Administrators often attribute the problems to "personality conflicts" and do not look for deeper issues. The constant recurrence of interpersonal conflict results in an organizational self-centeredness that saps energy and diverts time away from ministry and productivity. Leadership meetings seem to focus more on working out relationships than on actually working toward their intended mission. On the other hand, a veneer of peace and smooth relationships may hide seething resentment and fear. Manipulation may be covered by a facade of caring, compassion and spirituality.

■ For example St. Ambrose Church presented itself as a growing, family-friendly congregation where all people were loved and valued. However, staff meetings often degenerated into competition for scarce funds and blaming one another or others for low attendance. Their pastor insisted that the way to judge ministry success was by counting "bucks and butts." Any programs that did not draw a large attendance and significant funding were dropped.

■ The Food Bank saw themselves as the only people in town who really cared about the poor. Each congregation would try to top the others in the gifts and services they provided. Each would compete for the loyalty of the people they served. Members of one congregation would frequently denigrate the other churches in casual conversations with clients, friends and colleagues under the guise of their concern for excellence. ■

The "scarcity model"—a sense that there is not enough to go around of funds, personnel, material goods or attention—leads to playing one person against another to gain power, control and affection. Relationships become exclusive and competitive. The illusion of control becomes evident as those leaders abusing power move from one victim to another, while others inadvertently enable the behavior.

■ The senior pastor of St. Ambrose Church felt jealous of the attention that the youth group advisors received from the group members and their parents. He kept his ears open for any complaints from the congregation about the youth ministry and often exaggerated the concerns when he reported them to the youth advisors. He constantly criticized the youth leaders until they eventually quit and left the church. The youth and their families were forced to take sides, and most of those siding with the former youth leaders ended up leaving the church as well. The pattern repeated itself over and over.

■ The Food Bank volunteers saw scarcity all around them. There were always more people to feed than food to go around. Their fear of the food running out caused them to treat clients with suspicion, assuming that many were free-loading and did not really need the handouts. They also treated one another with suspicion. Frequently, someone would comment, "You have to watch Sue, she always gives clients more than they should receive." Sometimes one volunteer would step over to others to correct them in front of the clients. ■

A deep fear of emotion, especially loneliness, anger or loss may underlie the pattern of distrust and criticism. The constant criticism may shame the person under scrutiny. When people feel shamed, they seldom report the offense. So shame provides secrecy to protect the behavior from exposure—especially where sexual harassment or emotional abuse are involved. No one wants to admit they have been attacked, especially when the person attacking is a respected leader or when victims feel that they may have inadvertently provoked the attack. This, in turn, leads to ethical deterioration or spiritual bankruptcy as the problems are spiritualized in order to avoid dealing with them.

■ Years before the current pastor of St. Ambrose Church arrived, there had been an incident in which a well-liked youth advisor had been caught fondling a teenage girl in the church. He admitted to having an affair with her for several months. The incident was covered up. The girl's parents were not sympathetic with their daughter and accused her of flirting and causing the problem. She refused to attend church anymore and developed and eating disorder. This incident became indelibly impressed on the minds of the church board. Every new pastor was warned that this should never happen again. However, rather than dealing with the situation openly with the congregation, it had been kept silent. No one was allowed to speak of it openly. If they did, they were immediately told that this was gossip and it was sinful to spread such rumors. No one really knew exactly what happened, but it became part of the church's whispered story. ■

Victims of clergy sexual abuse often suffer profound spiritual losses, including loss of the church as a safe haven, loss of the faith community, loss of confidence in church teachings and even loss of faith in God. The church's response must be to believe the victim, ensure confidentiality and discipline the abuser. If a minor was involved, the incident must be reported to proper authorities. Because most abusers have more than one victim, it is a high risk for the church to return a known abuser to a parish, or to allow abuse to go unreported.[52]

Most people think of abuse only as physical harm, or sexual aggression; however, it also includes verbal abuse, fear and intimidation, or any action that humiliates or destroys another's self-esteem.[53] The stress created by emotional abuse affects not only the immediate victims, but also the ability of the entire group to function effectively. As you look at the history of your church or organization, look for patterns where verbal abuse may have been passed down, either from within the organizational structure, or in the families of those involved in conflicts.

Abuse, when it comes from religious leaders, supervisors and counselors, can be especially damaging. Christian leaders often represent God to their victims. When a leader who has had a significant influence on someone's spiritual formation becomes physically, sexually or emotionally abusive, everything that leader represents may become tainted for the victim. Clergy sexual abuse has wreaked havoc in churches of all denominations, church-related schools and Christian organizations. Sexual abuse can range from sexual intercourse to erotic talk, seductive behavior, fondling and kissing. Sexual advances toward a parishioner or a supervisee are *never* appropriate because the impact of such behavior wounds at the deepest level, sometimes causing the victim to abandon her faith entirely. The consent of the other person is *not* a defense. Sexual advances or contact between a person in authority and supervisees is a betrayal of a trust relationship and an abuse of power and control.

■ The director of the Agape Food Bank abused volunteers by manipulating them against one another. He would call volunteers from one church into his office to tell them that volunteers from another church were accusing them of some inappropriate behavior, and then berate them for their alleged actions. Some of these wounded volunteers stopped helping at the Food Bank, but others continued because their strong commitment to the poor over-rode their pain. Instead, they buried their emotions and continued serving. However, negative attitudes and unspoken fears seriously interfered with the interpersonal relationships among the volunteers. ■

Churches and organizations can become abusive when the following characteristics conducive to exploitation exist:

- Homogenized values ("If you don't believe the way I do, you can't belong");
- Over-commitment by staff and volunteers (with expectations that parishioners/supervisees will maintain similar levels of commitment);
- High stress (which may lead to various forms of emotional abuse);
- Low support (and alternately being approached as "special" by a leader);
- Strong "no-talk" rules about sexuality (preventing reports of abuse).

Use these characteristics to assess where some of the roots of any generational wounding may lie in your own situation. As you become aware of these signs and symptoms, walk through the following healing steps with your own church or organization in mind.

209

Step 1: *Awakening to the present influences of the past and calling out to God*

At some point every church or organization will face a crisis that feels all too familiar. It may manifest as a rapid turnover of leadership, a series of leaders with widely divergent leadership styles, a pattern of recurring sexual indiscretions (often with different perpetrators and victims), chronic low morale within the congregation or organization, conflicts that seem to come out of nowhere, a surge of membership losses, frustration among lay leaders or middle management, or just a nagging sense of "why is this happening again?" This is the time to begin calling out to God, asking for wisdom and discernment about the root causes of these recurring patterns.

■ St. Ambrose Church had called five pastors over the past twelve years. Each seemed to be the direct opposite of the previous one. The first was socially and theologically liberal. When he finally announced that he could no longer believe in God, he was asked to resign. His successor was strongly fundamentalist and advocated home schooling to protect the children in the congregation from being influenced by the world. Almost every sermon contained an anti-abortion theme. It was during his tenure that the incident with the youth advisor's sexual indiscretion occurred. The pastor was asked to leave after two years. The next pastor was an academic who preached complex, scholarly sermons that no one understood. He was recently divorced, which had precipitated a forced resignation from his seminary professorship. He arrived at St. Ambrose with a girlfriend who wanted nothing to do with the church. She was frequently observed staying overnight at the parsonage and eventually moved into the parsonage. At that point the church council requested the pastor's resignation. During his tenure, the youth group disbanded and most of the young families left the church. The next pastor was a young woman with excellent pastoral skills and a deep desire to see the congregation healed, but she was constantly blind-sided and undermined by female leaders in the congregation. She stayed two years. By then the congregation was down to 35 and the denomination sent in an interim pastor who openly acknowledged that he had a borderline personality disorder. The church then actively began considering whether they should disband. They began crying out to God for guidance.

■The Agape Food Pantry found that whenever their ministry seemed to be flourishing the most, something would occur to create discord and division. The Agape Director was accused of siphoning off funds. A volunteer became involved with a drug ring and was selling marijuana to clients. Another volunteer was arrested for prostitution. Friction mounted among participating congregations. Several churches split off to form their own food pantries. The Food Pantry board members began to cry out to God, "Why is this happening?" Two board members committed themselves to pray together weekly. ■

In practical terms, this awakening may start with one individual becoming aware of patterns within the church or organization that indicate a deeper wounding. It may come to a small group or among the leadership. Prayer at this point can be a calling out to God about what is going on and asking for wisdom and discernment about how to proceed.

The church council at St. Ambrose began meeting weekly for prayer and called on the congregation to pray daily for their church. At the Food Pantry, a small group of concerned volunteers met weekly off-site to pray for discernment in their situation.

Step 2: *Seeking God's face (listening to God and community)*

Seeking God's face begins with appreciating who God is—worship. Before delving into an identified problem area, look back over

God's faithfulness in your corporate history. List the blessings you have experienced and thank God for them. Note the periods of fruitfulness and their relationship to the times of wounding. Praise God for his faithfulness in hard times and thank him for the positive effects of painful experiences, which may include deepening faith, character-building and strengthening of lay leadership.

☐ *Ask God to show you where negative spiritual influences linger from the sins of the past.* Pray through your facilities asking God to show you places that have been desecrated by sin. For instance, a room in which a sexual affair or conflict took place, a pulpit from which bullying messages were proclaimed, pews that were claimed and occupied by unwelcoming members or an office where intrigue was plotted, need to be blessed and reconsecrated for holy purposes. When evil spirits are discerned, they can be bound and sent to the foot of the cross. As Peter reminds us, "Discipline yourselves, keep alert. Like a roaring lion your adversary the devil prowls around, looking for someone to devour" (1 Pet 5:8). That prowling lion seems to show up whenever Christians are most fruitful.

☐ Generational healing is always a spiritual encounter—between the power of God and evil forces. *Pray for protection from spirits that seek to do harm* using wording similar to the example below. Pray especially for protection over relationships between leaders and members. Pray blessing on those who seem to be creating conflict and division, and for everyone involved in the healing process.

☐ *Respect the leaders God has placed over you* as much as possible. Listen carefully to what they have to say, even if you do not agree with them.

Binding and Covering Prayer

In the name of Jesus Christ and by the power of his blood, we bind all spirits in this place that are not of God. In the name of Jesus Christ we seal this room/building in the blood of Jesus. Lord, protect us by your Holy Spirit and surround us with your holy angels, through Christ our Lord. Amen

---

☐ *Pursue generational healing with humility.* Do not shame anyone or make scapegoats of individuals.

☐ *Work through the appropriate leaders, if possible.* Be careful that the generational healing process does not become a subversive movement. Even if leaders do not support the process, keep them informed and included unless it becomes counter-productive.

- If the clergy or organizational leaders appear to be causing or exacerbating the wounds, it may be necessary to work through the board and/or the next level of authority in your denomination or organization.

- If authorities shut down the generational healing procedures, wait respectfully and pray for the appropriate time to resume the process. Sometimes the road blocks protect you from unknown dangers or lead to better opportunities.

- Seek the Holy Spirit for direction regarding intercession for generational healing as you wait for readiness among leaders and members.

- Remember that God made the Israelites wander in the desert for forty years, even though the trip to Canaan could have been much shorter. Impatience can subvert the healing process.

☐ When possible, *gather leaders and members together to pray* for the ministry of your congregation or organization. Ask God to reveal areas that need healing.

- Make listening prayer a priority in your personal and corporate life.
- Pray together for the Lord's guidance and direction.
- Take time for silence in your group time, or send everyone out to listen to God individually, and then come back together to share what each has heard.
- You can also gather small groups to pray, and then share together as a larger group. If you are seeking healing for a dispersed organization, this can even be done long-distance via conference calls in which small groups meet in several locations and then dial in to share what they have heard. If all are listening well, there will be striking themes that recur as each one reports back.
- If individuals seem to be deeply wounded, listen to their concerns and provide opportunities for personal healing. As individuals experience healing, they will be more able to participate in the corporate healing process.

When you are searching for the truth in a generational lineage, keep in mind that Jesus, in praying for his disciples as he sent them into the world prayed, "Sanctify them in the truth; your word is truth" (Jn 17:17). Delve into the Scriptures looking for how God led biblical leaders when they dealt with similar situations. Ask God to open your eyes to the Scriptures in fresh ways as you read.

In both St. Ambrose Church and the Agape Food Bank, the designated leader (pastor and director), while not the root cause of the present crises, were culpable of perpetuating the destructive patterns. They were not the appropriate people to lead the healing process, or even to make the call to prayer.

■ At first, the St. Ambrose congregational president and church council led the healing process. They put out a call to prayer in the church newsletter and began to meet regularly to pray as a council without the pastor. Eventually, the discernment group narrowed to the congregational president and vice president. They met with denominational officials to inform them of the situation and seek direction. The officials appointed a liaison who met with the church council without the pastor and determined that it would be appropriate to request the pastor's resignation. The liaison also recommended that another denominational official come to the church after the pastor left to lead a few key leaders in an exorcism of the church building.

■ At the Agape Food Bank, the two board members who first began to pray together decided to invite one person from each participating congregation to pray with them for discernment. They asked the churches to each select a representative. There was so much friction among the group that formed that the board members reassessed and narrowed their discernment group to the board, while keeping the participating churches informed. Each church had at least one representative on the board anyhow. The board voted unanimously to terminate the dishonest director. The Board Chairman agreed to serve as the interim director. He planned a weekend retreat for the entire board so that they could listen to God in an undistracted environment.

Step 3: *Researching the sins, wounds and blessings of the past*

When a Christian community (or any organization) is in crisis, the sins of the past may not be immediately apparent, and assumptions that appear obvious may be inaccurate. The goal of generational healing is to discover the truth and bring it to Jesus for healing. As you delve into your common history, keep asking, "What is *God* doing here." As the corporate story develops, patterns and trajectories become apparent. Divide your group story into eras. The most obvious way to do that is by the tenure of key leaders, or you can simply use decades as the dividing points on your timeline. Look for events, people, issues, blessings and challenges that shaped the common story during each era. How were core beliefs, behaviors and attitudes influenced in each of these periods?

☐ *Begin by researching the written history* of your congregation or organization. Look for official minutes of the governing bodies, annual reports, collected written histories, scrapbooks and archives of church news in local papers.

Keep in mind the purpose and perspectives of these records. Every historian has a bias. Most histories are recorded by those in charge. You will have to dig harder to learn the history of the disenfranchised and the powerless, such as women, children, slaves, immigrants, or those who came and left disillusioned. Often when you review the recorded history with long-time members, someone will remark, "Well that was *their* history, but this is what really happened…" The written history is simply a starting point.

☐ *Look for patterns and inter-relationships* in the historical records.
- Who were the founding members? Were they community leaders or the powerless?
- Was this a "daughter church" of a neighboring congregation?
- Was it formed (or survived) from a church split?
- Was this an organizational spin-off?
- Was it merger with another church or organization?
- Did the members include professionals, farmers, blue collar workers, slaves?
- Was the membership diverse or homogenous?
- What personal wounds and/or blessings did each leader bring?

Each of these questions will lead to further questions because they require delving deeper into individual stories that contributed to the communal story. If founders were prominent community leaders, they might well bring different values and concerns from those of founders who were disenfranchised, such as migrant workers, slaves or former slaves, or the physically handicapped.

☐ As you move along in constructing your group story, *examine how the leadership developed*.

- How were leaders chosen? Were they appointed by denominational or corporate officials, selected by a small group of powerful people, or elected by the whole membership?
- How long did they serve? Did they serve long terms, or was there a rapid turnover?
- Why did they leave?

Many early American churches were served by itinerant clergy (some with little or no theological training), so strong lay leadership developed. That could result in tensions when fulltime clergy were called if lay leaders held tightly to their own power. Look for radical changes in leadership style and focus. Autocratic leaders may alternate with *laissez faire* ones. Liberals and conservatives may follow each other. Ask why these dramatic changes occurred. A series of leaders who were "asked to leave" may indicate a deeper problem in the corporate dynamics, rather than the sins of the resigning leaders. The behavior that precipitated the dismissal may have triggered generational fears or challenged the status quo.

☐ Next, *look at the group's characteristics*.

- How has the church or organization related to the surrounding community? Has it been inclusive and friendly, or an exclusive club?

- Were leaders politically or socially active or focused primarily on spiritual concerns? How did members respond to these activities?
- Was the spiritual climate more internal (personal relationships with God and one another) or external (defined by outward expressions such as activism, social causes and duties)?
- Was the general climate legalistic or grace-filled?
- How has the ethnic and racial balance of your parish changed? How did the changes come about?
- How has the average age of the congregation changed?

☐ *When and why was the church or organization founded?* Many early American churches were established so that members would have a place to bury their dead. Most early churches had their own cemeteries, but this purpose was hardly a recipe for growth. Some churches and organizations were founded around the leader's personality and passions, often making leadership transitions difficult. Others were founded to address a particular need or concern which may or may not continue to exist. For example, many churches in the 1950s were founded to meet the needs of young families in the post-war era. Today, most of the members may be elderly, with few young families left in the church. Other churches were founded to minister to a particular ethnic group, but the surrounding neighborhood has now changed. How has the mission changed or remained the same over the years? What precipitated the changes?

☐ *Look for gaps in the records.* In one church's board minutes, the treasurer had a long tenure and every board meeting recorded his strong opinions. Suddenly, there was a new treasurer and no mention of the former one in the minutes. Further digging revealed that funds were missing during that same period. Did the treasurer abscond with funds and leave without repenting or making restitution?

Also be aware of subtle references to indiscretions. One church history indicated that a well-liked pastor had been relieved of his duties rather suddenly, but no reason was given for his departure. Researching the denominational archives revealed that this man had later been arrested and convicted of child sexual abuse. The incident was significant because years later, during a generational healing session, it was discovered that seven generations of child sexual abuse had subsequently been passed down within that congregation. The victims, and in many ways the entire congregation, finally received healing in that session.

☐ Once the recorded history has been reviewed, *gather information from current members*. This may occur through one-to-one interviews that can be recorded in audio or written form, a series of small group gatherings with a trained facilitator, or an open forum in a public gathering. These large group sessions often create a feeling of safety to bring up "secrets" that have previously been communicated only through gossip. When sensitive issues arise, following up those sessions with a small group or one-to-one conversation with individuals affected can begin the healing process. Surround these sessions in prayer—before, during and after. Often, a traumatic memory will unexpectedly be triggered in someone and shared with the group. It is appropriate to stop and pray for that person in the group context and continue with more in-depth prayer afterward in a more private setting.[54]

In these listening sessions it is extremely important for the leader to remain nonjudgmental and encouraging. Keep your ears open for stories that indicate potential wounds. For example:

- Leaders with a history of sexual abuse or emotional manipulation;
- Leaders who develop relationships with staff or members that seem to involve unusual power and control;

219

- Antagonism between leaders, creating an "us versus them" mentality;
- Issues of personal power are disguised as ministry philosophy or policy;
- Denial occurs whenever someone tries to expose the issues;
- Management tries to fix the dynamics without understanding the true nature of the problem;
- Otherwise healthy victims begin thinking they are crazy;
- A deep enmeshment between the leader and victims occurs leaving those involved feeling confused, guilty and ashamed;
- Anyone questioning the dysfunctional system is viewed as violating Christian principles of love, forgiveness, reconciliation and peace;
- The emotional wounds lasting a long time.

Invariably, when discussions of traumatic past history take place, participants are hesitant to bring up unresolved issues. Someone may remark about the "elephant in the room," express fear that the discussion is becoming gossip, or indicate shame over the "skeletons in the closet." Constructing an accurate history of both the blessings and the wounds of the church or organization is different from gossip. Gossip occurs when shameful events are communicated as *secrets* without corroboration or appropriate follow-up. The purpose of uncovering the sins of the past is to set the stage for confession, repentance, reconciliation and healing.

Interestingly, the Bible does not hesitate to record the failings, as well as the glories of the people of God and their leaders. The Old Testament records Moses committing murder, David raping Bathsheba, Sampson's dalliance with Delilah, as well as a long line of evil kings and their deeds. In the New Testament Jesus openly dealt with prostitutes, adulterers, unethical tax collectors and hardened criminals, as well as abusive religious leaders. Paul confronted the early churches about their sinful practices—as well as being transparent about his own battle with sin (Romans 7). Paul warned Timothy:

> You must understand this, that in the last days dis-
> tressing times will come. For people will be lovers of
> themselves, lovers of money, boasters, arrogant, abu-
> sive, disobedient to their parents, ungrateful, unholy,
> inhuman, implacable, slanderers, profligates, brutes,
> haters of good, treacherous, reckless, swollen with
> conceit, lovers of pleasure rather than lovers of God,
> holding to the outward form of godliness but denying
> its power. (2 Tim 3:1-5)

Should we expect anything different today?

☐ Once the written and oral histories are collected, *put them before the Lord and seek the strength and guidance of the Holy Spirit to illuminate the collected data.* Attempt to visualize the historical events— especially major crises and high points. Engage your imagination, viewing each generation's story from the perspective of the period being examined. Consider the values and beliefs of each generation, rather than judging their history from your own values. For instance, if the church leaders held slaves at one time, or women were not allowed to vote or teach, or pews had to be rented by the occupants, look at how their generation justified these actions.

How to Handle the Elephants in the Room

1. Begin by talking one-to-one with the person describing this incident or pattern. Be sure to listen carefully, so that the person sharing feels heard and not condemned.

2. Determine if this person needs counseling and/or healing prayer and arrange for follow up, if the person agrees.

3. Ask if the person sharing would be willing to gather with other current members who were affected by this incident for a confidential small group sharing. If you do not feel competent to facilitate this meeting, find someone who has been appropriately prepared to work with you—a trained therapist or prayer minister.

4. Avoid pointing to a scapegoat or placing blame on anyone. Focus on the dynamics of the wounding and the effects upon the church/organization as a whole. If individuals need healing, that can occur one-to-one or in a small group with other victims.

Ask the Holy Spirit to provide insight into the subjective experience of the church or organization in each generation. Look particularly at their fears, resentments, prejudices, sense of entitlement, experiences of failure, talents and blessings. For example, how would living through a church fire affect the emotions of the congregation—especially if caused by arson? What if people died in the fire? What if it were racially motivated? Put yourself in the situation. How would the experience color your attitudes, emotions and values? How would it affect your relationship with God?

As generational story lines begin to develop from the objective and subjective information, they will reveal emotions, vulnerabilities, attitudes, identities, beliefs, resentments, idolatries and addictions, interpersonal alienations and relationship patterns that underlie the concerns for which you are seeking healing today. As the stories unfold, consider who and what have been silenced, denied, mystified, not sufficiently voiced or admitted in this church/organization both currently and historically?

What harm needs to be seen, heard, understood, and admitted, currently and historically?

- Whose injuries need to be voiced and stood for, currently and historically?
- What injuring actions need to be confessed and repented? What and whose strengths and contributions need to be owned and appreciated in this story?

☐ *Own your belonging to the corporate history*, even if you have no direct connection other than your current membership. Simply belonging to this group makes you a part of its history, even if you or anyone in your ancestry did not participate in it prior to joining.

☐ *Identify your complicity with harm done* by past wounding, your own part in continuing the attitudes and patterns that resulted from past events, including how you have continued to participate in such harm or failed to name the harm and challenge it. Ask, "Why are we doing this?" when traditions seem to restrict health and growth.

☐ *Examine the wounds suffered during each leader's tenure* and consider how these injuries continue to affect your life together—both positively and negatively. For instance, becoming aware of a series of leaders who were sexually abusive may have awakened the need for safeguards outlined by church or organizational policies, including police checks and training for leaders, glass windows placed in doors and setting procedures for safety. On the other hand, a continuing lack of trust toward leaders may need spiritual healing.

☐ *Speak and own what has come to your awareness*—both positive and negative. For example, you may realize that the periods of conflicted leadership were also times when other leaders stood in the gap and mentored new people into leadership positions. Rather than focusing on the old bitterness, a sense of strength and spirit of thankfulness can develop.

■ St. Ambrose's constructed their congregational story using the Sunday morning Adult Forum. About one third of the congregation participated in at least part of the sessions, which took place over a two-month period. People shared eagerly and freely about both the blessings and the challenges of each era. In the process, the healing began as secrets were aired, data clarified, and patterns became evident. New members and those who had grown up in the church gained an appreciation for the history and for each other. During the discussion of a particularly difficult pastoral era, a new couple visited the Forum, but the discussion progressed unabated. After the class, the couple came forward and told the discussion facilitator that they had been deeply wounded by the same pastor being discussed in a subsequent church. They were so relieved to know that they were not alone in their pain.

■ The Agape Food Pantry limited their discussion of the corporate story to the board. They used their retreat time to tell their personal stories and weave them together into the organizational story line. A deep trust developed, as well as new sense of hope. They worked together on a plan for making the Food Pantry a healthy and effective organization that included listening to the pain, offering grace to one another and developing trust. The board ended with a worship service focusing on repentance and reconciliation. The board chairman agreed to call a meeting of all the volunteers from the participating churches in order to repent openly to them and ask for their forgiveness. ■

In both cases, participants in the process were struck by how evident the work of the Holy Spirit became throughout their histories. Surprisingly, it was during the difficult times that both groups had grown stronger in their faith and become more open to change.

Step 4: *Searching the heart of God for our lineages.*

Often this step flows naturally from the story-gathering process. If it does not, attempt to visualize the historical events—especially major crises and high points. Engage your imagination, viewing each generation's story from their perspective. Consider the values and beliefs of each generation, rather than judging their history from your own values.

☐ *Ask the Holy Spirit to provide insight* into the subjective experience of church or organizational members in each generation. Look particularly at their fears, resentments, prejudices, sense of entitlement, experiences of failure, talents and blessings, and at their concept of God and their mission in the world.

☐ *Seek the Holy Spirit to infuse you with God's love* for your church or organization. Then identify your identification with its wounds, shortcomings, longings and desires.

☐ *Identify your authority* to represent this church or organization based on your belonging, role or position within it, or your call by God to intercede for it. For example, you may drive past a church or ministry headquarters for which God places on your heart to pray— even if you do not know anyone in that place.

❑ Review the collected objective and subjective histories of the church or organization, *listing the good done* that has positively influenced both past and present generations. Look particularly for strong Christian values that passed from generation to generation, such as care for the poor, openness to strangers, love for one another, or a heart for evangelism. Thank God for these blessings and praise him for his faithfulness. Gather as a congregation or organizational team to worship together, giving the glory for all the good done to God.

❑ *Seek God's heart and perspective as you identify wrongs done*, wounds created and degrees of culpability. Focus on patterns or repeated behaviors such as entrenched bitterness, emotional or sexual abuse, brief tenures of leaders, or poor communication. Also identify major traumatic events that left lingering scars.

❑ *Ask the Holy Spirit to reveal any demonic powers* that may have been involved—and may still be present. For example, the former pastor of one church guarded the pulpit carefully and would not allow anyone else to preach from it. Each succeeding pastor, and even visiting clergy, remarked about a strange sense of evil around the pulpit and felt intimidated when entering it. One supply pastor even felt physically pushed back when trying to enter it. When a group of prayer ministers was invited to pray through the church, they sensed a spirit of fear surrounding the pulpit. They bound it and commanded it to leave. They also told the spirit of the former (deceased) pastor that he had no right to continue protecting that pulpit. After that prayer session, the pulpit no longer held the same power of intimidation.

■ St. Ambrose Church finished compiling their story shortly before Christmas. Once the Advent season began, other activities consumed the congregation. A small group of congregational leaders began

226

praying over the gathered material, as well as focusing on the transition to a new pastor. They used the gathered historical material in shaping the profile of the congregation for their pastoral search, but essentially tabled the generational healing process until the next pastor was in place.

■ The Agape Food Bank sensed that their task was complete after the leaders' retreat. They went back to normal operations with a new optimism. Their positive attitude became contagious and a healthy cooperative spirit prevailed among volunteers and staff for several years. About three years later, the same negative patterns began to develop and leaders again sought God's wisdom and discernment. Several key leaders started meeting weekly to pray, seeking the heart of God for this ministry.

Step 5: *Humbly confessing, personally and representationally*

Having become conscious your own sins and injuries as well as those of your church or organization and its predecessors, confess to God and others the generational sins and wounds and your personal complicity with continuing group transgressions. The sins and wounds may be both contemporary and historical.

■ At the Agape Food Bank, one participating church, Bethel Assembly, a predominantly African American congregation, had been historically treated with disregard and misunderstanding. The board felt that they were not fully participating, and often impeded the work of the Food Bank. Volunteers from Bethel were deeply committed, but had a different ministry philosophy from the other participating churches. Over the years a pattern of duplicity developed. Volunteers from Bethel appeared to be conforming to the overall organization's mission, while continuing to focus on priorities that the other churches did not value. If members of Bethel Assembly suggested new ministry approaches, others would make comments like, "Oh, that's just Bethel's hobby horse," and the suggestion would be disregarded. However, the Bethel volunteers would implement their plans covertly, creating more tensions. After an Agape board member confessed to Bethel volunteers and repented of their attitude toward Bethel Assembly, the Bethel volunteers felt safe in confessing their duplicity. After this time of mutual confession and repentance, the leaders representing both sides were able to share their concerns and values so that they could develop a healthy collegiality.

■ At St. Ambrose, the Merry Marthas Society, that served the church suppers, developed a critical spirit toward each pastor that served. Group members would keep written records of all their grievances and spread dissention through gossip among members of the congregation. When a church member confronted the problem in an annual meeting, she did not blame others, but confessed and repented of her own contribution to the spirit of negativity. Gradually, other members of the Merry Marthas began to confess and change their behavior. ■

When transgressions have spread within a church or organization, speaking aloud to others is essential, because sin cannot continue when exposed to the light. Speaking aloud often gives a sense of having opened your heart to God and completed an action. Also when confessing aloud to others in a spirit of humility, hesitancies to own material are more evident to yourself and to those listening and receiving the confession. Allow the Holy Spirit to prompt you as you express remorse and sorrow to God for wrong doing and its destructive consequences.

☐ *Ask the Holy Spirit to guide you* in representational confession.

228

☐ *Determine to whom and with whom* this confession should be delivered and where it should take place.

- If most of the collected history is unknown to the general membership, the corporate leaders may need to do the work within the leadership team. If only one particular group has been wounded, but others in the church or organization are unaware of the problem, airing the issue before the entire body can be confusing and potentially create more wounds.

- When individuals or a small group are affected, the representational confession may be done with the individuals or small group by current leaders representing previous leaders who are no longer present, as well as themselves, apologizing for the sins of their predecessors to those they wounded. When doing so, it is in the name of the church or organization, saying "*We* have sinned by..." and listing the offenses and how they will be prevented in the future.

Step 6: *Apologizing, asking forgiveness and forgiving*

☐After *apologizing to God and others* (where appropriate and led by God) on behalf of yourself and those you represent, *express remorse and awareness of hurts caused.* When you have listened carefully to those who have been wounded, you will be able to repeat back what they have expressed. For instance, several hurting parishioners might explain that they felt degraded and disheartened by a former pastor's blaming them for their own problems when they came to him for counseling. The current pastor could say to them, "As a member of the clergy I apologize that we have sinned against you by degrading and disheartening you. May the Lord give us grace to speak respectfully and encouragingly with you. Please forgive us."

☐ *Ask God's forgiveness for both personal and corporate transgressions and then ask the forgiveness of others* (where appropriate and led by God). Often those most wounded will have moved on to other churches or organizations. If those who were wounded are no longer present, a leader can ask forgiveness from those standing in for or representing the persons who were injured by previous leaders, asking God's intervention, release and blessing for all those affected. It may also be helpful to seek out the wounded who have moved on to ask their forgiveness.

■ St. Ambrose Church began sponsoring annual confirmation class reunions, serving a dinner after the worship service honoring the returning members and providing opportunities for reconciling conversations. Pictures of events during the time of their confirmation were displayed in the church hall. The sermon on those Sundays would focus on the importance of remembrance, of both the good times and the hard times, and express repentance for any wounds that may have occurred. Many of those returning for the celebrations continued to attend worship services and became involved in church activities again.

■ The Agape Food Bank began inviting former volunteers to their annual picnic. Board members intentionally sought out disgruntled former volunteers for one-to-one conversations. They listened carefully and when needed, they apologized for the way the volunteers were treated and asked their forgiveness. When the Board became aware of individuals who were deeply hurt and had not responded to the general invitation, they would call them to personally invite them and provide an opportunity for them to share their grievances, and then ask for their forgiveness. ■

Often those who caused historical wounds were so blinded by the culture of their times, they were unaware of the harm they did. They may never have thought about the rights of women, other ethnic or racial groups or children.

☐ *Offer forgiveness to those predecessors* and others where appropriate. For instance, early churches usually did not allow women to vote or serve in leadership positions. Many white churches opposed the Civil Rights movement. Some assumed that children should "be seen and not heard." They were acting on biblical interpretations and the values of their time.

☐ *Express gratitude for God's faithfulness* and for the additional blessings of the generations that have come to light, naming the strengths and values that have become evident.

Representational apologies to God, to previous generations in your history, and to those injured by you and your predecessors proceed naturally from opening your history to God. You can express remorse for injuries caused as a representative of the church or organization, trying to be as accurate as possible regarding your predecessors' awareness of wrong and their understanding of the injurious impact of their actions.

Step 7: *Repenting: renouncing the old and asserting the new*

☐*Repentance requires* more than feeling sorry for past sin. It demands *a change in behavior.* In a corporate setting *this may involve setting new policies, changing by-laws and renouncing old traditions.*

■ St. Ambrose Church instituted "safe church" policies, including screening leaders for past sexual indiscretions, installing glass panels in doors, training employees and lay leaders in safe-church policies and acting quickly when violations were reported.

■ The Agape Food Bank had been frustrated because few African-American Churches participated in the ministry. After they elected the African American pastor of Bethel Assembly as Chairman of the Board, several other black churches began to participate. ■

Often, even when the desire for change is sincere, old prejudices and emotional ties to old traditions may linger. Members may feel deeply unsettled about female clergy or reporting to a woman supervisor. Some may not welcome leaders of another race. Some may feel mistrusted, or that their privacy has been violated by newly required police checks of leaders. Many people take comfort in long-held traditions, even when they are no longer appropriate. Rational explanations for change do not address the emotional turmoil experienced by those who lose valued traditions. An on-going bondage to the past may continue, even when a group seeks to make positive changes. As one church leader expressed it, "Why do we keep doing things initiated by a bunch of dead people for reasons that no longer exist?"

Turmoil and conflict may arise at this point. In order to facilitate the bondage-breaking, prayerfully envision the cross of Jesus placed between each generation and between all persons in the lineage, absorbing and transforming all generation-to-generation influence. That can take place in the imagination, or literally gathering around a cross.

■ When the board of the Agape Food Bank was particularly conflicted they tried visualizing the cross, but that seemed to make things worse. Those who felt unable to enter into the visualization process accused those who did of "getting deceived by New Age practices." While some of those who were visualizing the cross gently explained that this was an encounter with Christ. Finally, one board member brought a standing cross to the next meeting and placed it in the center of the table. She told the group, "This represents the presence of Christ in our midst, let's listen to him together." This tangible symbol was acceptable to everyone present. The whole tenor of the discussion changed. Interestingly, the cleaning crew moved the cross after the meeting, at the next meeting it was missing. One of the non-visualizing board members searched for it and placed it firmly back in the middle of the table stating, "We need this." ■

☐ *It may also be helpful to visualize the blood of Jesus flowing throughout the group lineage,* healing all wounds and cleansing the stain and bondage of sin. The imagery can help the group to effectively articulate their prayer intention. If clergy are present, it would be appropriate to conduct a Holy Communion service in order to commit yourselves and your church's or organization's lineage to replacing old destructive patterns of thought, action and belief. Name the old and new patterns.

☐ *Renounce and revoke destructive patterns* and ask God's release from their hold on the lineage. Ask for wisdom to replace them with new, life-giving patterns, asking God's power and infilling.

Step 8: *Rebuking evil, breaking curses and restoring blessings*

Once sinful patterns have been identified and repentance occurs, you can cast out any evil that has lodged in the renounced sins and break any curses. This phase of healing can begin within the corporate leadership, but then extend to the larger body. When evil patterns linger long after they have been renounced, something or someone may be giving them permission to remain. For example, a particular tradition may have given privilege or status to an individual or small group. It may be as simple as who decorates the Christmas tree.

■ At St. Ambrose Church, new members were deeply hurt whenever they volunteered to help decorate the church for Christmas. Some had been so offended that they left the church. Members of the women's group who felt entitled to that job rudely refused their offers to help. The women's group proclaimed that no one else could ever decorate the church. They also insisted that only certain decorations could be used, even though the ornaments were falling apart. The tree was traditionally placed over a heat duct (that did not exist when the tradition began), and it had to be a cedar tree because, "That was the original Christmas tree." The crisis came to a head when the farmer whose family had always donated the tree died and his property sold. Although the women's organization had disbanded by this time, the former members maintained the right to decorate the church for Christmas. A relatively new church member donated a spruce tree and suggested changing the location of the tree, since its former location created a fire hazard. The Sunday school made new decorations for the tree. The privileged decorating group protested and seethed with anger.

The church council recognized that they had allowed evil to fester by allowing the group to own this aspect of the church's life. They apologized to those who were hurt and transferred responsibility for decorating the church to the Christian Education Committee. The previous decorating committee eventually repented and joined new group. In turn, the youth in the church invited the older ladies to help them bake cookies for the homeless. Once the curse of their pronouncement ("No one else can decorate the church") was withdrawn by the group, a new spirit of freedom and caring for one another developed.

■ In other cases the evil may be more serious. In another church, one of the lay leaders became involved in witchcraft. He eventually joined a coven, becoming a warlock, and vowed to destroy the pastor and cursed his marriage. He also recruited other church members to join the coven. Although the warlock was asked to step down from his leadership position and he eventually left the church, the pastor's marriage dissolved and he left the church as well. The whole matter was covered up and the church began a slow decline. An unusual number of marriages—especially around the warlock's former circle of friends—began to erode. In this case it would have been imperative to break any curses that the warlock and his coven sent against the church and individual members within it. The church members who dabbled in witchcraft, even if only briefly, needed to publicly confess and repent to rid the church of its continuing influence. Sin left hidden allows evil to fester. ■

However, once confession, forgiveness and repentance take place, the doors of welcome will be closed to evil. The roaring lion loses interest when its food supply is gone. At this point, church leaders can focus prayer on discerning any remaining evil influences that remain and curses that may still be in effect. Of course, these prayers for discernment and binding of evil may come into play at any point in the healing process when progress seems spiritually impeded.

Often in generational healing, at some point, it will seem like the process stalls. For instance, when seeking Jesus' presence in a hurtful situation that occurred in the past, people may report that Jesus' face (or his entire presence) is covered by a black blob. Ask those seeing this to describe what they perceive might be causing the blob—what else is going on in the scene they envision? Often a painful experience will come to mind. At other times, someone in the group may be withholding important historical information to protect himself or the reputation of someone else. Pray into this blockage and at the same time create an environment of safety in which people can share openly without repercussions. Sometimes God will put words into your mind, speak through dreams or visions, or provide the information through another source. Test these revelations by going to those involved and humbly reporting what you are sensing. Ask if this has any meaning to them, and if so, if it is accurate.

■ In working with one troubled organization, the healing process seemed blocked. After praying about the situation for several weeks the prayer minister leading the generational healing had a dream about an incident of sexual harassment that he knew nothing about. In the dream a supervisor was engaged in a sexual relationship with an employee. He heard a voice saying, "The wrong person was fired." The prayer minister told the department head about his dream and asked if the incident had actually happened. The shocked department head replied, "This is confidential information—and besides that supervisor repented and the supervisee was the aggressor." Whenever a person holds power over another, the one in the position of power is responsible for a sexual liaison—even if the victim seemed flirtatious or consented to the relationship. Once this situation was appropriately handled, the healing process began to move ahead again.

Step 9: *Praying for healing: inviting Jesus into our ancestral past to heal and restore*

The hard work of repentance and deliverance that you have done allows prayers for healing painful memories to flow freely. Healing may occur though times of concentrated healing prayer, while participants are meditating after receiving Holy Communion or sitting in the presence of Christ in a quiet place after a generational prayer session.

☐ *You can imagine those who were wounded in times long past and invite Jesus into those situations,* seeing, thinking or hearing him actively touch their wounds with healing, with understanding, with protection, or, at times, just outrage at what was done. Remember that they are still living in eternity, and Jesus can still touch them. These images of healing also may occur spontaneously after a repentance and deliverance period. And there is no strict order to these steps. Healing imagery, thoughts and words, at times, may precede repentance and deliverance as a strengthening prelude.

☐ *These prayer sessions can occur individually with those who have been personally wounded, or in small groups* who have shared a common history of wounding. They can also be conducted with whole departments, organizations or churches. The character of these sessions will be different in each situation. When praying with an entire congregation, you can lead from the front and ask people to sit with someone they trust to share their observations and concerns with one another. You could also ask people to silently go through the process, write down their impressions and provide opportunities to share one-to-one or in a small group afterward.

As long as we live on earth, none of us will experience full healing. It is always a process. There is no perfect church and no perfect organization. In fact, the way we deal with those who are disabled—whether physically, emotionally, mentally or spiritually— demonstrates the health of the body at large. The Lord puts us into imperfect communities so that we can learn to love one another with all our limitations and "provoke one another to love and good deeds, not neglecting to meet together, as is the habit of some, but encouraging one another" (Heb 10:24-25). A healthy body is one that continually works toward health.

The biblical understanding of health is represented by the Hebrew concept of *shalom*. The future new Jerusalem described in Revelation 21:2-4 illustrates the meaning of *shalom:*

> And I saw the holy city, the new Jerusalem, coming down out of heaven from God, prepared as a bride adorned for her husband. And I heard a loud voice from the throne saying, 'See, the home of God is among mortals. He will dwell with them as their God; they will be his peoples, and God himself will be with them; he will wipe every tear from their eyes. Death will be no more; mourning and crying and pain will be no more, for the first things have passed away.'

This is the type of healing we seek when working toward generational healing within the Christian community. Ultimate healing comes only through Christ. We can, however, look at health as a continuum. A healthy church or organization will be closer to the left on the following continua:

Peace	⬅———————➡	Conflict
Prosperity	⬅———————➡	Scarcity
Rest	⬅———————➡	Turmoil
Safety	⬅———————➡	Danger
Security	⬅———————➡	Insecurity
Justice	⬅———————➡	Injustice
Happiness	⬅———————➡	Despair
Health	⬅———————➡	Sickness
Welfare	⬅———————➡	Poverty
Wholeness	⬅———————➡	Brokenness

Assess your own church or organization according to these continua. Discuss with others where they see your group on this table.

Step 10: *Reconciling actions*

Reconciling actions may occur in several contexts: 1) between individuals, 2) in a small group of directly affected members, 3) among leaders (on various levels) and 4) with the full membership. These reconciling actions may further reveal patterns in the larger faith community that require additional reconciling actions.

As individuals recognize their personal wounds and seek counseling and/or prayer ministry, it often becomes apparent that a larger pattern is at work.

■ For example, Marilyn began seeing a spiritual director to sort through some of her lingering spiritual turmoil. Her former pastor had made sexual advances toward her ten years before, but she changed churches rather than confronting the problem at the time. Since then, several friends had come to her and confidentially confessed they had experienced similar advances, but also not reported the incidents. Another friend became involved in a sexual relationship with this man, after which she announced that she had lost her faith and succumbed to a lifestyle of promiscuity. As Marilyn grieved the ongoing effects of her former pastor's advances, she also feared for all the other victims.

First, Marilyn's spiritual director prayed with her with for healing of the wounds that occurred from her pastor's advances. Marilyn was able to confess her own inability to deal with the situation appropriately, as well as her bitterness toward the pastor and toward God. As she encountered Jesus in this prayer time, she was able to visualize his presence with her during the encounters, giving her strength and courage to refuse the pastor's advances. She also felt a deep compassion for the woundedness of the pastor and for her friends. She sensed that Jesus was asking her to share her new freedom with her friends.

Marilyn invited her wounded friends to dinner at her home. Afterward she shared her story, indirectly giving them permission to share their own. As they met in this small group, they prayed together for each other, the pastor and for the yet unknown other victims. Each one expressed how they had felt that they were the only one to have experienced this harassment, and how grateful they were to know that they were not alone anymore in their journey out of shame. Marilyn also planned a follow up meeting to which she invited her spiritual director so the others could learn more about resources available to them for healing.

Eventually, Marilyn went back to her former church. The pastor who harassed her had moved on to another congregation. Marilyn kept her ears open for hints that there might be further victims, and before long heard several similar stories. Without betraying any confidences, Marilyn went to the president of the church board to share her story. He listened carefully, and finally told her,

> You are not alone. There were others. The pastor was asked to leave for his indiscretions, but we never really told the congregation why he left. That's caused a lot of division in the church. Maybe we should have a retreat in order to minister to the victims, and then have a service of healing and reconciliation for the whole congregation.

Relieved to know she had been heard and understood, Marilyn relaxed and agreed to the proposed plan. Through these actions, the entire church repented of allowing the climate for abuse to continue for so long. Afterwards, they experienced a new sense of unity and commitment to mission.

The new pastor, who led the service of healing and reconciliation, invited the Bishop to attend the service. The Bishop then decided that since this was actually a much bigger problem than one pastor and one congregation, the issue should be addressed in the National Convention. This led to a national service of repentance for the church's role in perpetuating clergy sexual abuse. ■

The "Marilyns" in many denominations have spoken up on behalf of the victims of clergy sexual abuse so that safe church policies have been mandated in most of them today. Victims have been given a fair hearing and support, and perpetrators are rarely reassigned to other congregations. Many clergy have been brought to legal justice. The issue has become open and actively dealt with nationally and internationally, not only in the church, but in schools, businesses and government.

The issue and contexts will vary. The steps toward healing may not occur in the same order. Each situation is unique, but the same themes seem to appear and the same basic approach brings freedom and healing.

■ St. Ambrose Church began to train prayer ministers who were available for healing prayer during and after each Sunday service. As individuals learned to trust the prayer ministers, the prayer ministers received further training in inner healing so they could meet with individuals for more in-depth healing sessions. Small groups began to focus on spiritual disciplines, creating a safe environment to deal with deep wounds. The church also held a weekend conference on generational healing so that those who needed further healing could participate. Eventually, they held a congregational service of healing and reconciliation.

■ The Agape Food Bank became proactive in handling conflict as it developed, with prayer and humility. They instituted a grievance procedure that included listening, prayer, repentance and forgiveness. ■

In churches and organizations healing will always be an ongoing and multifaceted process. The variables are compounded not only by the number of individuals in the church or organization, but also by the complex family histories that are part of each one. Furthermore, healthy churches and organizations attract wounded people who come with their own painful legacies, seeking love, acceptance and support. As new members are grafted into the corporate story, new wounds will surface and the healing process continues as we bring people to Jesus, who invites us saying:

> Are you tired? Worn out? Burned out on religion? Come to me. Get away with me and you'll recover your life. I'll show you how to take a real rest. Walk with me and work with me—watch how I do it. Learn the unforced rhythms of grace. I won't lay anything heavy or ill-fitting on you. Keep company with me and you'll learn to live freely and lightly. (Mt 11:28-30, MSG)

For Reflection

Read the following portion of 2 Corinthians, chapter four, prayerfully considering the role of suffering in Paul's ministry. In what ways do you identify with what Paul is experiencing? How are some of these same concerns present in your own situation?

> [1]Therefore, since it is by God's mercy that we are engaged in this ministry, we do not lose heart. [2]We

have renounced the shameful things that one hides; we refuse to practice cunning or to falsify God's word; but by the open statement of the truth we commend ourselves to the conscience of everyone in the sight of God... [5] For we do not proclaim ourselves; we proclaim Jesus Christ as Lord and ourselves as your slaves for Jesus' sake. [6] For it is the God who said, "Let light shine out of darkness," who has shone in our hearts to give the light of the knowledge of the glory of God in the face of Jesus Christ.

[7] But we have this treasure in clay jars, so that it may be made clear that this extraordinary power belongs to God and does not come from us. [8] We are afflicted in every way, but not crushed; perplexed, but not driven to despair; [9] persecuted, but not forsaken; struck down, but not destroyed; [10] always carrying in the body the death of Jesus, so that the life of Jesus may also be made visible in our bodies. [11] For while we live, we are always being given up to death for Jesus' sake, so that the life of Jesus may be made visible in our mortal flesh. [12] So death is at work in us, but life in you.

[13] But just as we have the same spirit of faith that is in accordance with scripture—"I believed, and so I spoke"—we also believe, and so we speak, [14] because we know that the one who raised the Lord Jesus will raise us also with Jesus, and will bring us with you into his presence. [15] Yes, everything is for your sake, so that grace, as it extends to more and more people, may increase thanksgiving, to the glory of God.

[16] So we do not lose heart. Even though our outer nature is wasting away, our inner nature is being renewed day by day. [17] For this slight momentary affliction is preparing us for an eternal weight of glory beyond all measure, [18] because we look not at what can be seen but at what cannot be seen; for what can be seen is temporary, but what cannot be seen is eternal.

1. Prayerfully consider your own church or organizational environment. Can you see troublesome relational patterns that persist, even when the people involved in the initial situation are no longer present?

2. Bring this observation before the Lord in a time of worship and meditation. Ask God to show you relevant Scripture passages that will give you insight. Praise God for his sufficiency to bring healing and reconciliation.

3. Research the history of this pattern by reading through old documents that might demonstrate previous relationship issues, talking with long-standing members and leaders who were formerly associated with the church or organization and talking with individuals involved in the present issue. Recognize the good that was accomplished despite the problems.

4. Search the heart of God on this pattern. Ask God what he wants in this situation. Pray about whom to invite to work on this process with you.

5. Humbly confess, personally and representationally in regard to this problem. Ask God to show you how you may be contributing to the dysfunction. Using corporate language, confess the sin of the whole group—including those who have gone before—in allowing the dysfunction to continue.

6. Apologize to anyone you may have wounded in this situation, forgive anyone who has wounded you and ask their forgiveness

7. Repent of your collusion in this pattern and ask God to show you how to change your behavior or attitude.

8. Rebuke any evil forces that you may have discerned, break any curses and bless everyone involved.

9. Pray for healing, inviting Jesus into the situation to heal and restore. Look at the continuum in this chapter. Where on the continuum of healing does your church or organization fall on each point?

10. Determine what reconciling actions might bring healing and prevent recurrence of this problem. Make concrete plans to carry them through.

Chapter 10

Enlarging the Focus

At times we have been moved to intercede for healing with a focus that reaches beyond our specific family lineages, churches, or organizations to which we belong.

Everyone and everything has a history—persons, families and organizations, as well as nations, ethnicities, professions and locations. The impact of past events continues to bear powerful influence through both conscious and unconscious memories. Past events and their consequences echo in persons, on the land, in buildings and through national, ethnic, professional and occupational loyalty ties.

We transition from life stage to life stage, job to job, in a sense through generations of our own personal lives. We enter, participate, age and pass the baton to the next, usually younger, participants in every arena of life. Land is used, occupied and then passed to the next inhabitants, whether by war, by the movement of people or by sale. Similarly, nations, professions and trades have histories and generations. We even speak of the whole human society having generations.

This consciousness is imbedded in our language. We categorize the generations: the *Lost Generation*, the *Greatest Generation*, the *Silent Generation*, *Baby Boomers*, *Generation X*, the *Millennials* and those currently being born as *Generational Z*. Each is named according to shaping influences of the times in which the generation was born and raised. They each bear the influences of their times and pass forward what they have done with these influences. The memories of each generation imbue the whole society.

The following stories provide a few illustrations of the generational healing process in broader arenas or those which cross or combine the personal, familial, occupational, institutional, ethnic/racial, and/or governmental arenas. The illustrations represent the authors' areas of interest and experience. Our hope is that they will stimulate you to address healing concerns in the broader arenas that God may lay upon your heart.

☐ *Before reading on, however, make note of some the broader arenas that have already come to mind and concern you and for which you may be called to intercede for generational healing. Then as you read the following illustrations and how the healing concerns were approached, you might note the insights you glean for your own concerns.*

Generational healing for the consequences of legislative actions in healthcare practice

John was besieged by unrelenting anxiety, nightmares and night terrors, awakening suddenly in a terrified state. These only intensified as sleep deprivation mounted. He was concerned about the effects of his sleep deprivation and anxiety on his wife and son. "I hate the way I am so tired and preoccupied in the evening after work. I want to enjoy them."

John initially assumed that his anxieties had root in his early family life. His father had been physically abusive, taking the belt to him frequently. "My father would become angry and take out his belt and I had no idea what I had done. Mom would try to intervene.

That just made things worse. He would lash me harder and longer."
However, when John focused more specifically on the content of his
nightmares his understanding shifted markedly. "I am haunted by the
homeless on the streets of the city." This was not simply symbolic of
his childhood feelings of homelessness, no place to rest. For several
years John had spent his nights searching for certain homeless persons on the streets of the city and spending time with them. "I followed them all the way to the morgue." Now, at night, they haunted
him. He could not get them out of his mind. They visited him in his
nightmares, as if wandering homeless in the next life.

John's story:

> I was an orderly at the state mental hospital. Because
> I related well to the patients and they trusted me, they
> would seek me out and talk to me. The treating psychi-
> atrist incorporated me into his treatment team. I would
> be part of his sessions with certain patients and follow
> his assignments to spend time with them on the floor.
> With the advent of new medications and the com-
> munity mental health movement, the state decided
> to close the hospital and move the patients to rooms
> in the city. They were then to report to a community
> mental health clinic for psychotherapy, medication
> evaluation, prescriptions, occupational therapy and
> other treatments. I and other orderlies were assigned
> the task of tying the patients to their beds, loading
> them into vans, driving them into the city, carrying
> them into their rooms, placing them on their beds and
> then untying them. We would give them a paper with
> instructions and explain to them what they were to
> do. Many of these patients had been in the hospital
> from ten to twenty years. They had no idea how to

navigate the outside world. They became homeless
street people. I knew them, so I spent nights tracking
them down on the streets of the city, making sure they
were fed and warm. I was devastated by what we, I,
had done. Some committed suicide, jumping from
bridges. Others simply died on the streets. I followed
them all the way to the morgue and prayed for them
there. There were no requiems or memorial services.
I can't get them out of my mind. They haunt me as if
wandering and directionless. They seem to be asking
me for help and I don't know what to do.

Step 1: *Awakening to the present influences of the past and calling out to God*

John prayed for direction. He felt urged to contact the other order-
lies who had been involved in removing the patients to rooming
houses and to invite them to participate in a requiem service. He
was able to reach five of them and they eagerly agreed to participate. They all expressed their remorse and anxiety over what had
been done and what had happened to these people. The chapel at the
former state hospital was still open and used by a treatment program.
John obtained permission from the program for use of the chapel for
the service.

Step 2: *Seeking God's face (listening to God and community)*

They scheduled a Saturday morning requiem from 9 AM until
noon, allowing enough time to reconnect with the events, with each
other and to listen well. Six gathered, including John and the five
others. They began with a prayer seeking God's presence, leading
and blessings.

Step 3: *Researching the sins, wounds and blessings of the past*

After a brief few minutes of quiet, they each shared, one at a time, their experience of transporting the patients and the grief, remorse and anxiety they carried. They were all aware of the impact of those events on their current lives. They together recounted the blessings of the work they had done with patients and the history of the closing of the hospital. As they each spoke about their experience additional memories poured forth from the others.

Listening to each other and hearing their common distress seemed to unite the group, giving a sense of, "We are in this together."

Bonds from their years of working together were rekindled. "Remember when you...." "We used to...."

All reported their loneness in carrying this pain. Several had found it difficult to tell their stories in their current worlds. Friends and family seemed uncomfortable with their pain, with hearing of the terrors patients experienced. Others simply tired of hearing about it. "My wife says, '*Enough, let it go!*' But I haven't been able to. I hate burdening her and my kids are too young for this."

Each former employee felt angry with state legislators and bureaucrats who had conceived the scheme and carried it out from a distance without coming close to experience the actual unintended consequences.

"The new medications were expected to be magic."

"How were these former patients going to get themselves to the clinics when they had been institutionalized for years and were habitually passive?"

"I felt like a murderer taking them to their execution."

Step 4: *Searching the heart of God*

Together they sought God's perspective. After a prayer for opening to God's heart and mind in all matters being examined, they took time to articulate their confessions.

Step 5: *Humbly confessing, personally and representationally*

Because the whole liturgy was engaged in the context of prayer, much had been confessed during the time of sharing with each other about what they had experienced and suffered. Yet, beginning a time of confession and explicitly naming blessings and transgressions helped each focus on what now seemed most important to say to God.

> Lord I need to tell you that I did this and hated doing it at the time. I was so used to following orders. I just didn't see a way out. I believed my job was at stake. Yet I was losing my job anyway. The hospital was closing. I now can feel how trapped I was between compassion for the patients and my responsibility for my wife and kids. I was hard-working and dutiful like my mom and dad.

"I am so angry with the state government, those who conceived this and enforced this process. There had to be a better way. Patients were not screened well as to their actual capabilities. There were no gradual steps of preparation and training for them."

"I am grateful to the administrators and psychiatrists who fought this and the way it was done. They tried and were overridden."

"I dream about the patients who have died. They haunt me. I want to help them. They look so lost and confused. And I feel responsible. What we did put them there."

Step 6: *Apologizing, asking forgiveness and forgiving*

"Lord forgive me, forgive us, all of us, top to bottom, for placing these patients in a situation they could not handle. Inexcusable. I am so sorry! I was so scared myself that I didn't object."

> Alex [one of the patients who committed suicide], I am so sorry for what was done to you. I saw how you looked when I tied you to that mattress, when I left you in that room in the city. God please forgive me. Alex, I ask your forgiveness. Lord please take Alex to be with you. Give him your peace.

> Jesus I have been so angry with the state legislators and bureaucrats, for their ignorance and money focus. I realize that many of them felt caught as well, doing what they were told to do. But others conceived this scheme. They imagined that this would work, that patients could handle this 'if they wanted to.' Lord forgive them. They seemed clueless and cut off from the real consequences for these patients. I will forgive them in time. I give to you the revenge I think about, what I want to do to them. I am not yet able to wish them well, but I am willing to get there."

> Lord Jesus, forgive the family members who stopped visiting and the patients who screamed at them or refused to talk when they did. I could see the pain on both sides. I imagine the shame they each carry. And forgive those therapists who failed to reach out to the families and attempt to include them in treatment. I got tired of hearing therapists' complaints

252

about family members. Also forgive me. I just realized what an attitude I built up against family members who refused to visit.

Step 7: *Repenting: renouncing the old and asserting the new*

"I will no longer be silent about what happened. I will do what I can to voice the real need of the severely mentally ill. I will listen to what you lead me to do and I will join with others to do it."

> Lord, I didn't realize that I could pray for these souls, that I could ask for their forgiveness, or that I could ask you to meet them and bring them 'home.' I pray specifically for Joe and Gina and Rick. I will not let my anxieties go undefined and remained unfocused. I will also speak where I can about what happened and I will pray for state legislators and mental health administrators and professionals. I know what they have to deal with and I can identify with them in their work. Lord have mercy. Teach us, teach them, your ways.

John, who had subsequently been ordained into the ministry, then led the group in Holy Communion. Together they prayed for the consecration of the elements, bread and wine, that they become the body and blood of Jesus. They reflected together on the body of Jesus broken for the healing of all wounds, their wounds, the wounds of the patients, the wounds of those who ran the systems and passed the legislation. John spoke of the blood of Jesus as cleansing all of our sin and flowing through all of the events being recounted and the systems in focus to free them of all evil and bondage to destructive and hurtful patterns.

Step 8: *Rebuking evil, breaking curses and restoring blessings*

After all had received Communion, John then prayed to bind and rebuke the spirit of evil in all of these events. He prayed for release from evil for each person present and their families, for the political and mental health systems involved and for the rooms and streets and bridges in the city where these patients had lived and died. Several other participants added their own binding prayers to John's. "Lord Jesus, in your name, I bind all evil spirits from my house, home and family, especially my children. I bind all spirits of anxiety and guilt from myself, my wife and children and send them to the foot of the cross of Jesus."

John continued, "I break all curses on this land from the transgressions committed here. Lord loose this place, this land, from all destruction to again receive your blessing and to thrive. We consecrate this land to you for your purposes."

Step 9: *Praying for healing: inviting Jesus into our past to heal and restore*

After Communion John invited those present to sit in silence for a while and inwardly imagine what Jesus was doing, his healing touch, wherever their imagination took them, asking the Holy Spirit to lead.

Then he prayed a general healing prayer for those patients who had died or were still homeless on the streets of the city and for the healing of guilt and anxiety carried by those present and their fellow hospital colleagues who had been involved. He also prayed for all legislators, state bureaucrats and those who had conceived the plan and administered its implementation, that they be forgiven and raised to consciousness about the consequences of their decisions and healed of any wounds they carried.

After expressing their own requests for healing, they spent an hour simply sharing what they had been experiencing. Remarkably, all shared a feeling of peace and rest, as if a burden had been lifted.

"I feel free. The anxiety is gone. I can see Alex with Jesus. He looks peaceful and happy."

"I am so happy that Joe and Gina are home with Jesus. I see that they are okay."

"I feel empowered to speak up. Those guilt feelings are not as strong. It seems like we have really done something."

"I am remembering some good times. When Rick and Alice had moments of clear thinking and sanity, they would talk to me, even laugh. They would share their deeper thoughts and feelings with me."

"I am so happy that we did this. I want to stay in touch. I would like to pray and see what else the Lord would want us to do. No pressure, just a desire."

Step 10: *Reconciling actions*

Several others in the group agreed that they would also like to stay connected and to meet again to pray. All committed to continue to pray, seeking God's leading as to next steps.

John had no further night terrors and felt at peace and free from these anxieties. Three months later he still reported no reoccurrence of haunting nightmares or intense anxiety. The others also reported continued peace and freedom. They all agreed to not be silent about what had been done and to meet in several months to talk about their follow-up experiences and what each felt led to do now.

Healing with Native American Nations: Addressing the consequences of physical and cultural genocide in the United States

The following confession, apology and call to repentance were spoken in year 2000 for the Bureau of Indian Affairs (BIA) by the leader of that agency, Kevin Gover, then Assistant Secretary-Indian Affairs, Department of the Interior. This confession and apology is a part of the broader arena of healing a nation, the United States of America. The Bureau of Indian Affairs is a United States Government agency, part of the United States Department of the Interior. In its founding it was part of the United States Department of War.

While this representational confession, apology and repentance were spoken by the head of the BIA, for the office of the Assistant Secretary and for all present and former employees of the agency, a similar confession, apology and repentance could be made by any employee of the BIA, standing for her/himself and for all present and former employees.

And a similar confession, apology and repentance could be spoken by any USA citizen moved to do so, albeit from a different position, one of the complicity of a citizen with the actions of the agency, such as failing to be knowledgeable about and take action to make known the actions of the agency. Most United States citizens of European descent benefitted economically from the BIA's participation in the removals of Native peoples and attempts to destroy their cultures, and therefore are beneficiaries of what was taken. We will look at a similar citizen's confession after studying Mr. Gover's statement.

Kevin Gover's representational confession for the transgressions of the BIA

This bold representational confession, apology, contrition and call to repentance were spoken by Mr. Gover at a ceremony, September

8, 2000, acknowledging the 175th anniversary of the establishment of the Bureau of Indian Affairs. The full written statement can be found online.[55] As you read Kevin Gover's confession, look and listen for the various steps of generational healing.

> In March of 1824, President James Monroe established the Office of Indian Affairs in the Department of War. Its mission was to conduct the nation's business with regard to Indian affairs. We have come together today to mark the first 175 years of the institution now known as the Bureau of Indian Affairs...
>
> Before looking ahead...this institution must first look back and reflect on what it has wrought, and, by doing so, come to know that this is no occasion for celebration; rather it is time for reflection and contemplation, a time for sorrowful truths to be spoken, a time for contrition.

Mr. Gover has been researching the sins, wounds, and blessings of the past (**Step 3**). He continues by confessing his findings (**Step 5**).

> We must first reconcile ourselves to the fact that the works of this agency have at various times profoundly harmed the communities it was meant to serve. From the very beginning, the Office of Indian Affairs was an instrument by which the United States enforced its ambition against the Indian nations and Indian people who stood in its path. And so, the first mission of this institution was to execute the removal of the southeastern tribal nations. By threat, deceit, and force, these great tribal nations were made to march

1,000 miles to the west, leaving thousands of their old, their young and their infirm in hasty graves along the Trail of Tears.

...it must be acknowledged that the deliberate spread of disease, the decimation of the mighty bison herds, the use of the poison alcohol to destroy mind and body, and the cowardly killing of women and children made for tragedy on a scale so ghastly that it cannot be dismissed as merely the inevitable consequence of the clash of competing ways of life. ...We will never push aside the memory of unnecessary and violent death at places such as Sand Creek, the banks of the Washita River, and Wounded Knee.

Note Mr. Gover's owning of this history here, in committing, "We will never push aside the memory."

After the devastation of tribal economies and the deliberate creation of tribal dependence on the services provided by this agency, this agency set out to destroy all things Indian. This agency forbade the speaking of Indian languages, prohibited the conduct of traditional religious activities, outlawed traditional government, and made Indian people ashamed of who they were. Worst of all, the Bureau of Indian Affairs committed these acts against the children entrusted to its boarding schools, brutalizing them emotionally, psychologically, physically, and spiritually.... the legacy of these misdeeds haunts us. The trauma of shame, fear and anger has passed from one generation to the next, and manifests itself in the rampant alcoholism, drug abuse, and domestic violence, that plague Indian country... So many of the maladies suffered today in Indian country result from the failures of this agency. Poverty, ignorance, and disease have been the product of this agency's work.

Here we have confession (**Step 5**) of the generational story lines, the impact of transgressions generation to generation.

"...These things occurred despite the efforts of many good people with good hearts who sought to prevent them. These wrongs must be acknowledged if the healing is to begin."

Transgressions must be acknowledged and spoken if "healing is to begin."

I do not speak today for the United States. That is the province of the nation's elected leaders, and I would not presume to speak on their behalf. I am empowered, however, to speak on behalf of this agency, the Bureau of Indian Affairs, and I am quite certain that the words that follow reflect the hearts of its 10,000 employees.

Here Kevin Gover stays within the bounds and authority of his office and belonging to the agency and speaks representationally for the history and members of the agency. Next he expresses sorrow and apology (**Step 6**).

Let us begin by expressing our profound sorrow for what this agency has done in the past... our hearts break... We desperately wish that we could change this history, but of course we cannot. On behalf of the Bureau of Indian Affairs, I extend this formal apology to Indian people for the historical conduct of this agency.

And while the BIA employees of today did not commit these wrongs, we acknowledge that the institution we serve did. We accept this inheritance, this legacy of racism and inhumanity. And by accepting this legacy, we accept also the moral responsibility of putting things right.

Again we see here ownership, and belonging to the history and to the people who enacted that history of the agency. This belonging and ownership is reiterated as he prepares to enter into repentance (**Step 7**).

We therefore begin this important work anew, and make a new commitment to the people and communities that we serve... Never again will this agency stand silent when hate and violence are committed against Indians. Never again will we allow policy to proceed from the assumption that Indians possess less human genius than the other races. Never again will we be complicit in the theft of Indian property... Never again will we allow unflattering and stereotypical images of Indian people to deface the halls of government or lead the American people to shallow and ignorant beliefs about Indians. Never again will we attack your religions, your languages, your rituals, or any of your tribal ways. Never again will we seize your children, nor teach them to be ashamed of who they are. Never again.

This is repentance (**Step 7**) turning away from a destructive way and toward a new life enhancing way: "Never again will this agency stand silent," and toward "renewed hope and prosperity for Indian country."

> We cannot yet ask your forgiveness, not while the burdens of this agency's history weigh so heavily on tribal communities. What we do ask is that, together, we allow the healing to begin.

> Together, we must wipe the tears of seven generations. Together, we must allow our broken hearts to mend. Together, we will face a challenging world with confidence and trust. Together, let us resolve that when our future leaders gather to discuss the history of this institution, it will be time to celebrate the rebirth of joy, freedom, and progress for the Indian Nations. The Bureau of Indian Affairs was born in 1824 in a time of war on Indian people. May it live in the year 2000 and beyond as an instrument of their prosperity.

Note here the importance of not yet asking for forgiveness, recognizing that changed action for the good must precede such a request. Asking for forgiveness cannot be cheap or manipulative.

And then he initiates **Step 10**, reconciling action, asking for trust and a renewed viewpoint. Success depends on true repentance, a real turning of the agency. He is counting on future generations to act on this repentance and hope and earn the trust of the tribes. And the heart of this hope is an appeal to do this together. Healing is a reconciling action between peoples.

Kevin Gover has made a remarkable confession, apology, repentance, step toward healing and call for reconciliation. As different in form as his confession is from Nehemiah and Ezra[56], the conveyed intent and heart is one with them.

Firstly, the facts are faced, admitted and owned. There is no attempt to soften or diminish the violence and injury that the agency has committed or failed to prevent.

Secondly, the agencies destructive legacy is accepted and owned. Although new to the position of director there is no attempt to separate himself or his staff from the past actions of the agency, as in condescending judgment of those who committed these wrongs.

Thirdly, responsibility is accepted and owned on behalf of those who have gone before. Owning responsibility means confessing past wrongs (committed by and through this agency by past members of the agency), as one belonging to and now responsible for the agency, therefore owning the responsibility to research past actions.

Fourthly, he confesses what is unearthed. The agency has its own continuity and active legacy as a human institution and those who serially occupy agency positions of authority and responsibility inherit the history of the given office and the whole agency and responsibility for addressing that history and the affected communities.

☐ *Take a moment to reflect on Kevin Gover's representational confession. How does his confession speak to you as you engage or anticipate engaging generational healing with respect to the larger arenas that concern you? Make note of the insights that you want to use and implement.*

When Jeffrey, a United States citizen, read Kevin Gover's statement in the newspaper, he felt both startled and moved. He was startled that a government official could and would make such an honest statement about the actions a government agency. Being startled brought to his awareness that he was accustomed to leaders feeling compelled to color the historical actions of their predecessors, to put history in a positive light. He did not expect honesty about dark deeds. He realized that he had accepted such cover up as necessary. He was moved to tears, grieved by the stark realities of genocide, attempts to eliminate Native nations and their ways of life. And he was awakened to the reality that his ancestors, pioneers moving west, had occupied the land from which Natives Americans had been forcibly and illegally (in violation of treaties) removed. Jeffrey became aware that his ancestors and many like them had benefitted greatly from the removals (**Step 1**: *Awakening to the present influences of the past and calling out to God*).

> Jeffrey prayed: Lord Jesus, I bring to you my awareness of my own ignorance about the BIA and government policy regarding Native peoples and tribes. I have been aware of some of the wrongs committed by the US military against Indian peoples, but have never investigated the actions of the BIA, an agency of my government, or exposed myself to the details of the historical and more recent actions of the military against Indian people. Knowing the little I have known, I confess that I have resisted learning more. I have maintained a blind eye, in order to avoid facing what has been done, and how such knowledge might weigh on me. I imagine that my ancestors did similarly, for they were closer to the actions of genocide and benefitted directly and immediately from these actions. Yet they passed none of these stories forward. It became as if the tribes had not been there. Lord I am ready to become aware and to act as you lead me.

Jeffrey wanted to know more and to know how God was leading him in this regard. So in his own way he sat in God's presence (in his special prayer chair) asking for greater awareness, and for God's heart in the matter of these injustices and devastating consequences (**Step 2**: *Seeking God's face—listening to God and community*).

As he listened in prayer, he became aware that his grandparents, and most certainly his great-grandparents (on his mother's side) were most likely well aware of the devastation that was happening to Native nations. As they moved west this was happening all around them. He also became aware that, most likely, their sensitivity and felt remorse and entrapment had seeped through to him. He and they (must have) felt caught between carving out their own lives and opposing government policy from which they were benefitting economically. "I am the same," he realized. "I want gas prices down but realize that huge US oil fields lie under Indian land. Lord have mercy. What is your lead here?"

Jeffrey then set his course on discovery to determine what happened and what is still happening (**Step 3**: *Researching the sins, wounds and blessings of the past*). He sought out and listened to Native people. He inquired of his cousins. Did they carry stories from common grandparents and great-grandparents? From his Native inquiries in North Dakota he received an earful. Yes, they were being pressured to allow drilling and fracking on their lands. They themselves were now caught between being guardians of the land, a sacred trust given by the Creator, and escaping poverty with the monies being offered. And, yes, their tribes were in court seeking redress for several of the many broken treaties. Through oral traditions, they carried many stories of the rich and tragic history of their peoples. Randy White Owl wanted to talk about his tribe's trail of tears, how they had also been marched from their tribal lands to a reservation, pregnant women being knifed in the belly to kill their forming offspring. Deep pain. Jeffrey's genuine desire to listen earned a modicum of trust, and White Owl wanted to tell these stories to a white man and to be heard.

Jeffrey's cousins knew little more than he did but did want to share with him all they had been told. Great-grandfather had supplied horses to miners in the west and certainly interacted with the plains tribes and benefitted from removals, the slaying of the buffalo herds and military protection. Also he must have traded with the plains tribes to obtain worthy horses to sell. These stories they imagined together but nothing specific regarding family interactions with Native tribes had been passed along. Jeffrey shared with them what the North Dakota tribesmen had spoken to him.

Two of his cousins were sympathetic to his inquiry, though they did not share his faith. Because he sensed that they were "with him," in his lament and hunger for truth and justice, he chose to voice his prayers in their presence. Having immersed himself in listening enabled him to imagine what had occurred and to build on all he had heard and remembered. He asked for God's heart and perspective for his ancestors and for the Native tribes whose land and way of life had been taken and destroyed (**Step 4:** *Searching the heart of God*). His prayers were forthright and to the point.

Father, thank you for my mother's family, who carved out a life in difficult circumstances. They persevered and invested their talents and educated themselves. I am very grateful to them. They have given me life and a heart for justice. I also bring to you our silence regarding the taking of tribal lands, the removal of peoples and our benefitting from the way opened to us. We were close to these events and said nothing about this to our descendants even as we fought for justice for ourselves and told those stories. I have avoided knowing this until now. I and we have never, to my knowledge, acknowledged the undeserved privilege that these removals provided for us (**Step**

5: *Humbly confessing, personally and representationally*). Lord have mercy. Please forgive us for our silence (**Step 6:** *Apologizing, asking forgiveness and forgiving*). As I see in prayer that certain of my ancestors, most probably, knew and felt the wrong of these injustices and felt impotent to oppose them, I am further haunted by their silence. Lord I will be silent no more. I will speak these facts to my children and grandchildren, to my friends and colleagues (**Step 7:** *Repenting: renouncing the old and asserting the new*). I will tell my Native friends that I now know this and am sorry for our silence and that we will be silent no more. Lord Jesus in your name I break the power of this pattern of silence and self-protection. It has become like a curse to us. I bind from this pattern the forces of darkness that speak lies to us saying that silence protects us and that we were justified in taking Native land (**Step 8:** *Rebuking evil, breaking curses and restoring blessings*). I ask you to restore Native peoples and cultures. Raise them up in your resurrection. They need their identities and ways. I need their love for the earth and all of creation. Bless us with the power and joy of truth telling. Lord, heal all of these wounds, our habit of silence, the ravaged Native identities and ways (**Step 9:** *Praying for healing*). And please give us our next steps of action (**Step 10:** *Reconciling actions*). I want to do my part of honoring what has been lost and calling forth the reconciliation and new life that you are imparting to this land and its peoples in this day.

Jeffrey knew that his cousins were with him. He felt their silent assent as he prayed.

Healing the consequences of slavery

In 2012 an intercessory group met in Philadelphia, Pennsylvania, to intercede for historical wounds at the foundation of the United States of America. This band of intercessors gathers annually, moving sequentially, year to year, in a circle to the four directions, East, South, West and North. The group was formed in a Native American tradition of tribal societies. The core group is composed of persons from a variety of Native tribes, Cherokee, Kiowa, Potawatomi, Navaho, Apache, several of European decent, German, Russian, English and several of African American lineages. The core group are followers of Jesus, and see Jesus at the heart of their traditional cultures and practices allowing him to center their traditional practices in him. Participants pray in their own way and teach the others their ways of prayer. Members of other religions, who worship a God who is Love, are welcome and invited to pray in their way with mutual respect for others. When the group gathers in one of the four directions, others in the immediate area join the gathering and intercessions. The gathering attends to personal healing and generational healing of historical wounds that still grip the nation and the places and communities where they gather. Historical research precedes the gathering as part of preparations for prayer. During the gatherings the group moves from place to place in order to pray at the specific sites where significant historical wounding occurred.

When the group met in Philadelphia, Pennsylvania, in 2012, the intercessors spent the morning studying the impact of slavery through the generations and the historical trauma that continues to impact present generations. An African American psychotherapist and educator discussed, with the intercessors, research and clinical experience regarding inherited patterns, continued racism, and deep, inherited interior residuals of centuries of shaming, control, fear, and deprivation.

Digesting this data and processing personal reactions and reflections provided preparation for the afternoons intercessions to be engaged in Historic Philadelphia, at the Presidents House and the slave auction site. The intercessors also read documents about the Presidency of George Washington, the enslaved who served the President and the Country in the first President's House, and the slave trade and slave auctions.

Bill's prayers and experience of this intercessory gathering

We are at the boarded up ruins of a tavern where the London Coffee House once stood. I am across the street, imagining the historical scene: Men enjoying their morning coffee. Light conversation and business dealings. Then inspecting naked Africans and bidding for their bodies.

My mind flashes to a moment from childhood when our Baptist minister took my family on a ride into the Black ghetto of the city. He laughed at and mocked the people. I'm in disbelief, thinking, "Mom, *say* something! You *must* be sick at heart." She is silent.

The site is also silent. It, too, should speak out. Why is this place dead? Why has it been discarded? Why is this spot abandoned, alone, unredeemed? Can anything thrive here?

Is the grip of slavery still that strong? I imagine a platform in the middle of Market Street. Human beings naked. Every orifice inspected. The image is grisly, dehumanizing, difficult to hold.

Slowly the prayer warrior group gathers. I want us together. Yet, I know we are each in our own space with our own sense of the moment. At this moment I feel distant from yesterday's heartfelt imaginings of what we would do here. I feel unsteady, "Have I called us to a trivial act? Is this really as important as I felt it yesterday?" The only way forward is to trust what I felt yesterday and what we had agreed to do. Members of our group were moving in different directions, a few standing under the historical marker (about the slave auctions here)[57] on the sidewalk in front of the abandoned tavern, a few standing where I am hoping we will gather, across the street from the boarded up tavern. What to do?

I call for all to gather across the street. "I want us to gather over here." A few come. Others continue what they are doing. Steve is photographing Dale at the historical marker. I am shaken and angry. "This is not a spectacle, a cheap exhibition. We are here to remember, to allow ourselves to be addressed by this history, by the persons changed forever at this place." I walk to Steve, "Stop, not now." He stops and joins me with others in an open area across the street.

I voice my intentions.

> "Please stand and pray here with me. Feel this place, imagine what took place here. I want to cry aloud our grief, to confess our present complicity, to ask to be changed. I want the ongoing wounds from slavery to be healed and the hold of persistent racism to be broken. I want us to stand here together, to speak what has occurred here and to pray for healing of this place, the legacies, the consequences."

Now I feel such a clear representation within me. I know guilt, with no guilt feelings. I am me now and I am them then.

I turn to Dale, an African American. "Dale would you begin the prayer?"

He starts to pray and then goes silent. "I have no words," he says.

I have no words either; none come that seem to speak the moment. A few minutes earlier I had wondered at the value and import of our gathered voice. Now I feel the insufficiency of words. Becca, also African American, is sobbing, being held by Kris and Dale. I imagine, "Too brutal, overwhelming." Becca's ancestors had stood in such a place and been inspected and sold. I am moved and shout, "Change me. Change me. Change me. Change us." This is my prayer.

We are in a circle, Dale, Becca, Kris and the others holding onto each other crying and shouting our prayers. Gary is seeing and feeling the fear of those brought in chains from the ships to be examined and sold here. We all seem to be feeling deeply, some angry, others remorseful and contrite. Some are grieving for the plight of their slave ancestors. Some are grieving our complicity in tolerating racism. Some grieve the actions of our slave owner ancestors. We each speak what we imagine in this place. Some ask God's forgiveness for the torment committed here. Another binds evil in this place in the name of Jesus. Another asks God to cleanse the evil history in this place. One senses that this will take many and repeated prayers. So much human pain and abuse has accumulated here. Several prayed for the healing of all who were enslaved and abused in this place and for the healing of their progeny.

As the prayers ended and the group began to disperse to other locations, I approached Becca whose tears had quieted and said, "I am so sorry." I meant it. I felt it.

She was silent for a time and then spoke honestly from her soul. "I have heard this too often, without real change."

I responded simply, "Yes."

In the days subsequent to this prayer event, the words, "Change me, change us," continued to reverberate in my mind. Racial prejudice rose up in me, as if my generations were surfacing their poison for me to confess for us all in my lament and cry. Then suddenly there was an inward clearing in my soul. The ancestral racial prejudice that had gripped my soul and plagued me, despite my conscious and chosen beliefs and personal repentance, suddenly cleared. Prejudicial images ceased to plague me. My perceptions of others seemed clean, simply person to person. Months later this clearing has sustained. Praise God. ∎

In preparation for these generational prayers on location in historic Philadelphia, the intercessors had read and discussed documents on the history of these places. We had prayed to be centered in Jesus, filled with the Father's love and guided by the Holy Spirit.

In this example **Step 1**: *Awakening to the present influences of the past and calling out to God*, had occurred as the planning for the gathering took place, some eight months prior to the gathering. Those planning the gathering felt the tug of the Holy Spirit to visit the President's House and the place of slave auctioning and to pray at these places for generational healing. This was communicated to all those preparing to attend the annual meeting, so that they could begin to pray and seek God's leading.

As those planning the gathering found historical documentation of the places to be visited (**Step 3**: *Researching the sins, wounds, and blessings of the past*), we distributed the documents, to those preparing to gather, for study and prayer. Also **Steps 2 and 4**: *Seeking God's face (listening to God and community)* and *Searching the heart of God* were ongoing for those planning the gathering, for those preparing to attend, and for the entire group together as the gathering commenced. These are prayer actions and attitudes that are an ongoing part of the practice of this group of intercessors.

Then the intercessors absorbed relevant history, imagining the lives of the enslaved and the generational impact of these historical traumas, as they listened to and conversed with the African American psychotherapist.

In the outpouring of prayers at the slave auction site many steps for generational healing took place. These steps poured out of the intercessors in a cascade of utterance and emotion. Some confessed their own attitudes, their silent complicity with racism. Others confessed what they felt and imagined took place at this place in 1754 (**Step 5: *Humbly confessing, personally and representationally***). Becca sobbed, feeling the horrors suffered by her ancestors and the enslaved in this place. Gary saw and felt the slaves' terror. 1754 became present to him. I imagined the grisly scene, men transacting business and inspecting naked bodies as if they were cattle. Several cried to God for forgiveness in remorse for the inhumanity of slavery and slave trading and for their felt complicity with continuing racism (**Step 6: *Apologizing, asking forgiveness and forgiving***). Bill cried out his repentance (**Step 7**), "Change me. Change us." Another intercessor bound evil (**Step 8**). Several intercessors prayed for healing of those bound and sold here and their progeny. Another prayed for cleansing and healing of the ground, the building, the street (**Step 9**). Bill spoke his sorrow to Becca (**Step 10: *Reconciling actions***).

In this case steps for generational healing could flow spontaneously because there had been so much preparation and because those present had prayed together for generational healing many times in many different situations. The steps were familiar and understood through repeated experiences.

☐ Take a moment to reflect on these prayers at the slave auction site in Philadelphia. *What does this confession, repentance, and healing speak to you as you engage or anticipate engaging generational healing with respect to the larger issues that concern you? Make note of the insights that you want to use and implement.*

Healing our religious traditions

Religious loyalties and the identities and the belonging that they provide run deep. This makes it difficult to admit transgressions and departures from the gospel of Jesus in our own religious traditions.

Christians often fear that facing and owning their faith traditions' historical dark sides, and the hurtful consequences of ancestors' attitudes and actions, will bring dishonor and disgrace to revered heritage and crippling shame to the present generations.

There is no question that honest appraisal of our ancestors' and our own attitudes and actions will bring moments of shame and infect ambivalence into our identifications and belongings. Those who have been idealized will at least temporarily fall from favor and the culture and history we have trusted will lose its luster. As destructive attitudes and actions are revealed and our consciousness is struck, we will each, at least momentarily, want to deny or minimize what is being revealed. It may spark anger, or make us want to disassociate ourselves from our traditions and their legacies. I have witnessed these reactions in myself and again and again among Christians as the historical role of our churches in the genocide of peoples and cultures is exposed to our contemporary consciousness. Or, if terrible abuses to our familial and religious ancestors are made more explicit for us, we may find ourselves filled with deep outrage and a fierce resistance to seeing the offending others as real struggling human beings as well.

Because religious loyalties run deep, they have a way of surprising us, of suddenly showing up. That to which we are loyal through our religious belonging resists critique and tends to be felt as *right* or *wrong*, *superior* or *inferior*.

Aspects of religious cultures and practices that have been known as right belief and faithful action in one generation may be revealed to subsequent generations to be only one way, or as having left destructive consequences. Historical actions believed at the time to be faithful to God, now may be revealed to have been grossly unjust and injuring or to have been fueled by un-forgiveness. Denominational and cultural loyalties believed to be faithful to God have incited much violence, prejudice and intolerance.

273

Humanly, a conviction of superior belief combined with intolerance of differences comes from intolerance of true otherness, and intransigent un-forgiveness. These convictions may even fuel spiritual, psychological and physical violence. Historically peoples' resistances to Christian conversion have often been treated by Christians and their churches as resistance to God, rather than as adherence to deeply held convictions, resistance to the cultural forms of faith expression being demanded or reactions to Christians demonizing other peoples' faith practices without understanding. Many times Christians have had no grasp as to how their witness has been perceived and to what extent others were looking to see if their actions matched their gospel.

Pope John Paul's confessions

During his tenure as Pope of the Roman Catholic Church, John Paul II faced the dark side of his faith traditions and made many representational confessions on behalf of Catholics and Catholic leaders, taking these actions for generational healing of the Body of Christ and the healing of the wounds between the Catholic Church and other churches and cultures. These confessions are collected in a book by Luigi Accattoli entitled, *When a Pope Asks Forgiveness*.[58] This collection covers a range of historical events, peoples, issues, and places. Chapters include the Crusades, the Jews, Women, Galileo, the Inquisition, Hus, Calvin, Zwingli, the Indians, Islam, Luther, Racism, Eastern Schism and more.

The following illustration of his actions toward repairing relationships with Calvin and Zwingli, and their Swiss descendants in the faith, gives a window into the attitude and method he employed in his representational confessions. Here he laid the ground work for developing joint work toward mutual confession, forgiveness, repentance, healing and reconciliation.[59]

Pope John Paul II spoke of John Calvin and Huldrych Zwingli during his visit to Switzerland in June of 1984. At an ecumenical gathering (Meeting with the Federation of Protestant Churches, Kehrsatz, Switzerland, June 14, 1984), he honored the two reformers for their intention "to make the Church more faithful to the will of the Lord."[60]

John Paul spoke of the zeal which animated these two outstanding religious leaders in Swiss history. He went on to recount their accomplishments and their impact then and now, sustained across history. "The legacy of the thought and ethical convictions particular to each of these two men continues to be forcefully and dynamically present in various parts of Christianity" (p. 155).

He spoke clearly that the theology and spirituality of these two men both contributes to deep ties today between Christian denominations through their profound faith in Jesus and desire for a faithful church, and remains a challenge to unity, given differences of understanding and conviction.

Then he focused the work of generational healing between the Catholic Church and these Protestant traditions, acknowledging that each church and tradition reads the history between them differently. He asks that memories of the damage done by the events of the past and judgments regarding responsibility for the damage not prevent attempts to repair the damage between them and to pursue healing, saying,

> The cleansing of our memories is an element of capital importance in ecumenical progress. It implies the frank acknowledgement of reciprocal wrongs and errors committed in the way of reacting toward each other when indeed each one wanted to make the Church more faithful to the will of the Lord. (p. 155)

John Paul II called for research (**Step 3**) and confession (**Step 5**) and apologies and forgiveness (**Step 6**), that includes mutual admission of wrongs committed in reacting to each other. There is a claim here for mutual, reciprocal, fair, responsible representational action toward each other for healing divisions and forging unity in the Body of Christ. To do this he suggests collaborative research. Then he sees the possibility that together, representationally, the past could be submitted to the mercy of God, without reservation, and together we could freely seek God's will.

Notice that John Paul II begins his address, to the spiritual descendants of John Calvin and Huldrych Zwingli, by lifting up the positive contributions of Calvin and Zwingli, first their intention "to make the Chuch more faithful to the will of God." So often we caste our adversaries into the sea of bad intentions, focusing on the defective motives motivating the beliefs and actions we believe have hurt us and hurt our people, our church, or missled many, therefore harming the body of Christ. Many of us also tend to blame historical leaders for the destructive, injuring actions of their loyal adherents. So important to healing the generational wounds within and between nations, and religious denominations and traditions, is the action of identifying with the other, with the persons and peoples who have injured us, and exploring their motoves, their intentions, from their perspective. Motives are never pure and singular, but they always contain some good, if only the good of survival or loyalty or attempts to right wrongs. In effect John Paul II is saying to the people he is addressing, "I recognize the good they, Calvin and Zwingli, were trying to do. Therfore I credit their intentions and am joined with them in motive as I act also 'to make the Church more faithful to the will of God.'"

As we research the roots of the larger concerns that any of us have (**Step 3**), we encourage investigating and imagining the multiplicity of motives on all sides. John Paul II does this. He refers to the influences that remain deterrents to unity, "makes our ecclesial divisions always present" (p. 155) and those that reinforce unity, "maintain deep ties between us" (p. 155). These influences are stated generally here but refer to the impact of specific beliefs and actions. Assessing motives and intentions, and searching historical roots (**Step 3**), must therefore include honest appraisal of constructive and destructive influences on all sides.

John Paul II then goes on to reflect the heart of God (**Step 4**), "that all will be one." The different ways we see and interpret history and different understandings of faith "must not divide us forever" (p. 155). Jesus prayer, "That they may all be one" (Jn 17:21), is at the heart of John Paul II's generational healing work and the heart motive for all reconciliation.

☐ *Take a moment to make notes re: what you take from John Paul II's address to Swiss Protestants. Note anything that may be relevant to the generational healing work you are doing* or anticipating or thinking about with any "wider" healing arenas that concern you.

Generational healing at an international Christian conference

At an international conference of a worldwide Christian organization, held in Korea, the Japanese delegation asked to speak to the assembly. They came up on the stage and bowed to their Korean hosts. Then their leader read a letter of apology (**Step 6**) and repentance (**Step 7**) to all the Koreans for the way the Japanese had captured Korean women as "Comfort Women" for the Japanese troops during World War 2 (**Step 5: *Humbly confessing***). Then the whole Japanese delegation faced the audience as the leader said, "We want ask your forgiveness for our sin (**Step 6**) and pray a blessing on you (**Step 9: *Praying for healing***)." She suggested that anyone so moved come forward to offer their forgiveness and receive a blessing.

At first the Koreans poured forward, and then other Asians. Then Africans from warring tribes came forward to repent and forgive one another, followed by Eastern Europeans, and then English, Irish and Scottish delegates. Suddenly, the whole room erupted into individuals and groups confessing, repenting and forgiving one another. Tears flowed. After the activity subsided, a South African group began to sing, "We are marching in the light of God" as they grasped the hands of nearby delegates from other countries and began to circle the room, singing and dancing and pulling others into the dance.

The whole tenor of the conference changed to one of unity and celebration. The effect rippled outward as delegates went home with plans for international cooperation in research, publishing and joint ministries (**Step 10**: *Reconciling actions*). Out of those cooperative initiatives, a mission trip developed for North Americans to go to Africa to learn from their best practices in ministry. Articles from other countries were shared among national publications and ongoing international ministry research studies sought to better understand each other's cultures and ways of communicating.

☐ *Take a moment now to note what the actions taken by the Japanese and then the eruption of apology, forgiveness and reconciliation brought to mind. What does this illustration say to you as you think about any larger arenas that concern you? Make note of the insights that you want to use and implement.*

For Reflection

Read the portions of 2 Chronicles 6 and 7 below. Solomon prayed this prayer upon the dedication of the Temple in Jerusalem, after he had alienated most of the nation of Israel through his excesses and policies of harsh forced labor. The nation was resentful and divided.

6 [1]Then Solomon said, "The LORD has said that he would reside in thick darkness. [2]I have built you an exalted house, a place for you to reside in forever."[3]Then the king turned around and blessed all the assembly of Israel, while all the assembly of Israel stood. [4]And he said, "Blessed be the LORD, the God of Israel, who with his hand has fulfilled what he promised with his mouth to my father David, saying,[5]"Since the day that I brought my people out of the land of Egypt, I have not chosen a city from any of the tribes of Israel in which to build a house, so that my name might be there, and I chose no one as ruler over my people Israel; [6]but I have chosen Jerusalem in order that my name may be there, and I have chosen David to be over my people Israel." [7]My father David had it in mind to build a house for the name of the LORD, the God of Israel. [8]But the LORD said to my father David, "You did well to consider building a house for my name; [9]nevertheless you shall not build the house, but your son who shall be born to you shall build the house for my name." [10]Now the LORD has fulfilled his promise that he made; for I have succeeded my father David, and sit on the throne of Israel, as the LORD promised, and have built the house for the name of the LORD, the God of Israel. [11]There I have set the ark, in which is the covenant of the LORD that he made with the people of Israel.

[12]Then Solomon stood before the altar of the LORD in the presence of the whole assembly of Israel, and spread out his hands... [14]He said, "O LORD, God of Israel, there is no God like you, in heaven or on earth,

keeping covenant in steadfast love with your servants who walk before you with all their heart— [15] you who have kept for your servant, my father David, what you promised to him... [21] And hear the plea of your servant and of your people Israel, when they pray toward this place; may you hear from heaven your dwelling place; hear and forgive. [22] If someone sins against another and is required to take an oath and comes and swears before your altar in this house, [23] may you hear from heaven, and act, and judge your servants, repaying the guilty by bringing their conduct on their own head, and vindicating those who are in the right by rewarding them in accordance with their righteousness. [24] When your people Israel, having sinned against you, are defeated before an enemy but turn again to you, confess your name, pray and plead with you in this house, [25] may you hear from heaven, and forgive the sin of your people Israel, and bring them again to the land that you gave to them and to their ancestors...

[31] Thus may they fear you and walk in your ways all the days that they live in the land that you gave to our ancestors...

[34] If your people go out to battle against their enemies, by whatever way you shall send them, and they pray to you toward this city that you have chosen and the house that I have built for your name, [35] then hear from heaven their prayer and their plea, and maintain their cause.

[36] If they sin against you—for there is no one who does not sin—and you are angry with them and give them to an enemy, so that they are carried away captive to a land far or near; [37] then if they come to their senses in the land to which they have been taken captive, and repent, and plead with you in the land of their captivity, saying, 'We have sinned, and have done wrong; we have acted wickedly'; [38] if they repent with all their heart and soul in the land of their captivity, to which they were taken captive, and pray toward their land, which you gave to their ancestors, the city that you have chosen, and the house that I have built for your name, [39] then hear from heaven your dwelling place their prayer and their pleas, maintain their cause and forgive your people who have sinned against you. [40] Now, O my God, let your eyes be open and your ears attentive to prayer from this place."

7 [1] When Solomon had ended his prayer, fire came down from heaven and consumed the burnt offering and the sacrifices; and the glory of the LORD filled the temple. [2] The priests could not enter the house of the LORD, because the glory of the LORD filled the LORD's house. [3] When all the people of Israel saw the fire come down and the glory of the LORD on the temple, they bowed down on the pavement with their faces to the ground, and worshiped and gave thanks to the LORD, saying, "For he is good, for his steadfast love endures forever."

7[12] Then the LORD appeared to Solomon in the night and said to him: "I have heard your prayer, and have chosen this place for myself as a house of sacrifice. [13] When I shut up the heavens so that there is no rain, or command the locust to devour the land, or send pestilence among my people, [14] if my people who are called by my name humble themselves, pray, seek my face, and turn from their wicked ways, then I will hear from heaven, and will forgive their sin and heal their land. [15] Now my eyes will be open and my ears attentive to the prayer that is made in this place."

1. In what ways does Solomon put into practice the steps in the generational healing process?
2. How does he teach the Israelites about this process?
3. How does God respond?

Chapter 11

Maintaining Generational Health

After experiencing a few joyous, problem-free years at St. Ambrose Church, Alice, a member who had received prayer ministry, heard from a friend that the prayer minister who prayed with her had shared her confidential story with several other people. Alice felt devastated and reported her sense of betrayal to the pastor. After confronting the prayer minster and hearing her confession, he explained that she could no longer serve in that role. She in turn became vindictive and began publicly criticizing both Alice and the pastor.

■ Several years after overcoming the problems at the Agape Food Bank, the Director retired. A new Director came in with fresh ideas and a cocky attitude that irritated many of the volunteers. Old patterns of dividing into factions began to reappear, but alliances also began to form to determine how to appropriately handle their dissatisfaction with the new Director's approach. ■

Racial unrest continues to fester in our nation, despite electing an African American President. Native Americans continue to live under unjust circumstances. International peace treaties seem to be continually broken. Terrorists continue to strike. Friendships and marriages fall apart. Churches split.

It seems that nothing stays fixed for long.

Once you have experienced generational healing, further questions quickly surface.

How can I help prevent generational wounds from developing in future generations?

- How can I be sure that I am not wounding others without realizing it?
- How can I safeguard those who come after me from suffering from wounds like those I experienced?
- How can I pass on a legacy of faith, truth, goodness, healing and blessing?

Even healed people are wounded and wounding healers. We are constantly learning to trust and to be trustworthy. Frustration, defensiveness and misunderstandings rise up to confront us with our humanity. However, if we view generational healing as a journey, we see that we are still moving forward, even as we learn new lessons along the way. The path will often be muddy, or steep, or rocky, or hard to find. Sometimes we fall flat on our faces, but each new obstacle helps us to trust God and to deal more competently with the next one.

We approach generational healing with humility, identifying with the sins of our ancestors and/or predecessors. However, we tend to fall into old patterns under stress, behaving toward our own children, supervisees and younger associates with wounding words and actions similar to those that hurt us.

The normal give and take of human relationships is always tainted by sin—insensitivity, bias, fear, defensiveness, personal ambition, pride and all those things that the Bible calls the "lusts of the flesh."

We just cannot escape from being human, regardless of our passionate desire to be good. The apostle Paul wrote,

I find it to be a law that when I want to do what is good, evil lies close at hand. For I delight in the law of God in my inmost self, but I see in my members another law at war with the law of my mind, making me captive to the law of sin that dwells in my members. Wretched man that I am! Who will rescue me from this body of death? (Rom 7:21-24)

We also cannot control the future, nor can we control how even our well-intended actions toward others will be received. Our outpouring of love and concern may be perceived as controlling or smothering. Efforts to extend help may be seen as patronizing by recipients. Attempts to forgive may be rejected. Old patterns may recur despite all our efforts to heal. Consider how quickly wounds developed in the early church. Most of Paul's letters involved sorting out the effects of sin in these young churches. In Jesus' messages to the seven churches in Revelation 2-3, five of the seven churches received strong words of rebuke for their failings. However, two of the churches were doing well. What made the difference? The churches in both Smyrna and Philadelphia had remained faithful to God in spite of severe persecution. Even so, the wounds from that persecution may well have affected the children and grandchildren of those early church members—even in the good churches. However, the trajectory of God's redeeming work continues to move toward healing and reconciliation, so we have hope.

What can we do to pass on generational blessing, rather than wounding? How do we become "blessers"? Primarily, by keeping short accounts in our personal relationships rather than letting anger fester into bitterness. Our everyday struggles constantly tempt us to move into defensive mode, justifying our responses instead of clarifying the issues and forgiving the perceived offense. Every leader faces situations that require making hard decisions that may hurt someone, confronting injustice or unacceptable behavior or choosing unpopular stands.

Just like eating the right foods, regular exercise and getting routine checkups maintains our physical health, we can maintain spiritual and generational health by following the generational healing process with preventive health care in mind.

Generational Healing Process

1. awakening to the present influences of the past and calling out to God
2. seeking God's face (listening to God and community)
3. researching the sins, wounds and blessings of the past
4. searching the heart of God for our lineages
5. humbly confessing, personally and representationally
6. apologizing, asking forgiveness and forgiving
7. repenting: renouncing the old and asserting the new
8. rebuking evil, breaking curses and restoring blessings
9. praying for healing: inviting Jesus into our ancestral past to heal and restore
10. reconciling actions

Calling out to God and seeking His face. Develop a habit of listening. Generational healing is never completely finished in this life. Wounds formed over generations take years to heal. As we listen carefully to God, to ourselves and other people, new dimensions of the wounds we carry may become evident and present themselves for healing. However, most of us do not listen well. Good listening requires us to put aside distractions (such as cell phones, other responsibilities, agendas, time limitations), identify the filters that prevent us from hearing what others are saying (making assumptions about motives, prejudice, lack of respect) and concentrate on what the other is saying.

Listening to God requires maintaining a healthy relationship with him. A daily discipline of prayer and Scripture reading, faithful worship and study with the body of Christ and developing an attitude of bringing God into the everyday routine fosters an ability to hear God when he speaks.

Listening for generational influences that may need additional healing requires staying in close relationship with God daily. Schedule regular times of retreat in a place where you can focus on your relationship with God and with others. If you live in a lively household, home may not be the best place to retreat. Find a local retreat center, a remote cabin or a nearby park for a one-day retreat, or get away to a "thin place" (where people have prayed for many generations) for a longer stretch.

When conflict or other potentially wounding dynamics become apparent, stop and pray. Ask God what he is doing in this situation. Times of turmoil often serve to alert us to forks in the road or a new direction in the healing journey or to additional generational influences that need attention and healing. As we do generational healing work our awareness of generational influences tends to expand and enlarge. Praying with others over their generational issues in an ethnic heritage where ancestors were frequently persecuted or even murdered made me curious about issues that may have been passed down by my own ancestors. One lineage suffered under the Clearances in Scotland and another experienced persecution and over-taxation as Non-Conformists in England. Interestingly, both lines seem to have passed on a spirit of forgiveness and inclusivity.

Admit personal sins and seek forgiveness. There are always two sides to a conflict—even when we feel confident that our indignation is righteous. The natural human response to threats is either *flight* or *fight*. Fleeing often involves just ignoring the conflict (and the persons involved). In such situations, injustice may be left to reign. The actual source of conflict may be left to fester when we flee before hearing the whole story. A family member may be shunned. Leadership in churches, Christian organizations or governments may have become encumbered by self-seeking opportunism. Evil can run rampant. For those who decide to fight, responding to conflict usually means rising to defend another side of the issue. Often that includes garnering support from other like-minded persons so that the conflict grows into a larger battle. We see this in family feuds, church splits, gridlock in congress and outright wars. God calls us instead to examine ourselves, look for the "log in your own eye" (Mt 7:5), to forgive (Mt 6:14) and to reconcile with those who have something against us (Mt 5:24).

Reconnect with those you have wounded, or have wounded you. This may seem counter-intuitive, or even unsafe. In a situation where contact is truly dangerous, such as with physical abuse, it is usually best to simply speak forgiveness out loud in the presence of someone else—a prayer minister, friend, counselor or pastor. However, we have numerous examples of people who took forgiveness and reconciliation seriously enough to act on it. The former Pope John Paul II sought reconciliation with the man who attempted to assassinate him, visiting him in prison to forgive and pray for him. Several years ago an Amish community experienced the massacre of their children at school, but they not only forgave the shooter, they cared lavishly for his family.

■ I (Judy) personally experienced the freedom of forgiveness after a session of healing prayer for a situation in which I felt had been seriously wronged. Following the session, the prayer minister suggested that I ask those who had hurt me for their forgiveness. At first that seemed strange, but as I asked God to reveal to me what I had done to offend them, I became aware of my own sin in each relationship. I went to the persons involved and asked for their forgiveness. To my surprise, almost all of them responded by saying, "I'm the one who should be asking for your forgiveness." Through those encounters, deeper friendships formed and hard feelings evaporated.

Avoid moving on to another setting without trying to heal the wounds of the present one. North America as we know it was settled by immigrants fleeing persecution, famine and other hardships. We inherited a generational legacy with a deep sense that if the present situation becomes difficult, we can always move on. If I don't like my current job, spouse, neighborhood, school or church, I can always find another one. However, in doing so, we take with us all the attitudes and behaviors that contributed to the conflict in our former relationships. Reconciling with those in our present situation is the only way we can successfully move on to a new venue to make a fresh start.

Furthermore, North America comes with another dark legacy — our persecution and abuse of Native Americans and African slaves, as well as other immigrants. Even though we may not have personally participated in that abuse, many descendants of those persecuted people still carry the wounds inflicted generations ago. The effects of people being demeaned, families divided, land taken, privileges withheld and rights violated leave consequences that are only now being uncovered. A field of research and healing has developed called historical trauma. We have a responsibility to reconcile with the descendants of those who were wounded by our ancestors or predecessors. That may involve listening to outpourings of rage, bitterness, accusation and attacks that may seem unfair. At this point, representational confession and repentance can open the door for healing at a deeper level.

Be an encourager to others. Speaking out about your own wounds can give "permission" to others who are wounded so that they feel comfortable sharing their pain. Pass on the blessings and gifts you have been given as you minister to others. You may want to obtain further training in listening, prayer ministry or generational healing. Build on the blessings of your ancestors or predecessors to bless others—spiritually, emotionally, educationally or materially.

Connect with others who can support and encourage you. The warm glow that comes with a healing experience can quickly fade if it is not continually fanned by encouragement from others. Look for, or form, an accountability group with others who share your commitment to healing. I meet weekly with a small group where we share how we have seen God at work in our lives in the previous week, as well as our points of discouragement so we can pray for one another. As new aspects of your generational wounding appear, you may want to reconnect with a prayer minister who can walk with you on your continuing healing journey. A soul friend or spiritual director may also serve in that role. If you get stuck in some dimensions of the healing process, you may want to consider finding a Christian therapist to work with you.

Generational healing is an ongoing journey. Generational wounds are complex and develop over many years; they won't usually be healed in an instant. New wounds may be revealed over time. The Lord usually waits until we are healthy enough to pursue further healing work. Do not be surprised if new wounds appear years after you thought everything was done. Take time for grief and mourning over the wounds and sins discovered. New information about ancestors may require reintegration. You may need to ask yourself questions like, *who am I in the light of this revelation? What does this make me aware of in my life?* Transformation is a process, not an event. Through it we learn deeper things about God's hand in history—including our personal and corporate histories. That process not only heals the past, it gives us hope for the future.

For Reflection

Read Jesus' hopeful words in Matthew 11:28-30 in the *Message* translation.

> Are you tired? Worn out? Burned out on religion? Come to me. Get away with me and you'll recover your life. I'll show you how to take a real rest. Walk with me and work with me—watch how I do it. Learn the unforced rhythms of grace. I won't lay anything heavy or ill-fitting on you. Keep company with me and you'll learn to live freely and lightly.

What word or phrase stands out to you in this passage? Take a few moments to meditate on what has caught your attention.

Again, review your personal case studies for the generational lineages you have been exploring. Ask God to show how you can incorporate the following maintenance actions into your life:

1. How am I listening to God? To myself? To others?
2. When was the last time I took a retreat?
3. How can I make space in my life to retreat in the future? Set a date.
4. Are there personal sins for which I need to seek forgiveness?
5. Who are the people I have wounded, or have wounded me with whom I need to reconnect? Seek the Lord about how to proceed.

6. Who has wounded my people, family organization, nation, who I may need to address, forgive, understand, and bless.

7. Which people do I continue to wound, families, ethnicities, races, churches, etc, through attitude and action?

8. Which people or situations am I avoiding because of unhealed wounds? How can I change this avoidance?

9. Where am I giving and receiving encouragement in my healing journey? Where can I find opportunities for encouragement if I'm not receiving it now?

Appendices

Appendix A:

The Genogram Format for Mapping Family Systems

Monica McGoldrick, LCSW, PhD

The genogram has been established as a practical framework for mapping and understanding family patterns. The word "genogram" is just a fancy term for a family tree that maps out who you belong to and some basic patterns of these belonging relationships. It is a language that has been established over the past 50 years to depict for clinicians some of the basic demographic, functioning, and relationship issues in families. Genograms include biological and legal members of a family but also pets, friends and other kinship relationships.

Genograms map out the basic biological and legal structure of the family—who was married to whom, the names of their children, and so on. Just as important, they can show key facts about individuals and the relationships of family members. For example, one can note the highest school grade completed, a serious childhood illness, or an overly close or distant relationship. The facts symbolized on the genogram also offer clues about the family's secrets and mythology, since families tend to obscure what is painful or embarrassing in their history.

A genogram includes multiple types of family information: the basic facts: who is in the family, the dates of their births, marriages, moves, illness, deaths; information regarding the primary characteristics and level of functioning of different family members: education, occupation, psychological and physical health, outstanding attributes, talents, successes and failures; relationship patterns in the family: closeness, conflict, or cut off. Once the primary family information is indicated on the genogram, it is possible to examine it from the multiple perspectives of all family members. One genogram might emphasize the relationship patterns in a family, another might highlight the artistic patterns, another the patterns of illness, and so forth. A genogram is generally drawn from the point of view of a key person or nuclear family, going back in time at least two generations and forward to the children and grandchildren of the key person or people. Other genograms may be drawn to show in detail various branches of the family or aspects of their functioning and relationship.

This standardized genogram format is becoming a common language for tracking family history and relationships. Despite the widespread use of genograms by family therapists, family physicians, and other health care providers, prior to the first edition of *Genograms: Assessment & Intervention* in 1985, there was no generally agreed-upon format for a genogram. Even among clinicians with similar theoretical orientations, there was only a loose consensus about what specific information to seek, how to record it, and what it all meant. The standardized genogram format offered here was worked out in the early 1980's by a committee of leading proponents of genograms from family therapy and family medicine, including such key people as Dr. Murray Bowen, Dr. Jack Froom, and Dr. Jack Medalie. They became part of a committee organized by the North American

Primary Care Research Group to define the most practical genogram symbols and agree on a standardized format. Since the format was originally published in 1985, there have been a number of modifications recommended by different groups around the world. We see this format as a work in progress. Expanded use of genograms will undoubtedly extend the format further. For example, computers have led us to begin development of standard color coding for names, location, occupation, illnesses, etc. The symbols will surely be further modified in the future as they have been modified over the years.

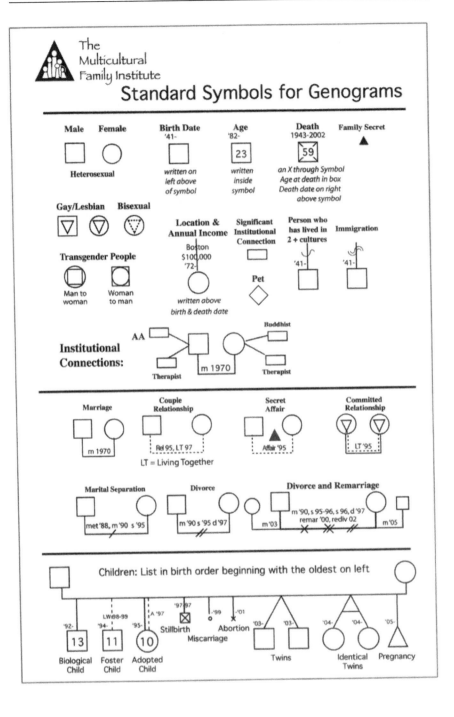

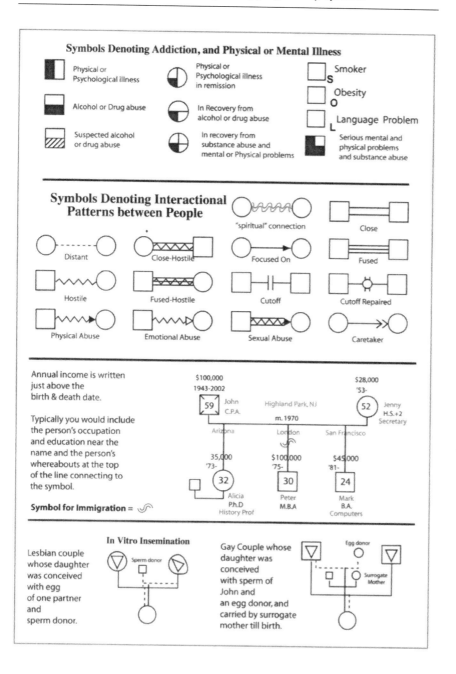

Symbols Denoting Addiction, and Physical or Mental Illness

Physical or Psychological illness

Physical or Psychological illness in remission

Smoker S

Alcohol or Drug abuse

In Recovery from alcohol or drug abuse

Obesity O

Suspected alcohol or drug abuse

In recovery from substance abuse and mental or Physical problems

Language Problem L

Serious mental and physical problems and substance abuse

Symbols Denoting Interactional Patterns between People

"spiritual" connection

Close

Distant

Close-Hostile

Focused On

Fused

Hostile

Fused-Hostile

Cutoff

Cutoff Repaired

Physical Abuse

Emotional Abuse

Sexual Abuse

Caretaker

Annual income is written just above the birth & death date.

Typically you would include the person's occupation and education near the name and the person's whereabouts at the top of the line connecting to the symbol.

Symbol for Immigration =

$100,000
1943-2002
59 John
C.P.A.
Highland Park, N.J.
m. 1970
$28,000
'53-
52 Jenny
H.S.+2
Secretary

Arizona
London
San Francisco

35,000
'73-
32 Alicia
Ph.D
History Prof

$100,000
'75-
30 Peter
M.B.A

$45,000
'81-
24 Mark
B.A.
Computers

In Vitro Insemination

Lesbian couple whose daughter was conceived with egg of one partner and sperm donor.

Sperm donor

Gay Couple whose daughter was conceived with sperm of John and an egg donor, and carried by surrogate mother till birth.

Egg donor

Surrogate Mother

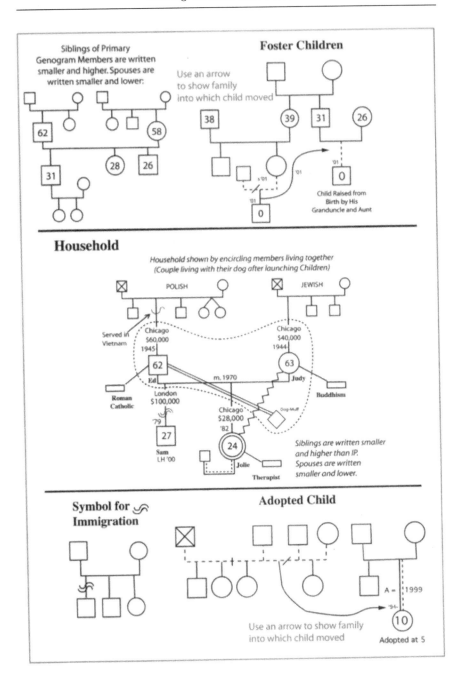

Siblings of Primary
Genogram Members are written
smaller and higher. Spouses are
written smaller and lower:

Foster Children

Use an arrow
to show family
into which child moved

Child Raised from
Birth by His
Granduncle and Aunt

Household

Household shown by encircling members living together
(Couple living with their dog after launching Children)

POLISH

JEWISH

Served in
Vietnam

Chicago
$60,000
1945

Chicago
$40,000
1944

Roman
Catholic

Ed

London
$100,000

m. 1970

Judy

Buddhism

Dog-Muff

Chicago
$28,000

Sam
LH '00

Jolie

Therapist

Siblings are written smaller
and higher than IP.
Spouses are written
smaller and lower.

Symbol for Immigration

Adopted Child

A = 1999

Adopted at 5

Use an arrow to show family
into which child moved

1. Husband, His Current Wife and his Ex-Wives (who are shown lower and smaller). Husband's wives may go on left to be closest to him. Indicators "1st," "2nd" etc. make clear the oader of his marriages.

2. Wife, Her Current Husband and her Ex-Husbands (who are shown lower and smaller). Wife's previous relationships are shown on left to keep children in birth order, since they remained in her custody.

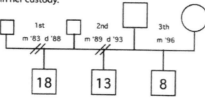

3. Couple with 3 year old, showing their previous spouses (smaller) and those spouses' new partners (even smaller)

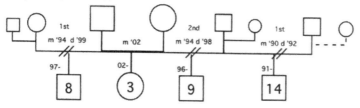

4. Couple living with their joint child and her child from a previous relationship. The other spouses of the partners are shown smaller and lower on either side of the present household, indicated by a dotted line.

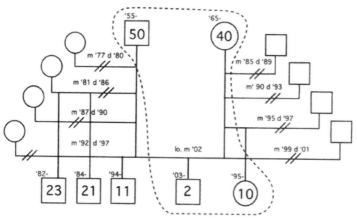

Genograms record information about family members and their relationships over at least three generations. They display family information graphically in a way that provides a quick gestalt of complex family patterns; as such they are a rich source of hypotheses about how clinical problems evolve in the context of the family over time.

Once you master this format you will want to learn the interpretive principles upon which genograms are based (see *Genograms: Assessment and Intervention*, W. W. Norton, 2008), and possibilities for software, which can record genogram information and store it for retrieval for research purposes. In our view the symbols make genograms the best shorthand language for mapping and summarizing family information and describing family patterns.

Genograms allow you to map the family structure clearly and to note and update the map of family patterns of relationships and functioning as they emerge in a clinical session. For a clinical record, the genogram provides an efficient summary, allowing a person unfamiliar with a case to grasp quickly a huge amount of information about a family and to scan for potential problems and resources. While notes written in a chart or questionnaire may become lost in the mass of information, genograms are immediately recognizable and can be expanded and corrected at each clinical visit as one learns more about a family. They can be created for any moment in the family's history- showing the ages and relationships of that moment to better understand family patterns as they evolve through time.

Genograms make it easier for us to keep in mind the complexity of a family's context, including family history, patterns, and events that may have ongoing significance for patient care. Just as our spoken language potentiates and organizes our thought processes, genograms, which map relationships and patterns of family functioning, help clinicians think systemically about how events and relationships in their clients' lives are related to patterns of health and illness.

Gathering genogram information should be an integral part of any comprehensive, clinical assessment, if only to know who is in the family and what are the facts of their current situation and history. The genogram is primarily an interpretive tool that enables the clinician to generate tentative hypotheses for further evaluation in a family assessment. It cannot be used in a cookbook fashion to make clinical predictions. But it can sensitize the clinician to systemic issues, which are relevant to current dysfunction and to sources of resilience.

Scanning the breadth of the current family context allows the clinician to assess the connectedness of the immediate members of the family to each other, as well as to the broader system- the extended family, friends, community, society and culture, and to evaluate the family's strengths and vulnerabilities in relation to the overall situation. Consequently, we include on the genogram the immediate and extended family members, as well as significant non-blood "kin" who have ever lived with or played a major role in the family's life. We also note relevant events (moves, life cycle changes) and problems (illness, dysfunction). Current behavior and problems of family members can be traced on the genogram from multiple perspectives. The index person (the "I.P." or person with the problem or symptom) may be viewed in the context of various subsystems, such as siblings, triangles, and reciprocal relationships, or in relation to the broader community, social institutions (schools, courts, etc.), and socio-cultural context.

Genograms "let the calendar speak" by suggesting possible connections between family events over time. Patterns of previous illness and earlier shifts in family relationships brought about through loss and other critical life changes, which alter family structure and other patterns, can easily be noted on the genogram.

Computerized genograms will soon enable us to explore specific family patterns and symptom constellations, which provide a framework for hypothesizing about what may be currently influencing a crisis in a particular family. In conjunction with genograms, we usually include a family chronology, which depicts the family history in chronological order. A computerized program for gathering and mapping genogram information with a data base will in the future make it a lot easier for the clinician to track family history, because a chronology will be able to show events for any particular moment in the family's history.

Genograms need to show not just the biological and legal members of a family, but also the network of friends and community essential for understanding the family. This includes current relationships, but also the relationships that came before and live in the person's heart, giving hope and inspiration in times of distress. It is also important to show the context around the biological and legal family in order to understand a family in context. Such people include those who live in one's heart, some long dead, and some in daily life, who could offer a loan, help your husband or children out, or give you strength and courage if you are in a crisis. It is this kinship network, not just the biological relatives, and not just those who are alive now, who would be relevant to know about if you want to understand clients or access their resources. Such genograms are important to illustrate in greater depth the context around the immediate family.

Family history always evolves in the context of larger societal structures: cultural, political, religious, spiritual, socio-economic class, gender, racial and ethnic structures, which organize each member of a society into a particular social location.

It is important always to think of the genogram in its broader context. At times we actually define the resources and institutions of the community to highlight families' access or lack of access to community resources (which can be noted around the genogram).

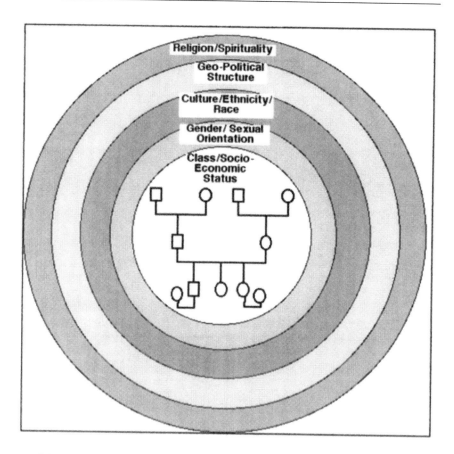

Many have been attempting to expand genograms to take these larger social structures into account in understanding genogram patterns. We look forward to the continued evolution of genograms to enable us to better illustrate the larger cultural levels along with the specific individual and kinship dimensions of family patterns.

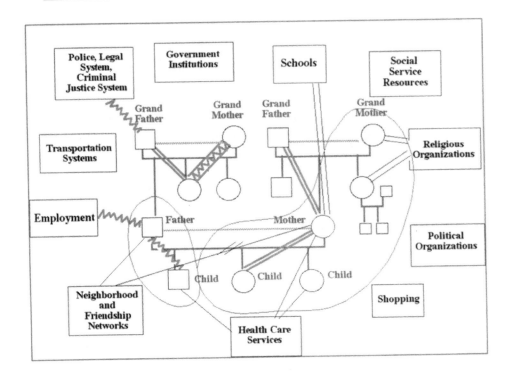

Appendix B:

Family Information Suggestions

Douglas W Schoeninger, PhD

Material to search for as you investigate family patterns from generation-to-generation includes various kinds of information, objective and subjective, useful for revealing family patterns generation to generation. Note that even names and dates can be revealing, such as the passing of names forward, the confluence of dates of significant events showing significant times of stress or celebration and the significance of events occurring near the anniversaries of births, deaths or major traumas.

Factual Data

For each person in each generation:
- Names, first and last;
- Date of birth;
- Date and cause of death (e.g. diseases, accidents, war, suicide, murder, crib death, suffocation, etc. Be as specific as possible.);
- Major moves and relocations and dates;

- Vocations and occupations/academic or educational field;
- Religious faith affiliation(s), religious/spiritual involvement(s);
- Dates of marriages;
- Separation(s) and dates;
- Divorces and dates;
- Remarriages and dates;
- Ethnic/racial identities;
- Countries of origin;
- Dates of immigration (from where to where).

Important Additional Information

- Major physical illnesses (cancer, heart disease, diabetes, seizures, asthma, arthritis);
- Major relationship and mental health issues (addictions: alcoholism, sexual addictions, gambling; eating disorders: bulimia, anorexia, obesity; suicide attempts, phobias, emotional imbalance, depression, anxieties and fears, rage and anger; mental illnesses: schizophrenia, paranoia, etc.);
- Physical strengths and blessings, healings, miracles;
- Spiritual dis-eases (greed, revenge, un-forgiveness, bitterness, materialism, control, extreme fundamentalism);
- Spiritual strengths and blessings, forgiveness, faithfulness;
- Died without being committed to God;
- Died without knowing God, knowing Jesus;
- Accidental deaths;
- Anyone alienated from the family;
- Disappearance of a family member;
- Abortions, miscarriages, still births;
- Violence and abuses: sexual, physical, verbal, rage and anger;

- Traumatic events (natural disasters, accidents, crash of transportation vehicle, witness of murder or terrible crime, victim of any kind of assault: physical violence, sexual abuse or rape, war, economic collapse, expulsion, inquisition, Satanic ritual abuse, other injuries);
- Major losses, such as property, wealth, family members (to diseases, plagues, epidemics, natural disasters);
- Major recovery from losses;
- Experiences of war (imprisonment, massacre, witness of buddy's death);
- Experiences of God and great love amidst conflict and tragedy;
- Investments of energy
  o strengths, gifts, interests
  o blaming, hatreds, revenges, prejudices
  o positive and negative identities, beliefs
  o unfulfilled gifts, talents, vocations, creativity;
- Occult or Satanic ritual involvement
  o Free Masonry
  o mixed pagan/Christian traditions/cultural practices
  o witchcraft
  o spirit-based alternative medicine (channeling "energy," calling on "angels" or other spirits, crystals, etc.)
  o voodoo, santeria, etc.;
- Curses and evidence of cursing;
- Blessings and evidence of blessings;
- Unusual psychological, psychic, and spiritual occurrences, psychic abilities;
- Coincidental dates/years (patterns);
- Relationships
  o positive (reconciliation, forgiveness, commitment)
  o conflictual (feuding within family, with other groups, families, nationalities; un-forgiveness, blame, scapegoating)

- o boundary problems (e.g. severe parentification, adults turning to children to parent them)
- o sexual or emotional incest, triangulation, fusion, possessiveness;
- Extreme cut off of relationships, disapproval, disappointment, unfulfilled expectations;
- Family secrets: hidden, not confessed, un-repented sins.

Appendix C:

Organizing Generational Information

Judith Allen Shelly, DMin

When you research the generational history of multiple lines on your family tree, or study a church or organization, the data can become overwhelming. The following chart (on the next page) provides a way to organize significant data by generations, giving a snapshot of where important patterns began and ended and who was most affected by these patterns. As you organize the data, repeated conditions become visible, such as diseases, relationship patterns, repeated losses, significant joys and celebrations.

On this chart the first column on the *right* shows the current generation, then as you move to the left each preceding generation of the lineages can be listed and described. The spaces below the column headings in the top row boxes are for era being explored. An *era* defines the division of time being investigated. It could be simply divided by decades, or by the tenure of a particular leader. In a family you might list the parents' names with their dates of birth and death in that space. For a church, list the pastor with dates of tenure. For an organization, list the president with dates of tenure. The chart gives a way of recording multiple strands of generational patterns within a family, church or organization.

Previous Generation 4	Previous Generation 3	People involved and wounding/blessing that occurred	Previous Generation 2	Previous Generation 1	Current Generation

For instance, in a family you may want to indicate parallel patterns in both the mother's and father's family lines, or inter-relationships among/between siblings. A simple example might be a strong history of heart disease passed down through both parent's lines, and/or several siblings in each generation with heart disease. Obviously, persons who span more than one era will be listed more than once. This provides a way to show inter-relationships and possible influences beyond a single line in a family-tree. You can indicate only the relevant linkages, or provide more details as needed, including both life-affirming and life-diminishing influences.

Families can use this method to collect information from each generation to examine the patterns that develop. Information can be gleaned through listening to the stories of each living generation, reading family and community histories, diaries, journals and whatever written records have been passed down through the family. Often these bits and pieces do not fit neatly on a family tree or genogram.

For a church or organization, you may want to add additional rows for sub-leaders of the group affected, such as associate pastors, youth pastors or department heads. This provides a way to show inter-relationships and possible influences beyond a single line in an organizational chart. In the large column, list the members of the particular group that appears to be wounded. In a church, this might be a youth group, clergy or lay leaders. In an institution or organization this might be faculty or staff in a particular department. You can also list significant relationships and events, both life-affirming and life-diminishing, within the group itself and in the surrounding culture.

Adapt the chart to your particular situation. The main point is to show patterns in relationships over the generations. You can use genogram symbols or your own designations for the patterns that you see developing within and between generations (see page 315). You could trace each continuing relationship with a different colored ink, or even use a different color to write each name that continues across generations in churches and organizations (such as group members who continue to serve under several different leaders). You may want to make a separate chart for each era at first, and then combine them into one after the patterns begin emerging. Be creative. There is no right or wrong method.

Begin by taking the patterns that drew you to explore the generational component. For example, you are realizing that one particular department in your organization has had a rapid turnover of staff in the past ten years. Exit interviews were consistently terse and evasive. You have heard rumors of sexual harassment, but no one has actually accused anyone specifically. As you begin to explore, your chart may look like this:

What relationship patterns do you see? Who would you want to interview? What would you want to know? Where else might you find background information? Why did Sally Lee leave? Why did she come back after a five year hiatus? Did she just have a baby and come back once the child started school, or did George Prince's departure have anything to do with her return? Why did George Prince and Jean Lemon stay when everyone else left? Why did the number of staff fluctuate?

Next, look for significant events that occurred within each era at all levels in the organization. Gather a group of those who were involved in these eras, or can speak with knowledge about events that occurred. Note things such as splits or mergers, scandals, financial crises, interpersonal conflicts, divorces, deaths or serious illness— but also note significant anniversaries, marriages, awards, new ventures, successful programs, growth and other positive developments or events.

1995	2000	2005	2010	2015

President: Joe Turner *(beloved—died in office, remembered fondly, personal and pastoral, knew everyone's name and family, but poor administrator, avoided conflict)*

Bill Warner *(impersonal and business-like with staff, strong administrator, made many needed changes)*

Mary Jones *(friendly, but distant, did not interact personally with staff, organized, authoritarian)*

Director of Communications: Bob Owens

George Prince *(highly competent in job, impersonal, critical and demanding, showed favoritism, fostered competition & division among staff)*

Jack Sprat *(asked for resignations of all staff and replaced them)*

George Prince *(charming, manipulative, engaged staff in collusion, sexually & emotionally harassed both male & female staff)*

George Prince *(increasingly ambitious)*

Staff: George Prince *(bright, high achiever)*

Kendra Jetson *(quiet, competent, SK's friend)*

Sue King *(manipulated against KJ by BO)*

Sally Lee *(worked mostly from home)*

Jean Lemon *(shared GP's vision, worked together with GP on special projects and began a sexual relationship)*

Tom Caplan
John Jeffries
Jean Lemon *(GP's obvious favorite)*
Felicia West *(stayed only two years and resigned, feeling angry and emotionally abused)*

Tom Caplan
John Jeffries
Jean Lemon *(married GP and resigned)*
Joelle Mason

Tammy Wilson
Glen Hoch
Amanda Blue
Sally Lee *(returned after children started school, worked on site)*

Pattern of manipulation and both emotional and sexual harassment began in this period.

The staff of two colluded against BO force his resignation.

TC and JJ became close friends. FW became the target of JL's jealousy and anger.

GP manipulated TC and JJ against each other, he otherwise communicated to staff via JL.

Initial commitment and enthusiasm among staff soon became sense of fear & distrust.

Figure 8: Generational Timeline for an Organization

What was happening in the surrounding culture during these times? How did these events or trends affect the organization? For example, look for the effects of the economy on the budget, employees being called up for deployment, returning disabled veterans, changing technologies, changing lifestyles of those served by the organization, national or local disasters.

This is a time of brainstorming, let the memories flow. Take each era on a separate flip chart page, looking especially for

- Life-affirming aspects;
- Life-diminishing aspects;
- Current events and trends in the culture.

Once you have summarized each era, compile it on a chart like the one on page 317 and look for patterns or trends. For example, one church noticed that in times of poor pastoral leadership, the lay leadership grew and continued through subsequent eras. Another church realized that their declining membership, which they had blamed on their pastors' performance, was a trend consistent with all churches in their area. An organization that used this process was surprised at how employees in each era thought they were the only ones experiencing such distress. Most of the abusive relationships were kept secret and employees rarely discussed their fears and concerns with others. When victims of sexual or emotional harassment did report their abuse, supervisors often blamed them or did not believe them. When given the opportunity to share as a group, victims will usually be more comfortable sharing their own experiences when they realize that they were not the only ones affected.

After examining all the material collected, determine when and where healing needs to take place. Sometimes the process of prayerfully discussing the issues will be healing in itself. It may also identify those not present who were wounded. In such situations, it may be helpful to sponsor a reunion of former staff, providing a safe environment for healing and reconciliation. Current leaders can express repentance for the wounds suffered with former leaders. Counseling and prayer ministry can also be offered to wounded individuals. Good memories can be celebrated and friendships restored.

	1995	2000	2005	2010
Life-affirming Aspects	Strong sense of vision and purpose / Felt affirmed & encouraged by president Joe T. / Began era with a sense of "family"	Jean & George enjoy working together, fall in love	New dept leadership brings hope / Bill Warner becomes new company president	George and Jean marry (both resign)
Life-Diminishing Aspects	Closeness became abusive / Friendships became competitive and hostile	Hostility between staff and supervisor / Joe T refuses to 'take sides'	Hostility continues, but with new players / Feels unsafe to develop friendships at work	IPR increasingly strained / General feeling of unrest and distrust / Fear of layoffs
Current Events & Trends in Culture	Oklahoma City bombing / Budget crisis forces federal govt shutdown / Clinton accused of sexual relationship Monica Lewinsky / Columbine HS shooting / Fear of Y2k.	Geo. W. Bush elected President / September 11th terrorist attacks / Space Shuttle disintegrates upon re-entry / Iraq War begins / GW Bush re-elected	Hurricane Katrina / Nancy Pelosi first female Speaker of the House / Va Tech & N IL school shootings / Stock market crash / Obama elected President	HIPPA Act passes / Hurricane Sandy / Obama re-elected / Supreme Court allows federal recognition of same-sex marriages

Figure 9: Summarizing the Patterns and Trends

References

Accattoli, Luigi. (1998). *When a Pope Asks Forgiveness*. New York, NY: Alba House.

Boszormenyi-Nagy, Ivan, and Krasner, Barbara. R. (1986). *Between Give and Take. A Clinical Guide to Contextual Therapy*. New York, NY: Brunner/Mazel.

Boszormenyi-Nagy, Ivan, and Spark, Geraldine M. (1973). *Invisible loyalties: Reciprocity in Intergenerational Family Therapy*. New York, NY: Harper and Row.

Dawson, John. (1994). *Healing America's Wounds*. Ventura, CA: Regal Books.

DeGrandis, Robert. (1989). *Intergenerational Healing*. Father Robert DeGrandis, S.S.J.

Epstein, A.W. (1982). Mental Phenomena Across Generations: The Holocaust. *Journal of the American Academy of Psychoanalysis. 10, 565-570.*

Fiore, E. (1987). *The Unquiet Dead*. New York, NY: Ballantine Books.

Hampsch, John H. (1986). *Healing Your Family Tree*. Everett, WA: Performance Press.

International Theological Commission. (1999). *Memory and Reconciliation: The Church and the Faults of the Past*. (See Vatican web site).

Kellermann, Natan P.F. *Transmission of Holocaust Trauma*. Retrieved January 22, 2015 from web site http://yad-vashem.org.il/yv/en/education/languages/dutch/pdf/kellermann.pdf.

Krasner, Barbara, and Joyce, Austin. (1995). *Truth, Trust, and Relationships*. New York, NY: Brunner/Mazel.

Kupperman, Karen. (2000). *Indians and English*. Ithaca, NY: Cornell University Press.

Lemonick, M. (1999). Smart Genes? *Time*. Sept. 13, 54-58.

Linn, Matthew, and Linn, Dennis, and Fabricant, Sheila. (1985). *Healing the Greatest Hurt*. Mahwah, NJ: Paulist Press.

MacNutt, Francis. (1995). *Deliverance from Evil Spirits*. Grand Rapids, MI: Chosen Books.

Maloney, George. (1980). *The Everlasting Now*. Notre Dame, IN: Ave Maria Press.

Mitton, Michael, and Parker, Russ. (2004). *Healing Death's Wounds*. Grand Rapids, MI: Chosen Books.

McAll, Kenneth. (1996). *A Guide to Healing the Family Tree*. Santa Barbara, CA: Queenship Publishing Co.

McAll, Kenneth. (1982). *Healing the Family Tree*. London, UK: Sheldon Press.

McAll, Kenneth. (1989). *Healing the Haunted*. London, UK: Darley Anderson.

McAll, Kenneth. (1984). Intercessory Prayer Format: Prayers for Departed Souls during Eucharistic Liturgy. *Journal of Christian Healing*. 6:1, 45-46.

McAll, Kenneth. (1993). North American Allergies: Healing Native American and Settler Legacies. *Journal of Christian Healing*. 15:4, 10-14.

McAll. Kenneth. (1983). Ritual Mourning in Anorexia Nervosa. *Journal of Christian Healing*. 5:1, 24-27.

McGoldrick, Monica, and Gerson, Randy and Petry, Sueli. (2008). *Genograms: Assessment and Intervention* (Third Edition). New York, NY: Norton.

McGoldrick, Monica. (1995). *You Can Go Home Again*. New York, NY: Norton.

McGoldrick, Monica. (2011). *The Genogram Journey: Reconnecting with Your Family*. New York, NY: Norton.

Parker, Russ. (2001.) *Healing Wounded History*. Cleveland, OH: The Pilgrim Press.

Pearsall, Paul. (1998). *The Heart's Code*. New York, NY: Broadway Books.

Prince, Derrick. (1990). *Blessing or Curse: You Can Choose*. Grand Rapids, MI: Chosen Books.

Schoeninger, Douglas. (1988). Tending Family Roots Part I: Foundational Concepts. *Journal of Christian Healing*. 10:1, 22-28.

Schoeninger, Douglas. (1989). Tending Family Roots Part II: Engaging the Resources of Our Family Legacy. *Journal of Christian Healing*. 11:4, 3-12.

Schoeninger, Douglas, and Schoeninger, Frances. (1993). Tending Family Roots Part III: Healing Inherited Tendencies. *Journal of Christian Healing*. 16:2, 3-15.

Sheldrake, Rupert. (1988). *The Presence of the Past*. New York, NY: Random House.

Smith, Patricia. (1992). Healing of Generations: An Ancient Connection. *Journal of Christian Healing*. 14:4, 3-10.

Smith, Patricia. (1996). *From Generation to Generation: A Manual for Healing*. Jacksonville, FL: Jahovah Rapha Press.

Ssemakula, Yozefu-B, (2011). *The Healing of Families*. Pensacola, FL: Yozefu-B. Ssemakula.

Stirling, Stuart. (2000). *The Last Conquistador*. Phoenix Mill, Gloucestershire, UK: Sutton Publishing Limited.

Taylor, Michael J. (1998). *Purgatory*. Huntington, IN: Our Sunday Visitor, Inc.

The New Jerusalem Bible. (1985). New York, NY: Doubleday.

Wallace, Anthony. (1999). *Jefferson and the Indians*. Cambridge, MA: Harvard University Press.

Zinn, Howard. (1995). *A People's History of the United States*. New York, NY: HarperCollins.

The Authors

D ouglas W. Schoeninger, PhD, is a clinical psychologist and President of the Institute for Christian Healing, a nonprofit organization dedicated to publishing, teaching, and training for Christian Listening, Healing and Reconciliation. He grew up in an American Baptist Church and joined a Presbyterian congregation in 1972, where he was introduced to healing prayer. His private psychotherapy practice integrates spirituality and prayer as healing resources and is focused on the healing of persons and relationships within an intergenerational perspective. He graduated from the University of Wisconsin with a PhD in clinical psychology in 1965. Doug studied Client Centered Therapy with Carl Rogers, has extensive training in Contextual Family Therapy with Ivan Nagy and Barbara Krasner, and worked with Kenneth McAll in the field of family tree healing. He has been a member of the Association of Christian Therapists (now ACTheals) since 1977, over the years serving as editor of *The Journal of Christian Healing*, Chair of the Spiritual Life Committee, and ACT President. He currently coordinates the work of the ACT Healing Manual Team, and edits *The Journal of Christian Healing*.

Judith Allen Shelly, DMin, served on the staff of InterVarsity Christian Fellowship for forty years, focusing on resource development, spiritual formation and prayer ministry. She edited the *Journal of Christian Nursing* and is the author or co-author of twenty books integrating faith and life, including *Called to Care: A Christian Worldview for Nursing* and *Spiritual Care: A Guide for Caregivers* (both IVP). She has also served as adjunct faculty at North Park Theological Seminary (Chicago) and Yonsei University (Seoul, Korea). She graduated from Virginia Commonwealth University (BS in Nursing, 1966) and the Lutheran Theological Seminary (MAR in Pastoral Care and Counseling, 1976, and DMin in Health Ministries, 1997). She was introduced to healing prayer through InterVarsity and the Christian Healing Ministries School of Healing Prayer. Judy has worked with individuals, churches and Christian organizations to facilitate generational healing. She coordinates the Healing Ministry at Christ Episcopal Church, Pottstown, PA, and co-leads a School of Healing Prayer with her husband Jim. She serves on the board of the Institute for Christian Healing.

Endnotes

1   Ryan Jones, "Are We Born Biased?" (an interview with Peter Hatemi), *The Penn Stater*, September/October 2013, 101(1), p. 36.

2   We are defining *occult* as magical practices that attempt to control the spirit world.

3   Powwow has roots in German occultism. It uses biblical formulas, and often the names of the Trinity, as magico-religious incantations. Many Powwow practitioners find an affinity with Native American healing practices and incorporate them as well. For an extensive scholarly explanation of Pennsylvania Dutch Powwowing see http://www.esoteric.msu.edu/VolumeIV/Powwow.htm.

4   www.infoplease.com/askeds/many-spoken-languages.html.

5   G. K. (Gilbert Keith) Chesterton, *Orthodoxy* (Public Domain Books: Kindle Edition,1994), p. 10.

6   Henri J. M. Nouwen, *The Wounded Healer* (New York: Doubleday, 1972).

7   In this reference the words "and fasting" appear in a footnote because the most authentic manuscripts do not include these words; however, the practice of fasting was integral in the lives of most Jews at the time of Jesus. Biblical examples include: Mt 4:1-17; Ex 34:1-35; 2 Sam 12:1-23; Ezra 8:21-36; Dan 10:1-21.

8   Nicholas Wolterstorff, "For Justice in Shalom," in Wayne G. Boulton, Thomas D. Kennedy and Allen Verhey, *From Christ to the World: Introductory Readings in Christian Ethics* (Grand Rapids: Eerdmans, 1994), 251.

9   Jürgen Moltmann, *The Spirit of Life: A Universal Affirmation* (Minneapolis: Fortress, 1992), 191.

10   Thomas A. Droege, "The Healing Ministry of Jesus as an Example of Wholistic Health Care" in Granger Westberg, editor, *Theological Roots of Wholistic Health Care* (Hinsdale, Illinois: Wholistic Health Centers, Inc, 1979), 19.

11   For a comprehensive study of the relationship between time and eternity, see Oscar Cullmann, *Christ and Time* (Philadelphia: Westminster Press, 1964).

12   Plato, *Phaedo, Part II*. Translated by Benjamin Jowett, (1817-1893), accessed at http://evans-experientialism.freewebspace.com/plato_phaedo02.htm (April 3, 2012).

13   George Santayana, *The Life of Reason*, Volume 1. (Amherst, New York: Prometheus Books, 1998).

14   Henry Nouwen, *Life of the Beloved* (New York: Crossroad, 1992), p. 69.

15   Monica McGoldrick, *You Can Go Home Again* (New York: Norton, 1995).

16   Matthew Linn, Dennis Linn and Sheila Fabricant, *Healing the Greatest Hurt* (Mahwah, NJ: Paulist Press, 1985). Kenneth McAll, *Healing the Family Tree* (London: Sheldon Press,1982). Michael Mitton and RussParker, *Requiem Healing* (London: Darton, Longman and Todd, Ltd., 1991)

17   John Dawson, *Healing America's Wounds* (Ventura, CA: Regal Books, 1994). Russ Parker, *Healing Wounded History* (Cleveland, OH: The Pilgrim Press, 2001).

18   Michael D. Lemonick, "Smart Genes?" *Time*, Sept. 13, 1999, p.57. Available online at http://content.time.com/time/world/article/0,8599,2053672,00.html. Also see Bruce Lipton, *The Biology of Belief* (Carlsbad, CA: Hay House, Inc., 2008).

19   Rupert Sheldrake, *The Presence of the Past* (New York: Random House, 1988), Chapter 17.

20   The idea that, through a telepathic effect or sympathetic vibration, an event or act can lead to similar events or acts in the future or an idea conceived in one mind can then arise in another. *Collins English Dictionary – Complete and Unabridged* , HarperCollins Publishers 1991, 1994, 1998, 2000, 2003.

21 Fields that play a causal role in morphogenesis. This term, first proposed in the 1920s, is now widely used by developmental biologists, but the nature of morphogenetic fields has remained obscure. On the hypothesis of formative causation, they are regarded as morphic fields stabilized by morphic resonance. http://www.sheldrake.org/Resources/glossary/index.html.

22 Ibid.

23 Paul Pearsall, PhD, Gary E. Schwartz, PhD, Linda G. Russek, PhD, "Organ Transplants and Cellular Memories," *Nexus*, Volume 12, Number 3 (April–May 2005). According to this study of patients who have received transplanted organs, particularly hearts, it is not uncommon for memories, behaviors, preferences and habits associated with the donor to be transferred to the recipient. For more information see http://www.paulpearsall.com/info/press/3.html.

24 Natan P.F. Kellermann, *Transmission of Holocaust Trauma*. Retrieved January 22, 2015 from web site http://yad-vashem.org.il/yv/en/education/languages/dutch/pdf/kellermann.pdf

25 Ivan Boszormenyi-Nagy and Geraldine Spark, *Invisible Loyalties* (New York: Brunner/Mazel, Inc., 1984), p. 67.

The therapy theory and method that grew from this seminal work became known as Contextual Therapy. Additional developments of Contextual Therapy can be found in: Ivan Boszormenyi-Nagy and Barbara Krasner, *Between Give and Take* (New York: Brunner/Mazel, Inc., 1986). Also see Barbara Krasner and Austin Joyce, *Truth, Trust, and Relationships* (New York: Brunner/Mazel, Inc., 1995).

26 An old Scottish prayer reads, "From ghoulies and ghosties and long-leggedy beasties and things that go bump in the night, Good Lord, deliver us!"

27 See McAll, Mitton and Parker, op cit.

28 Paul Tillich, *The Eternal Now* (New York: Scribners, 1963), pp 122 – 132.

29 Derek Prince, *Blessing or Curse, You Can Choose* (Grand Rapids: Chosen Books, 1990).

30 A stronghold is an obstacle to deliverance that is formed when a person believes a lie (often delivered through another person) which gives evil spirits permission to remain in a person. It controls behavior and tempts a person to sin repeatedly. Mt 12:29; 16:23; Rom 6:16; 2 Cor 10:3-5; Eph 6:12; 1 Pet 5:8.

31 The full text of this document is available online at http://www.vatican.va/roman_curia/congregations/cfaith/cti_documents/rc_con_cfaith_doc_20000307_memory-reconc-itc_en.html.

32 Karen Ordahl Kupperman, *Indians and English: Facing Off in Early America* (Ithaca, NY and London: Cornell University Press, 2000), p. 141.

33 International Theological Commission (1999), *Memory and Reconciliation: The Church and the Faults of the Past*, p.17. http://www.vatican.va/roman_curia/congregations/cfaith/cti_documents/rc_con_cfaith_doc_20000307_memory-reconc-itc_en.html

34 "The determination of the wrongs of the past, for which amends are to be made, implies, first of all, a correct historical judgment, which is also the foundation of the theological evaluation. One must ask: What precisely occurred? What exactly was said and done?" "What are the conditions for a correct interpretation of the past from the point of view of historical knowledge? To determine these, we must take account of the complexity of the relationship between the subject who interprets and the object from the past which is interpreted. (65) First, their mutual extraneousness must be emphasized. Events or words of the past are, above all, "past." As such they are not completely reducible to the framework of the present, but possess an objective density and complexity that prevent them from being ordered in a solely functional way for present interests. It is necessary, therefore, to approach them by means of an historical-critical investigation that aims at using all of the information available, with a view to a reconstruction of the environment, of the ways of thinking, of the conditions and the living dynamic in which those events and those words are placed, in order, in such a way, to ascertain the contents and the challenges that—precisely in their diversity—they propose to our present time... She [the Church] is inclined to mistrust generalizations that excuse or condemn various historical periods. She entrusts the investigation of the past to patient, honest, scholarly reconstruction, free from confessional or ideological prejudices, regarding both the accusations brought against her and the wrongs she has suffered." *Memory and Reconciliation* (1999), pp 17-19.

35 To illustrate, according to Karen Ordahl Kupperman in Indians and English: *Facing Off in Early America*, Chapter 1, the early modern English interfaced with Native Americans for the first time during a period when there was great concern in England with the blurring of social boundaries and their demarcations. Foreign influences were being increasingly felt, pressing at the foundations of 'good order'. Traditional gender distinctions were threatened. In this context the beginning and fragile dialogue with Native Americans was both a source for demonstrating the inherent nature of gender demarcations (through finding these in 'unspoiled' Native cultures) and a threat to traditional social hierarchies and distinctions should too much merging with Native culture take place. Grasping the motives and actions of our early American ancestors requires such imagining of their horizons and concerns.

36 While beliefs in racial superiority were propagated initially by powerful land owners to preserve economic control, these beliefs became part of our cultures and were even justified theologically (Howard Zinn, *A People's History of the United States, 1492-Present*, Chapter 9. (Harper Perennial Classics, 1995)). Likewise many subjugated in slavery fought hard to heal each day and to instill knowledge of dignity in their offspring, invisibly providing a cord of courage reaching forward down the generations.

37 Anthony F. C. Wallace, *Jefferson and the Indians: The Tragic Fate of the First Americans* (Cambridge, MA: Belknap Press of Harvard University Press, 2001).

38 Stuart Stirling, *The Last Conquistador, Mansio Serra De Lequizamon and the Conquest of the Incas* (Phoenix Mill, UK: Sutton Publishing, 1999), p. 141.

39 *Memory and Reconciliation*, p. 19.

40 Reported in *The Philadelphia Inquirer*, April 14, 2000.

41 *Memory and Reconciliation*, pp.17-18.

42 "What precisely occurred? What exactly was said and done? Only when these questions are adequately answered ... can one then ask whether what happened, what was said or done, can been understood as consistent with the Gospel, and, if it cannot, whether the Church's sons and daughters who acted in such a way could have recognized this, given the context in which they acted." (*Memory and Reconciliation*, p. 17) Also see Russ Parker, *Healing Wounded History: Reconciling People and Healing Places* (London: Dalton, Longman and Todd, 2001), p. 94.

43 In such a context, one can speak of a *solidarity* that unites the past and the present in a relationship of reciprocity. In certain situations, the burden that weighs on conscience can be so heavy as to constitute a kind of moral and religious memory of the evil done, which is by its nature a *common memory*. This common memory gives eloquent testimony to the solidarity objectively existing between those who committed the evil in the past and

their heirs in the present. It is then that it becomes possible to speak of an *objective common responsibility*. (*Memory and Reconciliation*, p. 21)

44 Kenneth McAll, "Intercessory Prayer Format: Prayers for Departed Souls During Eucharistic Liturgy," *The Journal of Christian Healing*, 6:1(1984), 45-46. See also Michael Mitton and Russ Parker *Healing Death's Wounds* (Keels Hill, UK: Arcadia Publishing Services Ltd., 2002), for an in depth discussion of praying for those who have died.

45 *The give and take between present and past in families.* The child is vulnerable to all that comes from and through each parent and is heavily shaped by the parents' own formative relationships. In fact, raising children tends to reawaken our own history at corresponding ages as we implicitly reach for resources from internalized parental care or find our own childhood experience re-stimulated.

Because of the vulnerability of childhood, early formative influences and the primary dialogue with caretakers at times of profound dependency lay a groundwork that is not easily budged by subsequent choices and subsequent experience. As adults, our formative past, including our ancestral legacies, can easily overcome present influences in their shaping and predisposing power. The effects of generations of maternal and paternal deprivations are not easily erased. My being cries out to be mothered by my mother and fathered by my father. I meet in them both strengthening presence and anguishing absence—rooted to be sure in their own foundations. Their presence and absence both elicit and limit my growth and shape my search for healing. And to some extent, the consequences are permanent for me.

Adopted children, raised by two parents, draw from 4 lineages, two relatively invisible yet powerful, biological lineages, and two shaping day to day life. These four lineages interact in ways hard to discern. However, the above discussion of the shaping power of generational strengths and weaknesses applies to the impact of each of these lineages. The lineages of the adopting parents may provide strengths not present in the biological lineages. Or the biological lineages may undergird the child in ways that the adoptive parents' lineages are weak. Also the wounding of felt rejection and hidden loyalty to invisible biological kin may make receiving love difficult for the adopted child.

The impact of ancestral and early injury and deprivation can be addressed, if not fully met. Corrective emotional experiences are possible. With help, longings can be reformed into claims upon an adopted child's history and committed relationships. A reparative drive exists within and between us.

Parenting can be sought from other quarters. God does provide us with fathering and mothering presence. Adults do learn to parent themselves, crediting their longings, asking for care and receiving what their parents truly have to give. Deprivations, even half met, can lead to a hopeful sensitivity to other's similar needs.

The terms of each person's life and common family terms have a layered quality, shaped as they are by each generation's life exchanges, deprivations, wounds and reconciliations. Sometimes core motivations reveal a drama spanning centuries, exposing benefits received long ago by ancestors, or injuries long forgotten yet still disquieting, unheard and un-calmed repeated generation to generation as if refusing to rest until their terms are met.

For example, in particular family lines, the consequences of parents' selling their children as chattel a century or more ago—sin not grieved, disowned souls unclaimed—haunt contemporary tendencies for abandonment. On the other hand, courageous deeds risked long ago, when appreciated, infect contemporary zeal as a hidden resource. Our pioneering ancestors, their vitality and resourcefulness appreciated, continue to encourage, even mandate, urges to venture into new frontiers. Thus our terms and conditions are both personal and ancestral.

The healing process reflects this dynamic. A son, strengthened through marriage and friendship, brought to the surface a deep longing for his father's care. A challenge to his father to hear his desire and its terms, ("I want you to know me.") awakened a deep inner appreciation for four generations of fathers and sons resounding, "Go for it. You do this for us all." The depth of meaning here transcends one lifetime, reconciling many through one. Likewise for his siblings, one voice of pain converted to a claim served as a catalyst of possibilities previously inconceivable.

We engage a give and take as well, although indirectly, with our ancestors as they speak to us through genetic inheritance. The seeming assets and liabilities passed to me genetically change their meaning for me across time, depending in part on how I am relating to those ancestors who passed this genetic heritage to me. A talent can be a curse or a blessing according to how I negotiate its place and expression in my life. Its terms will continue to speak a message to me through depression, through misuse or inattention, or from the exhilaration of wise and creative investment and implicit thanksgiving to those who previously carried and nurtured this talent. I cannot change one talent for another or alter my natural hair coloring and consistency. I do negotiate the use of a talent and its place in my life, and I do decide how I will work with the hair I have been given.

46 "What precisely occurred? What exactly was said and done? Only when these questions are adequately answered... can one then ask whether what happened, what was said or done, can been understood as consistent with the Gospel, and, if it cannot, whether the Church's sons and daughters who acted in such a way could have recognized this, given the context in which they acted." (*Memory and Reconciliation*, p. 17) Also see Russ Parker, *Healing Wounded History*, p. 94.

47 In such a context, one can speak of a *solidarity* that unites the past and the present in a relationship of reciprocity. In certain situations, the burden that weighs on conscience can be so heavy as to constitute a kind of moral and religious memory of the evil done, which is by its nature a *common memory*. This common memory gives eloquent testimony to the solidarity objectively existing between those who committed the evil in the past and their heirs in the present. It is then that it becomes possible to speak of an *objective common responsibility*. (*Memory and Reconciliation*, p. 21).

48 Linn, Linn and Linn, pp. 105-140.

49 Parker, *Healing Wounded History* p. 134.

50 Ibid., p. 60.

51 Ibid., p. 62-67.

52 Mary Ann Moller-Gunderson, "Victims of Clergy Sexual Abuse: The Church's Response," *Accent, A Resource Newsletter from Holden Village,* 7(2), June 1991.

53 Teri Randall, "Abuse at Work Drains People, Money and Medical Workplace Not Immune," *JAMA*, 267(11), (March 18, 1992), pp. 1439-1440.

54 For more specific suggestions for constructing your group story, see Russ Parker and Michael Mitton, *Healing Wounded History: The Workbook* (London: Darton, Longman and Todd, 2001), Session 4, "Church Group Story," pp. 47-56.

55 See http://www.tahtonka.com/apology.html; http://www.tribal-institute. org/lists/kevin_gover.htm). The full video recording of the statement can be viewed on YouTube at http://www.youtube.com/watch?v=zu52ig696L4.

56 *The Holy Bible*, Nehemiah, Chapter 1; Ezra, Chapters 9 and 10

57 The sign reads, "London Coffee House. Scene of political and commercial activity in the colonial period. The London Coffee House opened here in 1754. It served as a place to inspect Black slaves recently arrived from Africa and to bid for their purchase at public auction."

58 Accattoli, Luigi. *When a Pope Asks Forgiveness* (New York: Alba House, 1998).

59 Accattoli, p. 154 – 155.

60 Accattoli, p. 154.

61 *The Genogram Format for Mapping Family Systems* by Monica McGoldrick is available online at http://multiculturalfamily.org/ under PDF eBooks. It can be downloaded for $2.50. It is reprinted here with permission of the author.

CPSIA information can be obtained at www.ICGtesting.com
Printed in the USA
BVOW05s1038260616

453358BV00001B/2/P